Natural Hazards, Risk and Vulnerability

Different people handle risk in different ways. The current lack of understanding about this heterogeneity in risk behaviour makes it difficult to intervene effectively in risk-prone communities.

Natural Hazards, Risk and Vulnerability offers a unique insight in the everyday life of a group of riverbank settlers in Jakarta – one of the most vulnerable areas worldwide in terms of exposure to natural hazards. Based on long-term fieldwork, the book portrays the often creative and innovative ways in which slum dwellers cope with recurrent floods. The book shows that behaviour that is often described as irrational or ineffective by outside experts can be highly pragmatic and often effective. This book argues that human risk behaviour cannot be explained by the risk itself, but instead by seemingly unrelated factors such as trust in authorities and aid institutions and unequal power structures. By considering a risk as a lens that exposes these factors, a completely new type of analysis is proposed that offers useful insights for everyone concerned about how people cope with the currently increasing amount of natural hazard.

This is a valuable resource for academics, researchers and policy makers in the areas of risk studies, disaster and natural hazard, urban studies, anthropology, development, Southeast Asian studies and Indonesia studies.

Roanne van Voorst is a postdoctoral researcher and lecturer in the Anthropology of Development at the University of Amsterdam, The Netherlands.

Routledge Humanitarian Studies Series

Series editors: Alex de Waal and Dorothea Hilhorst
Editorial Board: Mihir Bhatt, Dennis Dijkzeul, Wendy Fenton, Kirsten Johnson, Julia Streets, Peter Walker

The Routledge Humanitarian Studies series in collaboration with the International Humanitarian Studies Association (IHSA) takes a comprehensive approach to the growing field of expertise that is humanitarian studies. This field is concerned with humanitarian crises caused by natural disaster, conflict or political instability and deals with the study of how humanitarian crises evolve, how they affect people and their institutions and societies, and the responses they trigger.

We invite book proposals that address, amongst other topics, questions of aid delivery, institutional aspects of service provision, the dynamics of rebel wars, state building after war, the international architecture of peacekeeping, the ways in which ordinary people continue to make a living throughout crises, and the effect of crises on gender relations.

This interdisciplinary series draws on and is relevant to a range of disciplines, including development studies, international relations, international law, anthropology, peace and conflict studies, public health and migration studies.

Disaster, Conflict and Society in Crises
Everyday politics of crisis response
Edited by Dorothea Hilhorst

Human Security and Natural Disasters
Edited by Christopher Hobson, Paul Bacon and Robin Cameron

Human Security and Japan's Triple Disaster
Responding to the 2011 earthquake, tsunami and Fukushima nuclear crisis
Edited by Paul Bacon and Christopher Hobson

The Paradoxes of Aid Work
Passionate professionals
Silke Roth

Disaster Research
Multidisciplinary and international perspectives
Edited by Morten Thanning Vendelø, Olivier Rubin, Rasmus Dahlberg

The New Humanitarians in International Practice
Emerging actors and contested principles
Edited by Zeynep Sezgin and Dennis Dijkzeul

Natural Hazards, Risk and Vulnerability
Floods and slum life in Indonesia
Roanne van Voorst

"Riverbank settlers in Jakarta face risk every day and, what Roanne van Voorst refers to as, 'normal uncertainty'. Power relations can drive this risk and people have developed strategies in order to deal with nature and the powerful elite. Readers of this highly informative book will have greater understanding and compassion the next time they see media coverage of bulldozers pulling down houses."
— *Ben Wisner, UCL Hazard Research Centre, University College London, UK*

"Uncovering just how differently people behave and why they behave differently in a crisis is the central concern of this study of a flood-prone community in Jakarta. Finding theory in daily life, Roanne van Voorst has written a masterful work of discovery, analysis and empathy."
— *Greg Bankoff, University of Hull, UK*

"This book is an outstanding account of how poor people strategize, in the confines of the limited resources at hand, to deal with recurring disaster. It conveys a powerful message to politicians and aid programmes about the crucial importance to build policy and intervention on grounded research into people's everyday realities."
— *Dorothea Hilhorst, professor of humanitarian aid and reconstruction at the International Institute of Social Studies of Erasmus University Rotterdam, the Netherlands.*

"This book fills strategic gaps in disaster studies, showing how vulnerable people see risks as part of regular life experiences. The author shows how the diversity of coping strategies reflects people's responses to existing structural constraints and their own agency. The book is excellently written and will appeal to academics, professionals and the wider public."
— *I.S.A. Baud, University of Amsterdam, the Netherlands and President of the European Association of Development Institutes (EADI), Germany*

"For these impoverished slum dwellers, flood risk is not a one-off natural disaster but a normal part of their daily struggle to survive. Roanne van Voorst's 'thick' account of their lives is peopled with unforgettable characters and written in a fluid, literary style. I found it deeply moving."
— *Gerry van Klinken, University of Amsterdam, senior researcher KITLV Leiden, the Netherlands*

"This is an innovative book about the urban poor that challenges simple categorizations. Based on fieldwork under very difficult circumstances, Roanne van Voorst applies a view from below which foregrounds the agency and the heterogeneity of various groups of people who try to determine their future."
— *Henk Schulte Nordholt, KITLV/Leiden University, the Netherlands*

Natural Hazards, Risk and Vulnerability

Floods and slum life in Indonesia

Roanne van Voorst

LONDON AND NEW YORK

First published 2016
by Routledge
2 Park Square, Milton Park, Abingdon, Oxon OX14 4RN

and by Routledge
711 Third Avenue, New York, NY 10017

First issued in paperback 2017

Routledge is an imprint of the Taylor & Francis Group, an informa business

British Library Cataloguing-in-Publication Data
A catalogue record for this book is available from the British Library

Library of Congress Cataloging-in-Publication Data
Names: Voorst, Roanne van, author.
Title: Natural hazards, risk and vulnerability : floods and slum life in Indonesia / Roanne van Voorst.
Description: Abingdon, Oxon ; NewYork, NY : Routledge, 2016.
Identifiers: LCCN 2015032563 | ISBN 9781138860537 (hb) | ISBN 9781315716411 (e-book)
Subjects: LCSH: Human ecology—Indonesia—Jakarta. | Hazardous geographic environments—Social aspects—Indonesia—Jakarta. | Floods—Indonesia—Jakarta. | Slums—Indonesia—Jakarta. | Poor—Indonesa—Jakarta. | Risk—Sociological aspects. | Environmental sociology—Indonesia—Jakarta.
Classification: LCC GF13.3.I5 V66 2016 | DDC 363.34/930959822—dc23
LC record available at http://lccn.loc.gov/2015032563

ISBN 13: 978-0-8153-5501-4 (pbk)
ISBN 13: 978-1-138-86053-7 (hbk)

Typeset in Baskerville MT
by diacriTech, Chennai

Contents

Acknowledgements

This book could not have existed without the inhabitants of Bantaran Kali. These people were my neighbours and my study participants at the same time, and, more than that, they often jokingly referred to themselves as my *orang tua adopsi* – my adoptive parents. They did not take on an easy task when they 'adopted' me. They soon noticed that I was so unexperienced and ignorant that I needed to be supervised in nearly all of the daily practices that they deemed crucial for a safe and comfortable life in their neighbourhood. My neighbours decided that I had to be taught how to bargain on the local market; how to sell a rice meal to bypassing customers on the street; how to attach the mattress to the ceiling or evacuate in case of a flood; how to treat stomach aches; and how to take care of a baby – just to name a few examples of the topics on which they lectured me tirelessly. It is therefore first and foremost the riverbank settlers of Bantaran Kali whom I should thank for enabling me to carry out this research project and write this book.

But how does one thank people who live in a neighbourhood that is not registered, and who are therefore considered 'illegal' residents of Jakarta by their government? They will, for instance, not find their names or even the name of their neighbourhood in this book: I have had to anonymize all of these names to avoid increasing the many problems that this marginalized group of people already have in their daily life in the slums of Jakarta, and hence I cannot honour them personally in this book. And, most problematically, how does one thank people whose houses may be soon evicted by the city government as part of a larger 'development' or slum-clearance project in Jakarta? The next time that I plan to visit my informants, it is likely that the riverbank settlement that I describe in this book may no longer exist. So, to my great regret, the following sentence might be the best I can do to thank my neighbours for their help, their care, their tips and advice, and their participation in this study: *teman-teman, orang tua adopsi saya, terima kasih banyak: buku ini tentang anda dan untuk anda semua.* Or, for those youngsters who so diligently followed my weekly English classes in the kampong: thank you, my dear friends, this book is about you and for you.

There were also other people in Jakarta who helped me greatly in carrying out my fieldwork: Charina Chazali proved to be an intelligent and skilful research assistant; Dr. Erwiza Erman and Yetti Rochadiningsih helped me to get through the lengthy, bureaucratic process of obtaining a research permit; Jan-Jaap Brinkman,

Sandyawan Sumardi, Ariel Shepherd, Ivana Lee, Ika Kartika and Rudolft Abdul Muiz became dear friends and were always helpful in providing me with whatever information about Jakarta or Bantaran Kali I needed.

I am extremely grateful for the financial support I have received during the research and writing period from the Amsterdam Institute of Social Science Research (AISSR) and the Moving Matters Research Cluster from the University of Amsterdam. Colleagues and friends affiliated in various ways with Indonesian studies, disaster studies and/or anthropology have provided crucial advice and encouragement. Some of the many people who I wish to thank include Willem van Schendel, Rosanne Rutten, Gerry van Klinken, Tina Harris, Laurens Bakker, Barak Kalir, Isa Baud, Ben Wisner, Helene van Klinken, Thea Hilhorst, Freek Colombijn, Dick Roth, Michel Handgraaf, Ward Berenschot, Gregory Bankoff, Henk Schulte Nordholt, Amis Boersma, Anick Vollebergh, Amalinda Savirani, Michiel Baas, Erella Grassiani, Yatun Sastramidjaja, Marije Cornielje, Jonna Both, Naomi van Stapele, Jacqui Baker, Ian Wilson, Jörgen Hellman and Benno Netelenbos. Sincere gratitude goes out to Mario Rutten and Gerben Nooteboom, who skilfully guided me through the various stages of my PhD dissertation. Gerben visited me during fieldwork in Jakarta, where he patiently listened to all my ideas, and made me reconsider them by enthusiastically posing questions I had not even thought of as yet. He was supportive and critical at the same time, and helped me find my position as a young scholar. Back in Amsterdam, I could not have asked for a more energetic and supportive PhD supervisor and mentor than Mario. He challenged my thinking on all levels while believing in my work, even at times when I did not. Right before this book was published, the devastating news of Mario's death arrived. It is heartbreaking that I can only thank him in writing and no longer in person.

On a personal level, my friends, family and partner were my main source of support, and the ones who always reminded me that there is more to life than work.

List of figures

Figure 0.1 The Island of Java and the location of Jakarta.

Figure 0.2 Jakarta. The research area of Bantaran Kali is located on the border between South and East Jakarta, along the banks of the Ciliwung River.

Get ready for the flood!

It is two o'clock early in the morning when the residents of a poor, flood-prone riverbank settlement in Jakarta are wakened from their sleep by loud human voices, screaming: 'The kampong will be flooded! Get ready for the flood!'

Floods occur frequently in this neighbourhood, which is called Bantaran Kali in this book.[1] Several times each year, inhabitants experience small floods that come and go within a day. They also regularly experience medium-sized floods when children can swim in the streets, and, once every few years, large ones that turn the kampong into a mud pool full of drifting waste, building materials, dead cats and chickens. To a certain extent, the inhabitants have grown accustomed to floods. They consider floods a part of life. They are a worrisome part of life because they damage goods, cause disease and make it hard to continue business, but one can even get used to worries. This is reflected in the saying, 'We're familiar with floods' (*banjir sudah biasa*), which is popular in the kampong.

But that does not count for all of the floods. Some are too large to handle. Too sudden. Too devastating. They often lead to the destruction or damage of property. Moreover, they have a negative impact on health. That is not only because strong currents and electrocution can cause injuries or death, but also because floods often pose a high risk of the rapid spread of communicable diseases, such as diarrhea, influenza and skin infections. Additionally, floods may induce severe mental stress and anxiety. Finally, the impact of floods on poor urban livelihoods can be disastrous – for people with informal occupations and no fixed income, the interruption caused by floods can be very costly (Green et al. 1991; Zoleta-Nantes 2002; Blaikie et al. 2003; Few 2003).

Residents never know when these 'sudden floods' (*banjir tiba-tiba*) come, but they are increasing in frequency and severity. There have been at least five of them in the past 15 years, and newspapers often carry scary headlines at the start of the wet season that suggest that another one may again be on its way. The flood for which inhabitants are warned this particular morning might well be such a large, devastating one.

Within minutes, the neighbourhood buzzes with activities. Bags are packed, zippers are pulled, televisions and refrigerators are stored on upper floors, bundles of clothing are attached to ceilings with strings and nails and windows are slammed. Several residents walk around at a fast pace and routinely bang on each and every front door to make sure all of their neighbours are awake and alarmed.

Yusuf (27 years old) is one of the residential volunteers. He feels that it is his task to assist the Jakarta government in helping residents to stay safe during floods. As he has done during former floods, he now instructs his neighbours according to the governmental safety advice that he knows by heart. 'Prepare yourselves for a big flood', he shouts at them. 'Get out of here as soon as you can! It is dangerous to stay inside your house! It might collapse! Quickly evacuate to the safe area!'

Everyone knows what Yusuf means by 'the safe area'. It has become usual during large floods for residential volunteers to gather on higher ground just outside the kampong. They count who is there and who is not, and cook rice and boil eggs on portable gas stoves for hungry flood victims. Later a team of rescue workers and civil servants working for the *kelurahan* (the kampong administration) will arrive to provide evacuees with more support and free facilities, such as a canvas evacuation shelter, public toilets, more food, drinking water, free medication, and a solid roof that protects them from rain.

But this morning, far from all residents make use of the provisions in the shelter. In fact, many of them do not even head in the direction of the safe area, hence disobeying governmental safety advice. Instead, if there is one description that portrays what happens along the riverbanks after the message warning of the risk of flood is spread, then it must be 'heterogeneity'. Some residents evacuate to the governmental shelter, but others clamber on top of their roofs with the help of rope ladders or the knotted hands of family members. Yet others evacuate to provisionary, self-built shelters, while some seem to take no action at all and remain inside their house.

The fact that different people respond to risk in divergent ways is in itself not noteworthy. In fact, 'heterogeneous risk behaviour' is a widely known phenomenon among social scientists. However, as I will discuss below, surprisingly little has been written about the reasons underlying divergent patterns of risk behaviour. My main aim in this book is to try to make sense of people's diverse risk practices and understand which circumstantial and psychological factors underlie them. Through its approach and subject, my study fills a gap left open by several disciplines dealing with the issue of risk behaviour. Before I explain what has hampered the academic explorations of this subject so far, I will make the issue of heterogeneous risk behaviour more concrete by describing in more detail the divergent practices that Yusuf and the other inhabitants of Bantaran Kali exhibited – practices I witnessed when I conducted anthropological fieldwork in the riverbank settlement in 2010 and 2011.

Within-group heterogeneity

The night that my neighbours and I woke up startled from the sound of loud banging on our front doors and the shouted flood alarms, I had been living and working in Bantaran Kali for several months. I had already witnessed several small floods, which came up to my ankles and inundated my house, but never before had I been alarmed for a large flood, like this one. Anxious and as quick as I could, I packed my most valuable belongings in a large backpack and accompanied my direct neighbour Ida, a widow in her forties.

'Come on up!' she shouted at me through a hole in the ceiling. 'You want to stay with me? Hurry, or else you'll get wet! Get ready for the flood!' After I had worked myself up to the rooftop of her house with the help of her self-built ladder, I could see that Ida was busy preparing a private evacuation space of about two square meters for herself and her four children (the youngest was 8 years old at that time, the eldest 13). I knew that Ida had built the tiny shelter herself during past years, from wood that she collected from the river. It was now stacked with her valuables, which would not remain safe downstairs during the flood. Her rice cooker and fan lay on top of a stack of clothing and shoes, furthest away from the side where water might enter.

Ida gasped, seemingly exhausted from her hard work. Drops of sweat ran along her face, but she did not allow herself a rest. She put batteries in a plastic flashlight, then tested the device, turning it on and off again. She carefully placed a paper bag with salted eggs aside – the cheap yet nutritious side dish that is known in Bantaran Kali as 'flood food' (*makanan banjir*). She stuck her birth certificate and identity card in her bra, as well as a little brown envelope filled with 300,000 Indonesian rupiah in cash, money she had saved in anticipation of expenses that usually come along with a flood.

'I am well prepared', said Ida, 'but I am worried nevertheless'. She had reasons to be concerned: earlier floods in the neighbourhood had damaged her house severely and caused injuries, illness and even death among co-residents. One look at the river, flowing a few meters from her house, and she predicted what would happen in the next hours:

> I won't keep dry here. I never do during large floods. My children might get ill from the water and the cold, and I will get scared for sure, because I can't swim, but I am ready to make it through yet another flood. I have learned how to survive all by myself. I have become clever at surviving floods.

But what about Yusuf's advice to evacuate to the government shelter, I asked her. I was planning to go there now; was Ida sure she did not want to join me? Ida shook her head and replied:

> I never make use of the help of the *kelurahan*. In fact, I refuse all help that is offered to me by others. If you are as poor as I am, it is better not to depend on anyone. We never know whether the government will give us aid or whether they will let us down. And even if an ordinary neighbour offers you help, they might want something in return that disadvantages you… That man Yusuf; maybe he helps me today, but tomorrow he might demand a favour in return! People who are as needy as we are in this neighbourhood only give in order to take. Therefore

I never owe anything to anyone. You can go to that shelter if you want, Roanne, but I would rather protect myself against the floods in my own way.

After I had left Ida's place, I learned that other neighbours appeared less confident than Ida that they could take autonomous action to protect themselves against floods.

Yati (34 years old), who lived around the corner from Ida and me, sat quietly on a plastic stool in her living room, cross-legged and seemingly unmoved by the flood alarms. Rain battered against the windows of her dwelling, and a part of her ceramic floor tiles was covered with floodwater that entered her house through cracks in the walls. Unlike Ida, Yati had not set up an evacuation space on the rooftop of her house. Neither had she saved any of the income she earned selling ice cream and cigarettes to other residents in the kampong for use during this flood; nor had she stocked foods, a flashlight, batteries or important documents.

'Are you coming?' I asked Yati when I walked passed her house, and I pointed my finger in the direction of the government shelter. Yati replied: 'No, I never go there during floods'. Instead, she proposed I take a seat in her house, and continued:

> Believe me, waiting for assistance from my house is our best chance to stay safe. All we must do is keep calm and be patient. I'm definitely not evacuating, like the government wants me to do. Instead I will be rescued by another team of rescue workers any time soon. This is how I always survive large floods.

With 'rescue workers', Yati was referring to employees of a local non-governmental organization (NGO), who had helped her to evacuate during former floods as well. When I asked her what she planned to do if the water rose even higher and no helping hand reached out to her in time, Yati laughed and confidently said:

> They will come to this house for sure, because they know that I always need them to survive floods. You just wait here with me and you will see that I am right: soon they will send out a boat to rescue us, and if this house gets damaged during the flood, they will even rebuild it to compensate for my loss. Whenever I suffer after floods, they help me. So all I must do now, is sit here and wait for their help.

Clearly Yati had a very different strategy to handle floods than Ida: the latter tried to find ways to survive a flood autonomously, while Yati acted as if she was completely dependent on external assistance. And both Yati and Ida had a very different way of responding to the flood than Tono (33 years old), who was the third person I met on my way towards the safe shelter.

Tono sweated and panted for breath under the weight of a stack of wood that he carried on his back. 'These are materials to build a shelter', he clarified. In a surprised tone, I asked him why he believed *another* shelter had yet to be built: 'The government is already setting up a big one for all residents; Yusuf and the others are instructing everybody to go there!' Tono explained:

> Yes, but that shelter is not a safe place for me. It's the *government*'s shelter, remember, and the Indonesian government always has a second agenda. No matter what Yusuf told you, don't trust him, he is a friend of the government. You better come and seek refuge in my shelter. It will be a small and simple one, but at least it's safe there.

Studying risk behaviour

One river. One settlement. One flood. Yet the local practices that were exhibited in the face of the coming flood were diverse. Some residents took autonomous and preventive measures; others felt dependent on external aid. Some followed up on government safety advice; others acted against it.

The heterogeneity in risk practices that I observed during my fieldwork in Bantaran Kali is not incidental or arbitrary. Instead, similar patterns of behaviour by the same people arise each and every time the settlement is flooded. The narratives of respondents indicate that riverbank settlers have developed typical ways of handling flood risk. For example, Ida *never* evacuates during large floods, while Tono *always* does – albeit not to the government shelter but instead to a self-built, provisional place of refuge. Yati has waited in her house for help to arrive during *each of* the past large floods, while Yusuf *invariably* assists others in evacuating during floods. My observations of riverbank settlers' behaviour during several floods that took place during my research confirmed that their risk practices are structured along lines of habit and strategy.

And, as noted earlier, these observations are in line with the findings of other scholars, who conducted research on human flood responses in other places of the world. Whether they conducted research in Europe, in Africa or in Asia, their studies all confirm that typically, different people handle flood risk in different ways (Zoleta-Nantes 2002; Few 2003; Grothmann & Reusswig 2006; Gaillard et al. 2008; Harries 2008; Texier 2008; Febrianti 2010).

A similar argument of heterogeneity holds true for human responses to non-natural hazards, such as smoking, drugs, medicines or economic risk. Studies about these types of hazard often emphasize that generally, different people exhibit heterogeneous practices to handling risk (e.g. Ryan 2000, on divergent risk-handling practices of mental health service users; Hair et al. 2009, on heterogeneous risky lifestyles among late adolescents; or Nooteboom 2015, on various behavioural patterns in relation to income and social security).

The question that remains unsolved in all of these studies is: why? If people share a similar risk, what explains the consistent heterogeneity of their responses? Or, linking this question to the cases of flooding in Bantaran Kali, why would Yusuf typically handle flood risk so differently than Ida, Yati or Tono? The social scientific literature on human risk behaviour does not provide an answer to such questions. One important reason for this gap in the academic understanding of human risk behaviour is that the topic of heterogeneity is usually discussed by anthropological and sociological scholars of risk to analyse differences between socioeconomic or cultural *groups* in a given society, not to explain for within-group heterogeneity. Hence, while much work has been done on the collective risk-coping mechanisms of a cultural group or a socioeconomic class in a given society, so far little emphasis has been put on the individual differences in risk behaviour that exist *within* groups.

In this book I want to contribute to the academic understanding of risk behaviour, by examining what brings about heterogeneity of risk practices within a flood-prone riverbank settlement. While my analysis is mainly based on empirical investigations, I have also been inspired by lessons from the literature on risk and risk behaviour. Therefore, in this book I start my exploration with a review of the relevant literature, showing which findings and lessons have served as building blocks for this study. Below I discuss first the two most dominant sociological/anthropological approaches towards risk behaviour, after which I turn to psychological theories, which are typically more interested in individual differences.

Vulnerability approach

An important stream in the sociological literature known as the 'vulnerability approach' has emphasized that contextual economic, social, and political structures limit people's ability to handle hazards – most notably economic deprivation, political marginalization and social isolation. To put that differently: poor and marginalized groups in a society usually have less means and options to cope with natural hazard than do wealthy and powerful residents (Torry 1979; Hewitt 1983; Chambers 1989; Burton et al. 1993; Cannon 1994; Blaikie et al. 2003). Hence, in this stream of literature, differences between people's responses to a risk are explained by the relative level of vulnerability of the cultural or socioeconomic group in which they are embedded. Social structural characteristics, such as gender, age, health, status and disability, ethnicity or race or nationality, and socioeconomic status are typically included in vulnerability studies, as these are considered the main underlying factors of risk-coping mechanisms among cultural or socioeconomic groups. Cultural factors such as caste or religion are also frequently included in vulnerability analyses, as these are believed to shape people's perceptions of risk (Adger 1999; Fordham 1999; Bankoff et al. 2004; Blaikie et al. 2003).

The vulnerability perspective is helpful to recognize structural inequality between socioeconomic groups in Indonesian society, and how these are lopsided by unequal division of risk. For example, a vulnerability analysis exposes that Jakarta's urban poor are not only extremely vulnerable to flood risk, but that they also have relatively few coping options. In Jakarta, 3,5 million slum dwellers live on highly flood-prone riverbanks because housing in safer areas of the city is unaffordable to them. While former large floods in 1996, 2002, 2007 and

2013 have inundated as much as 70 per cent of the city in past years, affecting millions of inhabitants, they occur most frequently in these poor riverbank settlements. Jakarta's poorest neighbourhoods were also affected most severely, as floods caused disease and damaged assets of people that have relatively little means to restore their losses (Caljouw et al. 2005; Schonhardt 2013a; Texier 2008; Vltchek 2013). The last major flood that occurred during the writing of this book was in 2015. The water engulfed large parts of the city, affecting nearly 16,000 people and displacing at least 6,000 (Sentana 2015). But again the poorest neighbourhoods were most severely affected. In the neighbourhood under study, the water level reached two to three meters high, and all houses were damaged by the flood. Many riverbank settlers lost their assets and became ill afterwards.

The above section shows that the impact of people's socioeconomic situation on their vulnerability to risk is undeniable. Nevertheless, my own findings in Bantaran Kali indicate that the vulnerability approach is not helpful to explain the heterogeneous risk practices that are exhibited by different members of 'the urban poor'. The main limitation of vulnerability studies is that they tend to treat a socioeconomic or cultural group as a homogeneous unit full of victims, overlooking internal variation and complexity. Such perspective is unsuitable for research with an explicit interest in within-group heterogeneity, such as the one I present in this book. Perhaps more problematic, even, my experiences in Bantaran Kali taught me that the factors that are typically considered by vulnerability scholars as determining for heterogeneous risk behaviour lose their explanatory strength as soon as they are studied in a research context where levels of wealth and marginalization are relatively equal, such as is the case in the area under study (I describe the research area's socioeconomic characteristics in Chapter 1).

While my study revealed some discernable differences in the ways in which riverbank settlers responded to floods, these differences could not be sufficiently explained by the social structural characteristics that are typically included in vulnerability analyses. They cut across people's income level, religion, ethnic background, gender, age, physical condition and socioeconomic status, pointing instead to psychological factors and individual differences that may seem unrelated to flood risk at first sight, such as people's daily life experiences, their future hopes and dreams, and the different individual opportunities and limitations that are shaped by the unequal economic and political structures in which riverbank settlers live. I will discuss these factors extensively throughout this book.

Cultural approach

The second dominant perspective on risk behaviour in the anthropological/sociological disciplines is known as the cultural approach. It emphasizes cultural adaptations of groups or communities to risk. Studies of risk and disaster that take this approach have revealed how frequent or consistent threats of natural hazards shape communal mechanisms of coping that help groups overcome the challenges of their environment (Oliver-Smith & Hoffman 1999: 3; Gaillard et al. 2007).

For example, research on disaster-prone communities in the Philippines has described architectural adaptation to environmental conditions that communities apply, specific agricultural practices practiced by groups and other types of behaviour that have become characteristic for people's 'cultures of disaster', most notably practices of reciprocity, solidarity, a particular sense of humour and an attitude towards disaster in which it is perceived as 'normal' (Bankoff 2003, 2007; see Lavigne et al. 2008 for similar observations on volcanic hazards in Java, Indonesia; or Dugmore et al. 2012 for an historical analysis of Greenlanders' cultural adaptation to climate changes).

There is no doubt that communities living with natural hazards establish cultural coping mechanisms. One example of such a cultural coping mechanism was mentioned in the beginning of this introductory chapter, when residents were quoted to say that they had become 'familiar with floods'. This popular saying indicates that residents share an attitude towards floods in which these risks have become an expected occurrence in their daily life. If we consider that these people are used to living with the constant threat of floods, it can be argued that floods must be perceived as a 'frequent life experience' (Bankoff 2007: 26). Therefore, in order to take into account people's cultural coping mechanisms with flood risk, in this book floods are regarded a type of risk that is, at least to some extent, 'normalized' (Bankoff 2004: 102, 109; Van Voorst et al. 2015).

Nonetheless, in this book I am most interested in highlighting the heterogeneity in risk practices that also exists within groups. Therefore it is necessary to discuss yet one other important stream of risk literature from which I derived insights relevant to my study, namely the stream that is built upon psychological risk research. Unlike the sociological/anthropological approaches introduced above, the psychological perspective shares my explicit interest in individual differences in risk behaviour; below I elaborate on the three insights that are of most relevance for this study.

Psychological approaches

Compared to sociological or anthropological approaches towards human risk behaviour, psychological risk theories are generally less concerned with circumstantial factors and instead emphasize individual or psychological factors. Most psychological theories indicate that human risk behaviour is partly determined by three main factors: personal life experiences, self-efficacy, and trust in other actors involved in the risk management (Slovic 2000; Bandura 1977a, 1986; Schwarzer & Renner 2000: 187; Paton 2003; Schwarzer & Fuchs 1995).

In psychological risk literature, the term 'personal life experiences' refers to a person's past experiences with a given risk and to the feelings of dread or familiarity that are associated with this risk on the basis of these experiences (Blais & Weber 2006; Olsen & Cox 2001; Slovic 1987). The idea is that the more familiar a risk is, the easier it is for people to cope effectively with it. For example, a riverbank settler who has already experienced many floods and remained safe and well during all of them is likely to cope better with a new flood than would be a newcomer with no experience of floods. This finding of the psychological risk literature suggests that a study of heterogeneous flood risk behaviour should take into account people's personal, past experiences with flood risk.

According to the psychological literature, another aspect of risk behaviour that should be taken into account in a study of heterogeneous risk behaviour is 'self-efficacy beliefs' (Ajzen 1998: 738). Self-efficacy can be defined in terms of perceived personal competence or confidence (e.g. 'I believe I can do X success-fully'.). The notion is closely related to what psychologists call perceived behav-ioural control, which pertains to a person's perceived barriers and difficulties in taking an action (e.g. 'Doing X would be difficult'.) (Abraham et al. 1998: 571). While some scholars distinguish between perceived difficulty and perceived con-trol, others use the term 'self-efficacy' to describe an overall sense of control and ability to succeed, including both personal resources and perceived barriers. For the purposes of this book I use the term in this latter, broad sense, hence meaning an individual's beliefs in one's capabilities to produce desired effects by one's own actions (Bandura 1977b: vii). This finding is particularly relevant for this book because psychologists have repeatedly demonstrated that people's self-efficacy belief in successfully performing an action is predictive of their actual behaviour. If someone's self-efficacy is low, it is likely that he or she remains inactive in the face of risk, convinced that it is impossible for him/her to do anything that might mitigate or take away the risk. In contrast, if a person's self-efficacy is high, the person will likely dare to act and hence the chance of successfully diminishing a risk becomes greater (Bandura 1992, 1997; Schwarzer & Fuchs 1996; Abraham et al. 1998: 571). To concretize that for the case of flood risk: if a riverbank settler believes he or she is capable of staying safe during a flood by taking autonomous action, he or she will probably act according to this belief. But if a riverbank settler perceives the risk of a flood as unsurmountable, not to be mitigated or avoided by any personal action whatsoever, he or she will most likely remain inactive in the face of floods.

The third main factor that underlies human risk behaviour is the trust or the confidence one has in others involved in a particular risk. The function of trust in situations of risk and contingency is widely acknowledged by social scientists studying risk handling (e.g. Folkman & Lazarus 1985; Luhmann 1993, 2000; Giddens 1990; Vaitkus 1990; Möllering 2001; Skinner et al. 2003). To risk some-thing means not knowing for sure what the outcome will be and doing it never-theless. To dare and take a risk, one needs trust in a good outcome. It is in this sense that Sztompka has argued that 'in situations where we have to act in spite of uncertainty and risk…trusting becomes the crucial strategy for dealing with an uncertain and uncontrollable future' (1999: 25).

In psychological studies, 'trusting' is usually described as positive cognitive restructuring or wishful thinking (Folkman & Lazarus 1985; Skinner et al. 2003). In the case of flood risk in Bantaran Kali, this function of trust becomes immedi-ately clear if we think of the communication of a flood risk warning message. If the messenger of such a warning is known and trusted by riverbank settlers, it is probable that residents take the warning seriously and follow the advice given by the messenger. If, however, the messenger is unknown or distrusted by riverbank settlers for another reason, it is probable that the warning is ignored, dismissed as untrue or perceived as misleading. It needs be remarked that the importance of the factor of trust in situations of risk is not just acknowledged by psychologists; several sociological scholars have also discussed this factor in their writings, albeit implicitly or by using a different terminology. These scholars commonly speak of 'confidence' (e.g. Luhmann 1993, 2000; Giddens 1990) or 'fiduciary attitudes' (Vaitkus 1990). My understanding of trust in risky situations resembles what Möllering has defined as 'a state of favorable expectations regarding other people's actions and intentions' (2001: 403).

In line with psychological theories of risk, I am convinced that factors such as personal life experiences, self-efficacy and trust can have enormous impact on people's risk behaviour and that therefore, they need be taken into account in any study on heterogeneous risk behaviour. Yet at the same time, it seems to me that the psychological approach in itself is too limited to define and analyse the within-group heterogeneous risk behaviour that I have observed in Bantaran Kali. That is because psychological approaches tend to elide the fact that people respond to risk while they are embedded in a social context. As the vulnerability approach and the cultural approach have taught us, scholars of risk must be cognizant of the fact that people are limited in their options due to social structures, and they may hold on to specific cultural beliefs or social habits that impact their practices. Furthermore, these approaches suggest that one's behaviour and the process of decision making is not a purely individual matter; it is often affected by interactions and experiences with other actors. For example, people are always involved in social or cultural networks which bring both obligations and advantages.

Psychological approaches pay little attention to such circumstances. Psychological studies are usually undertaken in the laboratory via self-reports and questionnaires, which makes it problematic to apply the theories in natural settings, where social norms and other structural factors affect psychological processes.

Therefore, it is my contention that a study of heterogeneous risk behaviour needs to take into account both the circumstantial and the psychological factors that underlie risk practices. To this extent my study combines psychological ideas about the topics of personal life experiences, self-efficacy and trust with more typical anthropological and sociological analyses of the cultural and socioeconomic circumstances in which riverbank settlers live. This interdisciplinary and holistic approach towards risk allows me to get a sense of individual differences without losing sight of the social context. As the next sections will make clear, such a research approach has high social and academic relevance.

Social relevance

Heterogeneous risk behaviour is a topic that is as complex as it is crucial to investigate, especially in an age when there is a growing academic and political consensus that people, communities and ecosystems face an increasing number of significant natural hazards such as floods, tsunamis and hurricanes as a result of environmental change in coming decades (Bankoff et al. 2004; McLaughlin & Dietz 2008: 99; DeltaDialogues 2008; Marfai et al. 2009; Wisner et al. 2004; Wisner & Caressi-Lopez 2012; World Bank 2011). Due to growing urbanization, these natural hazards will especially put the world's urban citizens at risk (World Bank & United Nations 2010). By 2050, the number of people exposed to natural hazards in large cities could more than double to 1.5 billion, with the largest concentration of at-risk people living in Asia and the Pacific (Kraas 2007; World Bank 2011: 3; United Nations 2014). Asia accounts for two-thirds of the world's urban population, and almost three-quarters of the region's total population live in so-called 'low elevation coastal zones' –areas located less than ten meters above sea level (Emilia 2009; Firman et al. 2011). As the vulnerability literature discussed earlier indicates, it will be the poor and marginalized population groups within these cities that are especially vulnerable to a variety of hazards. Often, their adverse economic situations oblige them to inhabit areas that are threatened by natural hazards or other risks – be they flood plains of rivers, the slopes of volcanoes or earthquake zones, railways or garbage dumps (Van Voorst et al. 2015).

This makes the topic of heterogeneous risk behaviour all the more relevant for policymakers and employees of NGOs who will be involved in future disaster management. Flood disasters in megacities such as Jakarta require large-scale infrastructural structures beyond the capacities of individual disaster victims, or the community (Douglass 2013). Therefore, urban authorities are increasingly concerned with the issues of risk, disaster and coping. This is also the case in Jakarta, where the issue of floods has become an important political concern. Nevertheless, the flood risk intervention programmes that have been developed and implemented by governmental and aid institutions in Jakarta could not prevent tens of Indonesians from dying during recent floods, while hundreds or even thousands fell ill, were injured or became homeless (Caljouw et al. 2005; Texier 2007; Haryanto 2009; Rukmana 2009a; Philip 2013; Schonhardt 2013b).

Most Jakartan politicians involved in flood management hold that these dramas occurred because flood victims often ignore or act against formal safety advice. As one Jakartan policymaker told me about the residents of the riverbank settlement under study: 'Many of them do not follow up on our safety advice. For example, we tell everyone to evacuate, but some stay put in their house or flee to their rooftops. They prefer their own way of responding during floods; we have no idea why!' Hence, according to this politician, victims fall as a consequence of their own obstinate behaviour.

I would like to consider another possible reason for the ineffectiveness of intervention programmes in Jakarta, namely, a lack of understanding about the factors underlying risk behaviour. In my opinion, the major problem that currently hinders effective responses of governmental and nongovernmental aid institutions to floods has to do with the fact that most interventions do not consider nor understand the heterogeneous behaviour of residents coping with flooding.

For aid interventions to be effective for *all* people in a given group, it is important that urban authorities are cognizant of the fact that different people tend to cope with risk in different ways, and for different reasons. Otherwise, the homogenous information that is usually provided in safety advice will only appear relevant to some people, but not to others.

My experiences and conversations with policymakers and NGO employees involved in flood management in Jakarta have led me to believe that heterogeneous risk behaviour is hardly ever taken into account in interventions. For example, during my fieldwork the government, in cooperation with a large NGO, spread an expensive looking, full-colour brochure among different communities living on Jakarta's riverbanks. The brochure contained one piece of safety advice, which was similar to the message Yusuf, whom we briefly met in the beginning of this Introduction, communicated to his neighbours: leave your house and evacuate to a government safety shelter as soon as possible. Staying inside the house is dangerous, so the brochure explained, as the house may collapse or residents may get ill from dirty floodwater entering the house. This information appeared hardly relevant to a majority of riverbank settlers.

During several floods that I myself experienced in my research area, I observed and have defined 82 different risk-handling practices exhibited by riverbank settlers before, during or after flood events. Some prominent examples are 'evacuating to a self-built shelter' (as Tono did); 'building an improvised evacuation shelter on the rooftop' (as Ida did); 'helping others evacuate in the neighbourhood' (as Yusuf did); or 'waiting in the house for help' (as Yati did). In other words, most riverbank settlers already evacuate their house during floods, only they don't always flee to government shelters, but instead to different places.

In line with my own observations in Jakarta, other scholars studying floods in Jakarta also found that riverbank settlers usually evacuate during floods, albeit not always to government shelters but instead to other places of refuge, such as the houses of acquaintances and family members (cf. Texier 2008; Spies 2011; Febrianti 2010). This means that the homogeneous information provided in the brochure was only relevant to a specific, relatively small segment of the targeted population: namely those few people who refused to evacuate and remained inside their house during the flood. For most other residents, however, the warning not to stay put in their house was redundant. Their alternative strategies were not acknowledged in the brochure and, more importantly, it seems that the reason for people's alternative strategies are not understood either. Without taking into account the heterogeneous ways in which different people cope with risk, it is obviously hard – if not impossible – for policymakers and NGO workers to develop and implement effective intervention programmes for risk-prone communities.

This is a highly concerning situation, considering the fact that, of all urban areas at risk worldwide, Jakarta is deemed one of the most vulnerable in terms of exposure to natural hazards (Marfai et al. 2009; Ward et al. 2013). Flooding (*banjir*) of the city's rivers is already one of its main risk problems and the number of floods is expected to increase in the near future. In this sense, the case of Jakarta and its flood-prone riverbank settlements may offer the clearest indication of what is to come in the next decades of ever-increasing natural hazards, and of what needs be done by scholars and urban authorities to help protect the most vulnerable people in society against these threats.

Flooding in Jakarta

In Jakarta, floods are now occurring more often and they are more severe than ever before (Steinberg 2007; DeltaDialogues 2008; Ward et al. 2013). Even in an average year, 10,000 to 15,000 inhabitants are forced to flee from medium-sized floods, but experts are predicting that the severity of floods will increase by about 5 to 10 per cent in the coming years as compared to earlier years. Simulations of possible future flooding events foresee inundations of up to a quarter of the city, thereby threatening the physical and social security of over five million inhabitants (Brinkman & Hartman 2009; Brinkman 2009: 50; Marfai et al. 2014).

Part of Jakarta's flood problem can be explained by its geographical exposure to natural hazards. Jakarta is prone to flooding from coastal tidal flooding, and also from water draining through the city from the hills in the south. About 40 per cent of the city, mainly the most northerly area near the Java Sea, is below sea level. The city is located in a deltaic plain criss-crossed by 13 natural rivers and more than 1,400 kilometres of waterways that were constructed at the orders of the colonial Dutch. Periodic floods were already a common phenomenon during colonial times; however, in recent years the severity and frequency have seriously increased, due to local environmental and infrastructural issues (Brinkman 2009; Caljouw et al. 2005; Kadri 2008).

There are four main reasons for the increase of flood risk. First, rapid urbanization has aggravated the situation over the course of time. In 1811, Jakarta had a population of about 47,000. By the early twentieth century the city had expanded further south, and that number had increased to about 500,000. In 2010, Jakarta had an official city population of almost ten million and a metropolitan area with more than twenty million inhabitants. In recent years the population growth rate has declined, but Jakarta's population is still estimated to increase by about 130,000 to 250,000 per year (World Bank 2011; BPS 2011).[2] These urbanization dynamics lead to more extensive use of the built environment, more garbage clogging the sewerage system, and greater numbers of humans potentially affected.

Second, the city's government services cannot keep up with the demands of the fast-growing population. One problem is that the provision of housing for the poor and lower-middle class continues to be inadequate relative to demand. Skyrocketing land prices and rampant private sector development that is under-regulated has resulted in a booming real estate market that excludes the poor. Consequently, large informal settlements such as the one under study have grown over many years along waterways, natural rivers, sluices and reservoirs, contributing to the pollution and clogging of these flood-prone areas. Another problem is that the city's drainage system has been poorly maintained by the government and hence cannot channel floodwater to the sea fast enough during heavy rains (Sagala et al. 2013). A final example of an area in which government services prove to be largely inadequate is the provision of piped water (Kooy & Bakker 2008: 383). The majority of inhabitants rely on informal suppliers of water (Kooy 2014). More problematic, the lack of piped water is driving large multiuse developments and small residential communities alike to drill wells to access groundwater. This extraction of groundwater is causing areas of Jakarta to sink, particularly in the north of the city. Along with a rising sea level, land subsidence is one of the greatest challenges facing Jakarta and further increases the risk of flooding.

A third cause of increased flooding in Jakarta is related to inadequate city planning or, more precisely, 'corporatization of urban spaces' (Douglass 2013: 10). Since the 1980s, policies have aimed at economic liberalization and attracting of international investment in manufacturing, services and property development (Radoki & Firman 2009: 4). Between 1980 and 2002, almost one-quarter of the land area of Jakarta was converted from non-urban uses (e.g. agriculture, wetlands) to urban uses for industry, commerce and housing (World Bank 2011). In 2004, there were over 306 hotels in Jakarta, as well as at least 1955 large and medium manufacturing companies, 116 department stores, 125 supermarkets and 151 traditional markets (Abidin et al. 2011; Steinberg 2007). The areas of shopping malls significantly increased from 1.4 million m^2 in 2000 to 2.4 million m^2 in 2005 (Firman 2009; Abidin et al. 2011). This strong increase in built-up areas has paralleled a decrease of green and 'open' water catchment areas. While in 1965 green areas still made up more than 35 per cent of the Jakarta region, they nowadays account for only 9.3 per cent of the area (Rukmana 2009b; Firman et al. 2007). Furthermore, megaprojects in Jakarta have pushed low-income residents out of their neighborhoods and into ever more precarious disaster-prone locations, such as flood-prone riverbanks.

Fourth, despite a growth of 5.2 per cent in Indonesia's economy in 2014, income distribution inequality is widening (Trading Economics 2015; Indonesia Investments 2014). Earlier I explained that marginalized and poor inhabitants of urban areas are generally the population groups most vulnerable to natural hazard. This means that at present, a growing, marginalized part of the Jakarta population is becoming increasingly vulnerable to flooding; in order to help them stay safe, it is crucial to understand more about heterogeneous risk behaviour. With this book I hope to contribute to such knowledge.

Academic relevance

Considering academic relevance, one of the main goals of this book is to improve the academic understanding of heterogeneous risk behaviour, by integrating anthropological/sociological and psychological insights. Although it has long been accepted in the social sciences that both social and psychological processes affect the ways in which human actors handle risk and that therefore, both these processes should be taken into account in an adequate analysis of human risk handling (Skinner & Zimmer-Gembeck 2007: 137; Taylor Gooby & Zinn 2006: 408); in practice, most risk research continues to be undertaken by separate disciplines in isolation from each other and results from various disciplines are hardly integrated.

However, there is a growing number of both psychologists and anthropologists/sociologists calling for a unifying, interdisciplinary framework (Eagly & Chaiken 1993; Jessor 1993: 125; Skinner & Zimmer-Gembeck 2007: 137; Taylor Gooby & Zinn 2006: 408). First attempts have recently been made towards this aim (Evans et al. 2012; Van Huy et al. 2013). This book might be regarded as another such attempt.

There are also two other goals of this book that add to its academic relevance. The first is to introduce an analytical framework to define and interpret heterogeneous risk behaviour within communities facing natural hazard. As noted, my focus is on within-group heterogeneity rather than on collective coping systems, as is more common in sociology and anthropology. At the same time, I explained that there is a need to move beyond purely individual, psychological approaches of risk behaviour. In order to expose individual differences while also highlighting patterns of behaviour that exist in Bantaran Kali, in the next chapter I propose a categorization of 'risk styles', which help me to define and interpret heterogeneous flood risk behaviour within Bantaran Kali.

A final aim of this book is to take a bottom-up approach towards risk, instead of the top-down perspective of risk that is applied in most other studies of risk, whether they be sociological, anthropological or psychological. Most often, scholars base the estimation of risk on the point of view of risk experts or other outsiders – not infrequently, on that of the researcher him or herself. This leads to what has been called a 'disaster lens' perspective – an epistemological lens of (mostly Western) social sciences (Bankoff 2001; Heijmans 2009).

A disaster lens perspective typically regards the impact of risk events on daily life as abnormal and irruptive. However, as became clear from this Introduction, for the inhabitants of Bantaran Kali floods have become an expected, frequent and recurring aspect of their daily lives and they have established cultural as well as individual coping mechanisms for handling them. Therefore, as explained earlier, I do not perceive floods as abnormal, unexpected occurrences – which would, in fact, appear as an outsider perspective – but instead as a 'frequent life experience' and a risk that is 'normalized' (Bankoff 2007: 26; Bankoff 2004, p. 102, 109; Van Voorst et al. 2015).

A disaster lens perspective also typically focuses on one single risk under study (the one defined by the researcher as most relevant), while neglecting the impact of other risks and uncertainties in people's lives. In contrast, a bottom-up study of risk departs from the risk perspective of study participants. For my study, this meant that I had to look beyond flood risk, widening the scope of this research towards other 'normalized' hazards that threaten riverbank settlers' well-being.

While I began this project intending to investigate flood risk only, it soon became clear to me that I could not concentrate on a single risk, as floods are by far not the only problem riverbank settlers face – nor are they necessarily their greatest concern. Informants' narratives suggested that they feel threatened not only by the risk of flooding, but also by a whole range of other hazards, such as police raids against illegal food-sellers, social problems such as the abuse of alcohol and drugs in the neighbourhood, violence among competing street gangs and gas explosions in people's houses that lead to fires, and an adverse economic situation which may at any time create or increase poverty-related risks, such as illness or evictions. Of all these risks, people rated the three risks of floods, poverty and eviction as most threatening. It is important to recognize that these risks are interconnected: people's adverse economic situation forces them to live on an illegal and flood-prone riverbank, and floods reproduce or even worsen their financial situation. During interviews and everyday conversations, again and again, these three different types of risk were brought up by people and described as the most pressing for their well-being.

These experiences in the field convinced me that a study that focuses on floods while not taking into account other pressing risks would offer an overly limited and top-down image of my informants' risk experiences. This argument becomes even stronger if we consider that most riverbank settlers exhibit risk practices that are useful not just for floods, but rather for different risks at the same time. For example, 'saving money as a buffer' is a practice that helps people cope with floods, but that is useful also in times of illness or unemployment or after evictions. A similar argument can be made about other risk practices that riverbank settlers commonly exhibit, such as 'socializing with a politician or an NGO employee so that he/she helps my family during difficult times', 'praying to Allah to protect me whenever disaster strikes', or 'lending out money to a family member when he needs it, as to make sure that he/she also helps me in return when I get into financial trouble'. All these practices can and are used by riverbank settlers when they are coping with the covariate risks of floods, poverty and eviction. Clearly, it would be unrealistic to envisage riverbank settlers' risk practices in the face of flood risk as a response to the one, isolated risk under study (in this example, floods). Rather, people's practices in the face of flood risk must be regarded as expressive of the heterogeneous ways in which people balance and overcome the multiple risks that are part of their daily lives.

Therefore, in order to emphasize a bottom-up perspective on risk, I propose that floods in Bantaran Kali must be regarded as part of what I call in this book 'normal uncertainty': a context in which threats such as floods, poverty-related problems and evictions are perceived by people as hazards that are normal and problematic at the same time. I elaborate throughout the chapters on this notion of 'normal uncertainty' with specific examples from my fieldwork, describing how people perceive and handle the different risks that characterize their daily lives.

Structure of the book

Thus far I have presented three ideas that form the spine of this book. Firstly, I offer an interdisciplinary approach to understanding within-group heterogeneous risk behaviour, which is sensitive to anthropological/sociological as well as psychological factors. Second, I take a bottom-up and holistic approach towards risk, instead of the top-down, disaster-lens perspective of risk that is applied in most other studies of risk. This means that, although my main interest remains with flood risk and the way people cope with that particular risk, I also take into account two other pressing risks that characterize daily life in Bantaran Kali: poverty-related risks and eviction. I call this holistic approach a 'normal uncertainty' perspective. Thirdly, I have argued that a categorization of 'risk styles' is useful for highlighting the diverse yet patterned practices and behavioural structures of riverbank settlers – in the next chapter I will introduce an analytical framework to define and interpret heterogeneous risk behaviour within communities facing natural hazard.

Throughout this book, this framework will help me to analyse and describe each of the four most common risk styles in Bantaran Kali. I explore the underlying factors of each of the styles in order to understand what creates the differences between them. In the conclusion of this book, I consider whether the proposed analytical framework is also likely to be useful for future risk research, particularly for systemic comparisons of human responses to natural hazard in other parts of the world. Yet first, in the next chapter, I introduce Bantaran Kali and its residents, and explain how I have conducted fieldwork in the area.

Notes

1 In order to protect the anonymity of my informants, I have chosen to use a fictive name for the research area. Bantaran Kali is the name that the participants of this study came up with. It translates to 'riverbanks'. In consultation with respondents, their names have also been changed.
2 The last formal census was carried out in 2010 by the Indonesian government. It needs, however, to be noted that the official census figures only tell part of the story. How many people actually live in Jakarta is a matter for speculation (McCarthy, n.d.).

References

Abidin, K., Budianta, M., & Farid, H. (2011). Runaway city/leftover spaces. *Inter-Asia Cultural Studies*, 12(4), 475–483.
Abraham, C., Sheeran, P. & Johnston, M. (1998). From health beliefs to self-regulation: theoretical advances in the psychology of action control. *Psychology & Health*, 13(4), 569–591. DOI: 10.1080/08870449808407420.
Adger, W.N. (1999). Social vulnerability to climate changes and extremes in coastal Vietnam. *World Development*, 27(2), 249–269.
Ajzen, I. (1998). *Attitudes, Personality and Behaviour*. Chicago, IL: The Dorsey Press.
Bandura, A. (1977a). Self-efficacy: toward a unifying theory of behavioral change. *Psychological Review*, 84(2), 191–215.
Badan Pusat Statistik (BPS) (2011). *Recent Migration in 1980, 1985, 1990, 1995, 2000, 2005, and 2010*. Retrieved 30 July 2015 from http://www.bps.go.id/linkTabelStatis/view/id/1273.
Bandura, A. (1977b). *Social Learning Theory*. New York: General Learning Press
Bandura, A. (1986). *Social Foundations of Thought and Action*. Englewood Cliffs, New Jersey: Prentice-Hall.
Bandura, A. (1992). Exercise of personal agency through the self-efficacy mechanism. In R. Schwarzer (Ed.), *Self-efficacy: Thought Control of Action* (pp. 3–38). Washington, D.C.: Hemisphere.
Bandura, A. (1997). *Self-Efficacy: The Exercise of Control*. New York: Freeman.

Bankoff, G. (2001). Rendering the world unsafe: Vulnerability as western discourse. *Disasters*, 25(1), 19–35.

Bankoff, G. (2003). Constructing vulnerability: the historical, natural and social generation of flooding in metro Manila. *Disasters* 27(3), 224–238.

Bankoff, G. (2004). In the eye of the storm: the social construction of the forces of nature and the climatic and seismic construction of God in the Philippines. *Journal of Southeast Asian Studies*, 35(1), 91–111.

Bankoff, G. (2007). Living with risk, coping with disasters: hazard as a frequent life experience in the Philippines. *Education About Asia*, 12(2), 26–29.

Bankoff, G., Frerks, G., & Hilhorst, D. (Eds.) (2004). *Mapping Vulnerability: Disasters, Development and People*. London: Earthscan.

Blaikie, P., Cannon, T., Davis, I., & Wisner, B. (2003). *At Risk: Natural Hazards, People's Vulnerability, and Disasters* (2nd ed.). New York: Routledge.

Blais, A.R. & Weber, E.U. (2006). A Domain-Specific Risk-Taking (DOSPERT) scale for adult populations. *Judgment and Decision Making*, 1(1), 33–47.

Brinkman, J. (2009). *Flood Hazard Mapping 2. Overview Main Report*. Delft: DELTARES.

Brinkman, J. & Hartman, M. (2009). *Jakarta Flood Hazard Mapping Framework*. Retrieved from http://www.hkv.nl/documenten/Jakarta_Flood_Hazard_Mapping_Framework_MH.pdf, last accessed 24 October 2015.

Burton, I., Kates, R.W., & White, G.F. (1993). *The Environment as Hazard*. London: Guildford Press.

Caljouw, M., Nas, P.J.M., & Pratiwo, M. (2005). Flooding in Jakarta: towards a blue city with improved water management. *KITLV*, 161(4), 454–484.

Cannon, T. (1994). Vulnerability analysis and the explanation of "natural" disasters. In A. Varley (Ed.), *Disasters, Development and the Environment* (pp. 13–30). Chichester: John Wiley.

Chambers, R. (1989). Editorial introduction: vulnerability, coping and policy. *IDS Bulletin*, 20(2), 1–7.

DeltaDialogues (2008). *The Jakarta DeltaDialogue*. Nijmegen: Royal Haskoning.

Douglass, M. (2013). *The Urban Transition of Environmental Disaster Governance in Asia*. Asia Research Institute Working Paper Series No. 210.

Dugmore, A., McGovern, T., Vesteinsson, O., Arneborg, J., Streeter, R., & Keller, C. (2012). Cultural adaptation, compounding vulnerabilities and conjunctures in Norse Greenland. *Proceedings of the National Academy of Sciences of the United States of America. PNAS*, 109(10), 3658–3663.

Eagly, A.H. & Chaiken, S. (1993). *The Psychology of Attitudes*. Orlando, Florida: Harcourt Brace Jovanovich Inc.

Emilia, S. (2009, December 16). Discourse: oceans, coasts. Our best assets in coping with climate change. *The Jakarta Post*. Retrieved from http://www.thejakartapost.com/news/2009/12/16/discourse-oceans-coasts-our-best-assets-coping-with-climate-change.html, last accessed 24 October 2015.

Evans, K., Schoon, I., & Weale, M. (2012). Life Chances, learning and the dynamics of risk in the life course. In D. N. Aspin, J. Chapman, K. Evans & R. Bagnall (Eds.), *Second International Handbook of Lifelong Learning* (pp. 245–267). Dordrecht, Heidelberg, London, New York: Springer.

Febrianti, F. (2010). *Flood Risk Perception and Coping Mechanism of a Local Community: A Case Study in Part of Surakarta City, Central Java Province, Indonesia*. Unpublished Master's thesis, Gadjah Madah University & University of Twente, Yogyakarta & Enschede.

Few, R. (2003). Flooding, vulnerability and coping strategies. Local responses to a global threat. Progress. *Development Studies*, 3(43), 43–58.

Firman, T. (2009). The continuity and change in mega-urbanization in Indonesia: a survey of Jakarta–Bandung Region (JBR) development. *Habitat International*, 33(4), 327–339.

Firman, T., Kombaitan, B., & Pradono, P. (2007). The dynamics of Indonesia's urbanization. *Urban Policy and Research*, 25(4), 433–454.

Firman, T., Surbakti, I. M., Idroes, I. C., & Simarmata, H. A. (2011). Potential climate change related vulnerabilities in Jakarta: challenges and current status. *Habitat International*, 35(2), 372–378.

Folkman, S., & Lazarus, R. S. (1985). If it changes it must be a process: a study of emotion and coping during three stages of a college examination. *Journal of Personality and Social Psychology*, 48, 150–170.

Fordham, M. (1999). The Intersection of gender and social class in disaster: Balancing resilience and vulnerability. *International Journal of Mass Emergencies and Disasters*, 17(1), 15–36.

Gaillard, J.-C., Liamzon, C.C, & Villanueva, J.D. (2007). 'Natural' disaster? A retrospect into the causes of the late-2004 typhoon disaster in Eastern Luzon, Philippines. *Environmental Hazards*, 7(3), 257–270.

Gaillard, J-C., Pangilinan, M., Rom Cadag, J., & Le Masson, V. (2008). Living with increasing floods: insights from a rural Philippine community. *Disaster Prevention and Management*, 17(3), 383–395.

Giddens, A. (1990). *The Consequences of Modernity*. Cambridge: Polity Press.

Green, C.H., Tunstall, S.M., & Fordham, M.H. (1991). The risks from flooding: Which risks and whose perception? Disasters, 15(3), 227–236.

Grothmann, T. & Reusswig, F. (2006). People at risk of flooding: Why some residents take precautionary action while others do not. *Natural Hazards*, 38(1–2), 101–120.

Hair, E. C., Park, M,J., Thomson, J,L., & Moore, K.A. (2009). Risky behaviors in late adolescence: co-occurrence, predictors and consequences. *Journal of Adolescent Health*, 45(3), 253–261.

Harries, T. (2008). Feeling secure or being secure? Why it can seem better not to protect yourself against a natural hazard. *Health, Risk and Society*, 10(5), 479–490.

Haryanto, U. (2009, November 19). Most money thrown at Jakarta flooding only going down the drain. *The Jakarta Globe*. Retrieved from http://www.thejakartaglobe.com/archive/most-money-thrown-at-jakarta-flooding-only-going-down-the-drain, last accessed 24 October 2015.

Heijmans, A. (2009). *The Social Life of Community-Based Disaster Risk Reduction: Origins, Politics and Framing* (Benfield Hazard Research Centre Working Paper). Retrieved from https://www.ucl.ac.uk/abuhc/resources/working_papers2, last accessed 24 October 2015.

Hewitt, K. (1983). *Interpretation of Calamity: From the Viewpoint of Human Ecology*. Boston: Allen.

Indonesia Investments (2014). *Higher Gini Ratio Shows Indonesia's Widening Income Distribution Inequality*. Retrieved 30 July 2015 from http://www.indonesia-investments.com/nl/news/todays-headlines/higher-gini-ratio-shows-indonesias-widening-income-distribution-inequality/item1526.

Jessor, R. (1993). Successful adolescent development among youth in high-risk settings. *American Psychologist*, 48(2), 117–126.

Kadri, T. (2008). Flood defense in Bekasi City, Indonesia. Flood recovery, innovation and response. *WIT Transactions on Ecology and the Environment*, 118(1), 133–148.

Kooy, M. & Bakker, K. (2008). Technologies of government: constituting subjectivities, spaces, and infrastructures in colonial and contemporary Jakarta. *International Journal of Urban and Regional Research*, 32(2), 375–391

Kooy, M. (2014). Developing informality: Jakarta's urban waterscape. *Water Alternatives*, 7(1), 232–243.

Kraas, F. (2007, April). Megacities and global change in East, Southeast and South Asia. *Asien: The German Journal on Contemporary Asia*, 103, 9–23.

Lavigne, F., Coster de, B., Juvin, N., Flohic, F., Gaillard, J.C., Texier, P., Morin, J. & Sartohadi, J. (2008). People's behaviour in the face of volcanic hazards: perspectives from Javanese communities, Indonesia. *Journal of Volcanology and Geothermal Research*, 172(3–4), 273–287.

Luhmann, N. (1993). *Risk: A Sociological Theory*. New York: A. de Gruyter.

Luhmann, N. (2000). Familiarity, confidence, trust: problems and alternatives. In D. Gambetta (Ed.), *Trust: Making and Breaking Cooperative Relations* (pp. 94–107). Oxford: University of Oxford Press.

Marfai, M.A., Sekaranom, A.B. & Ward, P.J. (2014). Community responses and adaptation strategies toward flood hazard in Jakarta, Indonesia. *Natural Hazards,* 75(2), 1127–1144.

Marfai, M.A., Yulianto, F., Hizbaron, D. R., Ward, P., & J. Aerts. (2009). *Preliminary Assessment and Modeling the Effects of Climate Change on Potential Coastal Flood Damage in Jakarta.* Yogyakarta & Amsterdam: Gadjah Mada University & VU University.

McCarthy, P. (n.d.). *Urban Slums Reports: The Case of Jakarta. Understanding Slums: Case Studies for the Global Report on Human Settlements.* Retrieved from http://www.ucl.ac.uk/dpu-projects/Global_Report/pdfs/Jakarta.pdf, last accessed 24 October 2015.

McLaughlin, P. & Dietz, T. (2008). Structure, agency and environment: toward an integrated perspective on vulnerability. *Global Environmental Change,* 18(1), 99–111.

Möllering, G. (2001). The nature of trust: from Georg Simmel to a theory of expectation, interpretation and suspension. *Sociology,* 35(2), 403–420.

Nooteboom, G. (2015). *Forgotten People: Poverty, Risk and Social Security in Indonesia, the Case of the Madurese.* Leiden: Brill.

Oliver-Smith, A. & Hoffman, S. (Eds.). (1999). *The Angry Earth: Disaster in Anthropological Perspective.* New York: Routledge.

Olsen, R.A. & Cox, C.M. (2001). The influence of gender on the perceptions and response to investment risk: the case of professional investors. *Journal of Psychology and Financial Markets,* 2(1), 29–36.

Paton, D. (2003). Disaster preparedness: a social-cognitive perspective. *Disaster Prevention and Management,* 12(3), 210–216.

Philip, B. (2013). Jakarta faces up to a high flood-risk future. *The Guardian.* Retrieved from http://www.theguardian.com/world/2013/feb/05/jakarta-floods-rising-sea-levels, last accessed 24 October 2015.

Radoki, C. & Firman, T. (2009). *Case Study Prepared for Revisiting Urban Planning: Global Report on Human Settlements 2009.* Retrieved 30 July 2015 from http://www.unhabitat.org/grhs/2009.

Rukmana, D. (2009a, February 13). *Jakarta Annual Flooding in 2009* [Weblog comment]. Retrieved from http://indonesiaurbanstudies.blogspot.nl/2009/02/jakarta-annual-flooding-in february.html.

Rukmana, D. (2009b, February 28). The best way to stem flooding. *The Jakarta Post.* Retrieved from http://www.thejakartapost.com/news/2009/02/28/the-best-way-stem-flooding.html, last accessed 24 October 2015.

Ryan, T. (2000). Exploring the risk management strategies of mental health service users. *Health, Risk & Society,* 2(3), 267–282.

Sagala, S., Lassa, J., Yasaditama, H. & Hudalah, D. (2013). *The Evolution of Risk and Vulnerability in Greater Jakarta: Contesting Government Policy in Dealing with a Megacity's Exposure to Flooding. An Academic Response to Jakarta Floods in January 2013* (Institute of Resource Governance and Social Change Working Paper No. 2). Retrieved from http://irgsc.org/pubs/wp/IRGSCWP002jakartaflood.pdf, last accessed 24 October 2015.

Saksono, B. (2012). 2012 – 2014 PROJECT: Phase I of Ciliwung normalisation needs Rp 6 trillion. *Investor Daily.* Retrieved from www.indii.co.id/index.php/en/news-publication/weekly-infrastructure-news/2012-2014-project-phase-i-of-ciliwung-normalisation-needs-rp-6-trillion, last accessed 24 October 2015..

Schonhardt, S. (2013a, February 20). After disaster, governor faced with challenge of keeping Jakarta dry. *New York Times.* Retrieved from http://www.nytimes.com/2013/02/21/world/asia/flooding-tests-jakarta-governor-joko-widodo.html?_r=0, last accessed 24 October 2015.

Schonhardt, S. (2013b, January 24). *Jakarta's Floods Painful for All, More Enduring for Some* [Weblog comment]. Retrieved from http://sschonhardt.com/2013/01/24/jakartas-floods-painful-for-all-more-enduring-for-some, last accessed 15 September 2015.

Schwarzer, R. & Fuchs, R. (1995). Changing risk behaviors and adopting health behaviors: the role of self-efficacy beliefs. In A. Bandura (Ed.), *Self-Efficacy in Changing Societies* (pp. 259–288). New York: Cambridge University Press.

Schwarzer, R. & Fuchs, R. (1996). Self-efficacy and health behaviors. In M. Conner & P. Norman (Eds.), *Predicting Health Behavior: Research and Practice with Social Cognition Models* (pp. 163–196). Buckingham, UK: Open University Press.

Schwarzer, R. & Renner, B. (2000). Social-cognitive predictors of health behavior: action self-efficacy and coping self-efficacy. *Health-Psychology,* 19(5), 487–495.

Sentana, I.M. (2015). Jakarta floods displace thousands. *The Wall Street Journal.* Retrieved 30 July 2015 from http://blogs.wsj.com/indonesiarealtime/2015/02/10/jakarta-floods-displace-thousands/.

Skinner, E. A. & Zimmer-Gembeck, M. J. (2007). The development of coping. *Annual Review of Psychology,* 58, 119–144.

Skinner, E., Edge, K., Altman, J., & Sherwood, H. (2003). Searching for the structure of coping: a review and critique of category systems for classifying ways of coping. *Psychological Bulletin,* 129, 216–269.

Slovic, P. (1987). Perception of risk. *Science,* 236(4799), 280–285.

Slovic, P. (2000). *Perception of RISK.* London: Earthscan.

Spies, M. (2011). *Deconstructing Flood Risks. A Livelihood and Vulnerability Analysis in Jakarta, Indonesia.* Unpublished Master's thesis. Free University, Berlin.

Steinberg, F. (2007). Jakarta: environmental problems and sustainability. *Habitat International,* 31(3-4), 354–365.

Sztompka, P. (1999). The idea of trust. In P. Sztompka (Ed.), *Trust. A Sociological Theory* (pp 18–41). Cambridge: University Press.

Taylor Gooby, P. & Zinn, J. (2006). Current directions in risk research: re-invigorating the social? *Risk Analysis,* 26(2), 397–411.

Texier, P. (2007, June 22). Les inondations de février 2007 dans les kampung pauvres de Jakarta [The 2007 floods in poor kampongs in Jakarta]. Retrieved from http://echogeo.revues.org/905, last accessed 24 October 2015.

Texier, P. (2008). Floods in Jakarta: when the extreme reveals daily structural constraints and mismanagement. *Disaster Prevention and Management,* 17(3), 358–372.

Torry, W.I. (1979). Hazards, hazels and holes: a critique of the environment as hazard and general reflections on disaster research. *Canadian Geographer,* 23(4), 368–383.

Trading Economics (2015). *Indonesia GDP Growth Rate 2005-2015.* Retrieved 30 July 2015 from http://www.tradingeconomics.com/indonesia/gdp-growth.

United Nations (2014). *Asia-Pacific report: World's most disaster prone region experiences three-fold rise in deaths.* Retrieved 30 July 2015 from http://www.un.org/apps/news/story.asp?NewsID=49642#.Vbo8F6PCSUk.

Vaitkus, S. (1990). *How Is Society Possible? Intersubjectivity and the Fiduciary Attitude as Problems of the Social Group.* Dordrecht: Kluwer Academic Publishers.

Van Voorst, R., Wisner, B., Hellman, J., & Nooteboom, G. (2015). Introduction to the 'risky everyday'. Editorial. *Disaster Prevention and Management,* 24 (4), 430–433.

Van Huy, N., Dunne, M.P., & Debattista, J. (2013). Modeling predictors of risky drug use behavior among male street laborers in urban Vietnam. *Public Health,* 13(1), 453–570.

Vltchek, A. (2013). *Jakarta's Killer Floods and the Elites* [Weblog comment]. Retrieved from http://www.counterpunch.org/2013/01/25/jakartas-killer-floods-and-the-elites, last accessed 24 October 2015.

Ward, P.J., Pauw, W.P., van Buuren, M.W., & Marfai, A. (2013). Governance of flood risk management in a time of climate change: the cases of Jakarta and Rotterdam. *Environmental Politics,* 22(3), 518–536.

Wisner, B. & Caressi-Lopez, A. (2012). *Disaster Management: International Lessons in Risk Reduction, Response and Recovery.* London: Earthscan.

Wisner, B., Blaikie, P., Cannon, T., & I. Davis. (2004). *At Risk. Natural Hazards, People's Vulnerability and Disasters* (2nd ed.). London and New York: Routledge.

World Bank & United Nations (2010). *Natural Hazards, UnNatural Disasters: The Economics of Effective Prevention.* Retrieved from http://www.gfdrr.org/sites/gfdrr.org/files/nhud/files/NHUD-Overview.pdf, last accessed 15 September 2015.

World Bank (2011). *Resettlement Policy Framework (RPF).* Jakarta Urgent Flood Mitigation project (JUFMP). Jakarta: Jakarta Capital City Government & World Bank.

Zoleta-Nantes, D.B. (2002). Differential impacts of flood hazards among the street children, the urban poor and residents of wealthy neighborhoods in metro Manila, Philippines. *Mitigation and Adaptation Strategies for Global Change,* 7(3), 239–266.

1   Doing research in Bantaran Kali

Conducting long-term anthropological fieldwork in the very poor, unregistered and flood-prone neighbourhood of Bantaran Kali had the advantage that it offered me highly qualitative insights. Living along the riverbanks enabled me to study people in their own risky living environment. I became familiar with the riverbank settlers (as they became used to my presence), and was able to co-experience some of the risks that threaten them in their daily lives. My life and work in Bantaran Kali was often as insightful as it was challenging. Perhaps the greatest challenge for me to overcome was to get access to the research area; another one was to establish relations of trust with the inhabitants. In this chapter I discuss these challenges and explain how I have dealt with them, after which I present a section on the specific methods that I have used throughout my fieldwork. Finally, I elaborate on the concept of risk styles and introduce an analytical framework to define and interpret heterogeneous risk behaviour.

Getting there

Had it not been for my unexpected meeting with Rio, a teenage street singer (*pengamen*) and an inhabitant of Bantaran Kali, I might not have been able to conduct an anthropological study along the riverbanks at all.

Rio and I met in the bus, a few weeks after I had arrived in Jakarta to start this research project. At that point in time, I was still trying to decide where to pursue my research. The aim of my study directed me towards a flood-prone, urban research area. Before fieldwork started, I had collected information about the most flood-prone neighbourhoods in Jakarta with the help of newspaper articles, academic literature and Skype interviews with experts in the field. I had learned that the most flood-prone areas were also the city's poorest neighbourhoods, and that they were generally considered 'illegal', as inhabitants generally own no legal documents for their houses or land. Hence, in theory, I knew exactly where to go. Only in practice, it appeared that it was not easy for a Western, female visitor to Indonesia to autonomously access these most marginalized communities in the city.

Despite my research permit, none of the government officials I interviewed was able or willing to help me to gain access. In fact, they consistently advised *against* pursuing my research in the neighbourhoods that I had planned to visit, warning me that these would be unsafe locations for me to enter. Riverbank settlers were overtly described as criminals and thieves; the riverbanks were called dangerous. Government officials would typically tell me: 'In slums like that, you will be harassed. Besides, you will be flooded all the time! Why would you want *that?*' Although I tried to explain to the government officials that actually, co-experiencing floods was exactly what I needed to do for this research, I soon came to realize that my attempts to convince them were futile. Jakartan officials would not help me get access to the riverbanks, not just because they were concerned about my safety, but perhaps even more because they felt embarrassed about the idea of me entering these poor areas of their city. Slums did not fit the image of the modern world city that they aspired Jakarta to be. To them, Jakarta's overcrowded riverbanks were spots that needed to be cleaned, or at least remain far out of sight of visiting foreigners.

I changed strategy, and decided to explore the flood-prone areas in Jakarta without the approval or help of authorities, using public transport and a city map. But I soon learned that the government officials weren't the only ones who disliked the idea of me working in riverbank settlements – many of the residents I met after entering their neighbourhoods appeared uneager to participate in my study as well.

Even though they were by no means aggressive or overtly disapproving of me, there certainly was a sense of distrust between us. All riverbank settlers I spoke to seemed afraid that I worked for the government, and that my data would be used to justify slum clearance or would have other negative consequences for interviewees. As a result of this sense of distrust, the residents that I autonomously approached would usually politely listen to my introduction, but then quickly cut off the conversation and head back to their daily lives, indicating that I should do so too. My questions about whether it would be possible for me to live among them for a while to learn more about floods and kampong life were consistently ignored or laughed away.

On the afternoon I met Rio, I was no longer sure I would be able to conduct the type of research I had designed beforehand. As I had done each day before, I had stepped into the bus that morning, determined to spend yet another day of exploring potential research areas, but this time my hopes were low.

Until I unexpectedly came across a boy named Rio. He entered the bus in which I was sitting and tried to make some money by singing songs for the passengers. He sang me a *dangdut* song and after I got out of the bus together with him, I bought him a coffee in return in a street kiosk. We talked about life in Jakarta and Dutch soccer players, my research plans, his parents who had both passed away and my diseased grandfathers. After three hours of talking and a shared plate of fried rice, he bluntly offered to take me to the neighbourhood in which he lived, not in a house but on the streets. 'That neighbourhood is extremely flood-prone', I said, recognizing its name from several newspaper articles that had reported on floods in the city. During several recent floods, the Jakarta media published images of its kampong residents wading through the water. In a rather unimpressed tone, Rio agreed: 'Yeah, we have floods all the time. We have so many of them that we already have found smart ways to protect ourselves against them'.

Five hours later, after Rio had made enough money for the day, he led me through the narrow hallways of one of the most flood-prone and poorest 'illegal' neighbourhoods of Jakarta: my research area, Bantaran Kali.

Introduction to Bantaran Kali

My first impression of Bantaran Kali consists not of images but rather of smells and sounds. That is because I entered the neighbourhood for the first time after dark, led there by Rio. I had lost my sense of location and direction during the long trip that Rio and I had made to get from the city center to Bantaran Kali. I remembered that we had taken a public bus, then a smaller one, then yet a smaller one, then a motor taxi, and finally we had walked for about ten minutes before arriving in the riverbank settlement that Rio had called 'home' throughout our conversation.

The kampong had hardly any lighting, so all I could recognize were the vague shadows of people in between food carts and small houses (from 2 × 3 up to 3 × 5 meters), made from wood, plywood, bamboo or cement. The houses were built close together side by side and stacked on top of each other, from the riverside to tens of meters further away from the bank. Rio told me that the residents share six public toilets and use shared or individually installed groundwater pumps. I also learned that there is no piped water in the kampong, nor is there a sewage system or a regulated garbage disposal system. 'Most garbage is thrown in the river', Rio explained, 'and most families use the river as a public toilet or washing place'. From the literature, I knew that due to this and other urban usage of the water, the river had become contaminated and smelly.

It was this smell that struck me most during my first visit to Bantaran Kali. Following Rio in the dark to the part of the street where he usually spends the night, I was overwhelmed by my unexpected arrival in a potential research area; but, most of all, I was affected by the intense experiences attacking my senses: a mixture of the strong odour of the river with the smell of garbage and motor oil, the feeling of the hands of the curious street children who had come out to accompany us during our walk and now one by one touched my white skin, the warm glow that came from small fires under cooking stoves. While walking, Rio shouted out to residents that he had brought a new friend along.

I could not see their physical reactions to that news. Trying to keep up with his pace, I could only make out some excited voices and questions plied to Rio about me. We entered the shack where Rio and five other homeless youngsters in Bantaran Kali sleep, and soon more people joined us inside. Men, women, children and the elderly sat down in a circle around us, demanding to know who the strange visitor was, and what I was doing in their neighbourhood. I tried my best to answer their questions and introduced myself as a researcher interested in getting to know life in a riverbank settlement. The circle of listeners immediately passed my explanations on to other arrivals who had in the meantime gathered outside. Yet more people entered – apparently they had been told by others to come and talk to me. The kampong leader joined the group, accompanied by his wife and children. He told me a few stories about the neighbourhood – the best food sold in the main street, the problem of flooding and how best to catch cockroaches to remove them from one's house. Before I dared to take out my notebook, the conversation had already turned to the Netherlands and my personal situation. Are there good dams in the Netherlands to protect residents from floods? Can you buy rice in the Netherlands? What does it cost per kilo? Are my parents still alive and in good health? Do children in the Netherlands sing in buses as well? Was I planning to adopt Rio? Or marry him? Why was my nose shaped in such a sharp way, did I have a nose job? Why was I so skinny, did I eat enough?

My positive answer to this latter question was hardly convincing – despite my polite refusal, food was brought in at this point, and I was ordered to eat a meal of rice and tofu before the conversation could continue. The atmosphere remained excited, but also had become cheerful by this time. Residents laughed and told jokes amongst themselves, and Rio and his friends were singing more *dangdut* songs. One by one, people left the shack and headed for bed. I stayed overnight in the shack of the street children and spent the next day there as well to interview neighbours. On my second evening in Bantaran Kali, I again met the kampong leader to ask him whether I could stay in the neighbourhood for a longer period of time to pursue my research; he kindly gave his permission.

Rio helped me to rent a small dwelling from inhabitants for a local rental price. It was located a few meters from the river and built from asbestos, wood and cement. The owners of the house used my rental money (which I paid, on their demand, in advance for the full year) to build themselves a flood shelter on top of what was now 'my' home. After settling in, I slowly started to get to know Bantaran Kali.

Bantaran Kali

Bantaran Kali is located on the border of East and South Jakarta, squeezed in between a railway and the banks of a branch of the Ciliwung River, the largest river in Jakarta. The Ciliwung has a length of approximately 476 square kilometres and runs downhill from Mt Pangrango in Puncak to the river mouth on the coast of Java in north Jakarta, passing by the cities of Bogor and Depok and crossing the provincial administrative regions of the Province of West Java and of Jakarta.

The Ciliwung riverbanks have been populated at least since the fourth century; the mouth of the river was instrumental in the founding of Jakarta. It functioned as a port, initially for the Indianized Kingdom of Tarumanagara, later for the Kingdom of Sunda and the sultanate of Banten. From the sixteenth century, it was used by European traders, who described the river as a 'paradise in the tropical hemisphere'. To them, the Ciliwung was beautiful, relatively wide and useful, as it allowed small boats to transport merchandise within the downstream area (Batavia 2002; History of Jakarta 2011).

It seems improbable that these traders would still speak in positive terms about the river, had they seen it in its current state. From the twentieth century, human settlement started to increase extremely rapidly and the river environment was severely impacted. While in 1970, only 33 per cent of the river basin was used for human settlement, industrial estate and trade services, by 2000 this percentage had nearly doubled. These dynamics were paralleled with worsening water quality of the Ciliwung River (Fachrul et al. 2007).

At present, approximately 3.5 million people have come to live along the banks of the Ciliwung. Of them, 759 have settled in the area under study (or 232 households, counted by the number of household heads (*Kepala Keluarga, KK*). The first inhabitants of Bantaran Kali settled down in the area in the 1950s and 60s after they found work nearby. Hired by Indonesia's Railway Corporation, these settlers were paid to construct railways and a large storage building in this part of Jakarta. The work would take nearly ten years. More and more construction workers were hired during this period, and most of them built their houses along the riverbanks. The neighbourhood 'Bantaran Kali' was established – and it would grow fast. Along with settlement came trade: a large night market developed right across the neighbourhood, which again attracted newcomers to Bantaran Kali. Many of them had travelled from Java's rural provinces to Jakarta, looking for a better livelihood in the capital city, and found work on the market of Bantaran Kali.

At present, about half of the inhabitants of Bantaran Kali are grandchildren and children of the railway construction workers. These *orang Betawi* or *orang asli* were born in Jakarta and they have either built their houses themselves on a vacant area of land or inherited it from former generations. The other half of Bantaran Kali's inhabitants consists of first- or second-generation newcomers (*pendatang*). They generally live in houses that are built and owned by *orang Betawi* and pay monthly rent to them. Most of them originate from the countryside in Central or East Java, while some come from other islands, such as Sumatra or Aceh. The large majority of *pendatang* has been living in Jakarta for ten years or longer; only a very small minority moved into Bantaran Kali less than five years ago – mostly youngsters, who have come to live with a family member.

As diverse as their ethnic backgrounds may be, most residents in the kampong share their Islamic religion. Over 95 per cent of both the *orang asli* and the *pendatang* are Muslim; the rest are either Catholic or Protestant. Another thing inhabitants have in common is the way they earn a livelihood. A large majority of both the natives and newcomers sell food or goods on the market or streets surrounding the neighbourhood; a small group works as motor taxi drivers (*ojek*), chicken butchers (*ayam potok*) or broom makers (*tukang sapu*). As was already noted in the Introduction to this book, natives and newcomers also form a rather homogenous group with respect to important vulnerability indicators, such as levels of education or income, citizenship status, and the levels of material vulnerability of their houses towards floods. I briefly elaborate on each on these vulnerability factors in the next section, which allows me to sketch the socioeconomic characteristics of my research area while also providing insights into the most pressing risks and problems that shape people's 'normal uncertainty'.

Normal uncertainty in Bantaran Kali

On average, residents of Bantaran Kali earn the equivalent of 3 to 5 US dollars a week, which is just enough to pay for housing costs and provide family members with food and clothing, but not enough to accumulate much money, which is problematic in case an emergency arises. There are several common, poverty-related risks that threaten the well-being of riverbank settlers. Teenage pregnancies or drug abuse are common fears for many impoverished families, not just because of the emotional aspects of these events, but mainly because of the possibility of high financial costs for family members. Similarly, people often worry about getting ill because of the possibility of high medical finances. Just to indicate how common these poverty-related risks are in Bantaran Kali: during my fieldwork, I attended 16 funerals. Fourteen of these were of riverbank settlers who had died of diseases; two others involved overdoses. All of their families struggled financially with both the financial demands of treatment as well as with the costs of the funeral. In some cases, the family was not able to pay for a funeral at all, and the deceased was buried not in a costly cemetery but in a hole in the ground next to a family member's house in the countryside.

Floods are, obviously, another major problem in people's lives. As noted earlier, newcomers and natives live mingled and mixed throughout the neighbourhood. Some live right next to the river, others a few meters away; but no one lives far enough from the river to stay dry during floods. Whenever the kampong flooded during my fieldwork, all houses were inundated and the water level reached a relatively equal height everywhere in the neighbourhood. These floods thus worsened the economic situation of the riverbank settlers, which in turn increased their vulnerability.

The 'illegal' status of inhabitants of Bantaran Kali creates yet another risk: that of eviction. As part of an enormous flood-prevention program called *normalisasi Ciliwung* (normalization of the Ciliwung river), the government plans to deepen and widen the Ciliwung River and clear its banks of settlements in the nearby future. Consequently, the houses of over 70,000 slum dwellers will be evicted over the coming years. These people will be displaced or forcibly resettled, including the large majority – if not all – informants of this study (Muhammadi 2013). At the time of writing this book in mid-2015, evictions had already begun in the north and east of Jakarta. As these and future evictees do not enjoy the right of legal access to housing, it is expected that many of them will not be compensated, or properly compensated, after their houses have been demolished (Haryanto 2009, 2010). Critical voices in the media and social sciences say that the flood control campaign is little more than cover for the forced removal of squatters (e.g. McCarthy n.d.).

This criticism refers to the fact that evictions are rather common in Jakarta: for example, urban squatters are often evicted from areas where the government plans to build new shopping malls and business offices (Human Rights Watch 2006: 10; Mariani 2003). What is certain is that the present flood-control campaign of the government puts riverbank settlers at risk of losing their houses and often their livelihoods as well.

Even though residents of Bantaran Kali (and this counts for *orang Betawi* as well as for *pendatang*) possess no written ownership documents to prove they own the houses and land on which they live, most of them believe that they have some sort of land rights, because of their acquired user's rights, or because of the fact that nearly all residents pay yearly taxes for land and buildings to the Jakarta government (*Pajak Bumi dan Bangunan, PBB*). Besides, many of them also pay for government-provided electricity in their houses, which increases their sense of being a rightful dweller. As a result, most riverbank settlers feel that their settlement is legitimate; hence, they are convinced that it would be unjust to evict them. At the same time, however, most riverbank settlers indicate that they deem it quite possible that the city government will some time soon dismiss or deny their rights and pursue evictions.

In Bantaran Kali, the prospect of eviction creates tangible concern and uncertainty. This became notable throughout my fieldwork. For example, many inhabitants habitually carry a tax-payment receipt in their pocket, which, they hope, will be able to help them prove, in cases of emergency, that they possess land rights. And when a helicopter flew above us neighbours remarked that it might be a government helicopter measuring the land in preparation for clearance. Moreover, many respondents indicated in interviews or informal conversations with me that they have regular nightmares about the upcoming eviction, or that they often worry about it during the daytime. Feelings of uncertainty and distrust towards the city government as well as to external actors associated with the government were also frequently expressed.

The next section of this chapter will discuss the topic of (dis)trust in relation to risk and uncertainty in Bantaran Kali. The issue of trust is not only important to discuss here because it influences people's risk behaviour, as became clear above, but also because people's perceptions of trust and distrust affected this research. In order to explore deeper the role that trust plays in situations of risk and uncertainty, below I offer three examples of issues of risk and distrust that I encountered in Bantaran Kali.

Establishing trust

The first example concerns the distrust that many residents of Bantaran Kali initially felt against me. Despite Rio's friendly introduction, many riverbank settlers that I tried to talk to were initially afraid that the information provided by them would be used against them. This seemed an understandable concern, especially considering the fact that we often discussed topics that are considered sensitive in Indonesia, such as illegality and social inequality. Whenever such topics came up in conversations during my first weeks of fieldwork, people would typically try to change the topic, or politely refuse to answer any further questions. Of course I tried to explain again and again that I was not working for the government but instead for a Dutch university and that I would protect their anonymity in all my writings, but the sense of distrust pertained and this was reflected in people's behaviour towards me. Being open to me was clearly regarded by most people as 'risky'.

This opinion radically altered, however, on the night a devastating fire occurred in Bantaran Kali, about three months after my fieldwork had begun. The fire broke out because of a short circuit. Over 500 people lost their valuables and homes, and one man died after he tried to save his children's school diplomas from his burning house. I spent my night and the following days as my neighbours did: desperately trying to save people's goods by carrying them away to safe places, cooking rice for victims, and talking about the trauma of the fire over and over again. However disastrous this fire was for the residents, it offered me the opportunity to become a co-resident, rather than just a visiting, untrustworthy *bule* (white person).

After the fire, it appeared to me that people started to treat me differently. They started to visit me in my house, looking for a chat or a listening ear about their daily experiences and concerns. They invited me to join them during workdays or trips to the market, where I was often proudly introduced as their 'adoption child' (*anak adopsi*). Several residents took it on as their task to teach me about their daily lives: women taught me how to wash and cook, men taught me how to play cards and children laughed at my awkward Indonesian accent and taught me slum slang. After a few months, I spent my time in Bantaran Kali largely with the following routine: in the mornings, I listened to the Imam's prayer in the local mosque, stood in line in the street for a bowl of porridge (*bubur*) from one of the local vendors and helped children to fetch water from the pump or joined women going to the local market to buy groceries. During the daytime, I chit-chatted with neighbours, joined men as well as women in selling their snacks or goods in the street, or accompanied housewives and the elderly who stayed in the kampong to look after small children. In the evenings, I often taught English to interested local teenagers and adults or just sat on the doorstep of my room or that of someone else's overhearing gossip or sharing anecdotes about daily life with other residents. On weekends, I joined newcomers going back to their families in other kampongs, travelling on motors, in trucks or on local buses. I attended many local events, such as funerals and weddings, observed several local elections, and was often given permission to participate in communal prayers, neighbourhood meetings and *arisan*. During these activities, people generally spoke more openly, and this often meant rather negatively, about the government. The huge difference between their initial hesitance to interact with me, and their later friendship and cooperation with me, made clear to me the general distrust that people feel towards the government, and towards outsiders in general.

Here is a second example of how issues of risk, uncertainty and (dis)trust are related. When I fell ill halfway through fieldwork from what appeared to be a combination of various bacterial stomach infections and enteritis, my neighbours did not allow me to go to a hospital. Instead, they tried to cure me with traditional healing practices and medicines, without effect. At first, I thought that the reason they tried to keep me away from the hospital might have to do with a mistrust of hospital *treatments*, but I realized only later that they mistrusted hospital *employees*. Indeed, while they agreed with me that hospital treatment could cure me faster than any of their own, traditional practices probably would, it appeared that residents seriously worried about how I would be treated in the hospital, if staff found out I lived in the slum 'Bantaran Kali'. This fear was fed by the fact that many residents have had direct and indirect negative experiences with hospital staff, which they believed to be a result of their marginalized position in Jakarta. 'Doctors in the hospitals do not treat poor people well, because they fear we will not pay for our treatment', neighbours typically warned me, 'so if they find out that you live with us, they will think you are poor too and might just let you suffer'.

It needs be stressed that such distrustful perceptions of riverbank settlers towards more powerful or elite actors are by no means irrational. They are the result of the fact that poor, 'illegal' Jakarta residents such as those living along the riverbanks have long been neglected, disadvantaged or even discriminated against by political institutions (Firman 1999: 453, 2009; Reerink 2006; Aspinall & van Klinken 2011: 5). Even though the Jakarta government has taken steps to create a more effective and just social safety net by offering subsidized health insurance to the poor, the poor are still frequently refused or treated with less care in hospitals (Vaessen 2014; Lumanauw 2015).

When my illness got worse after a week I was finally allowed to go to the hospital, but only under strict preventative measures. I was accompanied by a male resident who took me there on his motorbike and stayed with me while I talked to the receptionists, making sure that I gave up a fake address in an elite neighbourhood in Jakarta, which I had had to rehearse with my neighbours beforehand. When I returned home a few days later, people's reactions indicated that they were as equally relieved about my improved health as about the fact that they had 'protected' me well enough against mistrusted hospital employees. This situation, though not exactly comfortable during the period of illness, in retrospect helped me better to understand the deep rooted distrustful perceptions of riverbank settlers about elite actors in wider society and the way this impacts their risk practices.

A final example of the way in which people's perceptions of trust can have an impact on people's behaviour occurred when an unknown man in a police outfit entered the neighbourhood. I was in the middle of an interview with a female respondent but was immediately warned by residents that I had to cut off the conversation and go home. Residents feared that the man might be searching for me, 'because maybe the government does not like it that you live in a slum with us and has sent in the police to come and get you'. This, so I was told, was not a good thing: if the police arrest an 'illegal' resident of the riverbanks (in this case: me), they might mistreat or physically abuse him or her. Memories of former encounters with the police, in which residents had been arrested and mistreated, were still vivid. I only later learned to understand the enormous impact of these memories on the perceptions and practices of my respondents – at the time I underestimated their impact. I was flabbergasted and somewhat sceptical about my neighbour's suspicions of a police officer's harmful intentions towards me, and therefore I was hesitant to leave the place of interview. Next, the owner of the house, visibly nervous, shut and bolted the door and instructed neighbours 'not to tell him [the policeman] about Roanne'. I was locked with her in the house.

Only after a teenage girl came to tell us two hours later that 'the policeman is gone' would the female respondent open her door again. The man in the police outfit was not searching for me at all. In fact, he was not even a policeman, but an uncle visiting a young person who had recently moved into the neighbour-hood – apparently he liked to dress up in a fake police uniform. Again, even if this experience was somewhat uncomfortable, temporarily restricting my autonomous movement, it had the advantage that it helped me to understand the distrustful ways in which riverbank settlers perceive the intentions and actions of more powerful outsiders.

While the three examples above may suggest that I became, to some extent, a trusted neighbour in Bantaran Kali because I co-experienced some of the risks that threaten inhabitants, I do not believe or pretend to believe that I ever became an absolute insider. There remained, of course, enormous differences between the everyday life challenges that they faced, and experiences which were only tem-poral for me. Most importantly, during my fieldwork I was the only resident in Bantaran Kali who had access to a formal social security system. Therefore, when I became ill during fieldwork, the financial costs of treatment did not pose a large financial risk as it would have for them. Likewise, during the medium-sized floods that I experienced, my concerns about losing my laptop (and hence my data) can by no means be compared to the fear people have of losing all their possessions, including their house, without having an insurance policy or buffer that could help to restore or repair these. Hence, the main difference between my respondents and me was the range of possibilities that we had available to cope with or recover from risks in the daily life of Bantaran Kali.

Resultant of their many past and structural experiences with risk, and also of their frequent negative experiences with elite actors, over the years riverbank settlers had developed what I will call throughout this book specific 'risk styles' to deal with the most pressing risks in their lives (floods, poverty and eviction). In the remainder of this chapter, I first explain what I mean by the term 'risk style', and after I briefly discuss the methodologies that I have used to obtain relevant data about risk behaviour. Next, I introduce the four risk styles that are most commonly used by people in Bantaran Kali to handle normal uncertainty.

Risk styles

A risk style can be defined as an observable pattern in the actions and perceptions of people in dealing with the insecurities, threats and risks that endanger their safety and well-being. The notion of styles describes customary practices of people, which are shaped by a combination of circumstantial factors (structure) as well as by people's own decisions and actions (agency) (Nooteboom 2015: 144; Jong 2013).

In most anthropological studies of risk, scholars speak of 'coping strategies' or 'risk strategies'. However, for the specific aims of this study I prefer the concept of 'styles' over that of 'strategies', for two main reasons. First of all, strategies can refer to ad-hoc or constantly changing decisions, while the notion of 'style' refers to a type of learned behaviour that has become habitual. In the process of staying safe and well in a risk-prone living environment, people develop a specific style of doing things (Nooteboom 2015: 155). Notwithstanding the fact people may and do alter their behaviour under specific circumstances, risk styles tend to be constant and long-term. This difference is crucial to my study of risk behaviour in relation to floods in Bantaran Kali, because, as became clear in the Introduction to this book, floods have become to some extent a normalized and expected risk in the lives of riverbank settlers. Consequently, they have developed typical ways of dealing with them. As such, the notion of styles helps to explain structured heterogeneity.

Second, in comparison to the concepts of 'coping strategies' or 'risk strategies', the notion of risk styles allows for a broader scope. It does not relate behaviour to one isolated risk (floods, for example) but instead understands risk behaviour as being embedded in people's everyday life experiences. As such, the notion of 'styles' acknowledges that, in the daily life of respondents in a given research area, there might be covariate risks, as well as other problems and events, that have to be coped with, handled by or responded to – and not just the single risk scientists with a narrow 'disaster lens' find relevant. Such wide scope suits well the aim of this book to approach the topic of flood risk in a holistic way, that is, as one of the many risks that shape riverbank settlers' normal uncertainty.

Stressing that I distinguish types of decision-making and behaviour rather than types of people, from now on I employ the shorthand of 'risk styles' to describe common practices of Jakartan riverbank settlers facing the three most pressing risks that make up their normal uncertainty: floods, poverty and evictions.

Methodologies and data

My ethnographic fieldwork was a rich source of riverbank settlers' perceptions of, and experiences with, floods and other risks. As noted earlier, I was able to use participant observation: living alongside the residents of Bantaran Kali to share their experiences and explore their understanding of the normal uncertainty that characterizes their daily lives. During three floods that I experienced in the field,

I was able to observe study participants' responses to them. These observations offered me data which I draw heavily on in this book.

I supplemented the participant observation with more structured data collection. I obtained information about risk behaviour from in-depth interviews, a survey, and a qualitative analysis of nicknames and typifications that are widely recognized in the kampong.

I carried out in-depth interviews with 130 respondents about their behaviours in relation to flood risk and poverty-related risks in their daily lives. I selected my informants on the basis of age (no people of under 18 participated in this study; the eldest was 67) and through snowball selection. More females (N = 80) than males (N = 50) participated; hence, there was a gender bias in the sample that may have affected the outcomes. Respondents were asked about what they perceived to be the cause of floods or other particular risks discussed in the interview, what they believed might be a solution to the risk problem, what were the effects of these risks on their well-being, who they thought should intervene to solve flood risk (or other risks that were threatening to the respondent), and how they personally coped with these risks.

I also carried out a quantitative survey on risk practices among the same group of 130 respondents. In the survey, 82 items were included that described common practices that people used to cope with flood risk, as well as 30 items that described common practices that people used to cope with poverty-related risks or eviction. Examples of flood-risk responses include 'stocking food and water', 'building a ladder', 'evacuating', 'asking for financial assistance after a flood', 'laminating valuable documents so that they cannot be damaged during a flood', 'providing neighbours with food if they refuse to evacuate and have no food left in the house', 'investing in social relations with actors who might offer financial support after a flood' and 'praying to Allah'. These items were either mentioned by study participants, or referred to actions that I had seen people taking before, during or after floods. Study participants indicated which of the listed risk-handling practices they used, by answering yes or no.

As will become clear below, I have purposely chosen to let the labels of my styles follow the nicknames and descriptions that are commonly used and therefore recognizable in the kampong. In this way, I underscore that my categorization of risk styles has a strong empirical basis. Indeed, as will become clear in the empirical chapters, the ways in which riverbank settlers described themselves and other study participants turned out to largely overlap with the result of my qualitative and quantitative analyses. This strong empirical basis of the categorization must be regarded an important characteristic of this study because, it seems to me, that if we want to understand human risk practices from the 'bottom up' perspective of the actors at risk, it makes sense to grasp the ways in which these actors perceive their own practices in a social context and vis-à-vis one another, and how these are translated into practice. That having been said, it must also be clear that even though I have been inspired by the typifications and nicknames that are commonly used by inhabitants of Bantaran Kali, the categorization of risk styles that I propose in this book is eventually based on my interpretation of risk practices, not theirs.

There are two main differences between my interpretation of styles and study participant's emic insights. First, my categorization is more temporal and fluid than theirs. My study participants generally believe in a fixedness in behavioural clusters, which I did not necessarily recognize in the field. For example, in narratives of riverbank settlers specific actors were consistently portrayed as a certain 'type' of person, possessing 'typical' characterizing traits that were reflected in fixed kinds of behaviour in the face of risk. He just 'is' like that, people would often remark when reflecting on the risk practices of a neighbour; or, if talking about themselves, they would say that 'this is just the way I am'. In contrast, the risk styles that I describe in this book are not completely fixed over time. In particular circumstances, people may and do change their risk style, and I offer different examples of these alterations in behaviour in this book.

Second, while study participants tended to classify all of their neighbours into one of the four risk styles defined in this book, I found that some people did not fall, unambiguously, into only one category. As Figure 1.1 shows, I have therefore also categorized one group of people (27 per cent of the research population) as 'unclassified': most of the respondents in this category are people who do not use one of the defined risk-handling styles, but instead mix two or more of the four most common categories. These people could in my opinion not be unambiguously categorized into one of the four main clusters; at the same time, they did not represent a new, fifth style either. More correctly it seems appropriate to regard their risk practices as occupying a grey area – that is why I call this category 'unclassified'. A few other respondents were categorized in the 'unclassified' category as well. Their behaviour was exceptional and did not fit in with any of the most common risk styles in Bantaran Kali. Neither can it be said that these exceptional cases represent a fifth style, as their behaviour was highly uncommon in the kampong and hence does not fit in with any of the major patterns. For example, there was one woman who refused to act in the face of floods because she believed that it was up to Allah whether or not she would survive disasters.

Categorization of styles

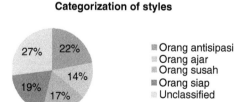

Figure 1.1 Categorization of risk styles in this study.

This behaviour was not mimicked by anyone else in the kampong; instead, people described it as 'weird' or 'crazy'.

On the basis of these four sets of data (observations, interviews, surveys and an analysis of local nicknames and descriptions), I was able to interpret my participants' perceptions of risk, as well as to define patterns in their risk behaviour.

Risk styles in Bantaran Kali

My analyses of these data sets indicated that there exist four clearly distinguishable behavioural patterns of handling risk in Bantaran Kali, which I further describe and analyse in Chapters 2, 3, 4 and 5: *orang antisipasi, orang ajar, orang susah* and *orang siap*. 'Orang' means person in Indonesian, and the following word is an adjective that describes a particular risk behaviour style. It will become clear in the coming chapters that the risk practices that characterize these styles differ considerably from one another; below I touch briefly upon these main differences and characteristics.

The practices of *orang antisipasi* (introduced in Chapter 2) typically reflect autonomous risk handling practices. With this I mean to say that people with this style do not make use of external aid. For example, during floods, rather than evacuating to a governmental flood shelter, the *orang antisipasi* survive in their own houses. And rather than accepting financial support from external aid institutions, these people reject such offers and seek other, often creative ways to collect money. I have categorized 29 out of 130 study participants as *orang antisipasi* in Bantaran Kali. That is about 22 per cent of this study's total research population.

In contrast, *orang susah* (Chapter 4) are highly dependent on external aid institutions. Their risk practices are not autonomous, but rather focus on socializing with wealthy actors who can support them financially in times of need. Twenty-three out of 130 respondents could be categorized as having a *susah* risk-handling style in Bantaran Kali. That matches about 18 per cent of the participants in this study.

The style of *orang ajar* (Chapter 3) is again very different. It involves cooperation with the city government in flood management as well as in other safety issues. *Orang ajar* establish and maintain reciprocal relationships with political actors, in return for social or financial support during floods or other problematic situations. Eighteen out of 130 respondents could be categorized as having an *ajar* risk style in Bantaran Kali. That is the equivalent of nearly 14 per cent of the participants in this study.

Finally, the style of *orang siap* (Chapter 5) is characterized by resistance towards the Jakarta government. People with this style typically engage in defensive practices, such as overtly expressing blame for floods and other risks on the government, experiencing and expressing anger and aggression towards bureaucrats, and refusing to cooperate with them in safety management or obey safety instructions. Twenty-five out of 130 respondents could be categorized as having a *siap* risk-handling style in Bantaran Kali. That equals about 19 per cent of the participants in this study.

In the coming chapters I will introduce people that represent in their risk behaviour specific styles. Yet before we get to know better the *orang antisipasi, orang ajar, orang susah* and *orang siap*, allow me to briefly summarize the key points of this chapter. The sketches of the neighbourhood that were presented here serve to concretize what I call in this book 'normal uncertainty': a context in which risks such as floods, poverty-related threats and evictions are perceived by people as hazards that are normal and problematic at the same time. Furthermore, they serve to show that natives and newcomers in the area are equally vulnerable to these risks. In my research I found that experiences of and responses to risk cut across people's income level, religion, ethnic background, gender, age, physical condition and socioeconomic status, pointing instead to psychological and individual factors that will be discussed in later chapters. This is an important point, as it strengthens the argument that was already made in the Introduction, namely that social structural characteristics that are typically included in vulnerability analyses cannot explain the heterogeneous risk behaviour in Bantaran Kali. Finally, from this chapter it became clear that central to this book is the idea that people follow different behavioural patterns that are guided by individual preferences and opportunities, which are again shaped within structural boundaries. I call these different trajectories 'risk styles'.

References

Aspinall, E. & van Klinken, G. (2011). *The State and Illegality in Indonesia*. Leiden: KITLV Press.

Batavia (2002). Online article from VOC website. Retrieved from www.vocsite.nl/geschiedenis/handelsposten/batavia.html, last accessed 25 October 2015.

Fachrul, M.F., Hendrawan, D., & Sitawati, A. (2007). *Land Use and Water Quality Relationships in the Ciliwung River Basin, Indonesia*. Paper presented at the International Congress on River Basin Management, 22–24 March 2007, Antalya, Turkey.

Firman, T. (1999). From "global city" to "city of crisis": Jakarta metropolitan region under economic turmoil. *Habitat International*, 23(4), 447–466.

Firman, T. (2009). The continuity and change in mega-urbanization in Indonesia: a survey of Jakarta–Bandung Region (JBR) development. *Habitat International* 33(4), 327–339.

Haryanto, U. (2009, November 19). Most money thrown at Jakarta flooding only going down the drain. *The Jakarta Globe*. Retrieved from www.thejakartaglobe.com, last accessed 24 October 2015.

Haryanto, U. (2010, January 6). Jakarta's new flood canal brings grief as riverbanks soften. *The Jakarta Globe*. Retrieved from www.thejakartaglobe.com/archive/jakartas-new-flood-canal-brings-grief-as-riverbanks-soften/

History of Jakarta (2011) Online article from Jakarta.go.id. Retrieved from www.jakarta.go.id/v2eng/news/2011/03/history-of-jakarta#.VciGUqPCSUk, last accessed 25 October 2015.

Human Rights Watch (2006). Condemned communities: forced evictions in Jakarta. Retrieved from www.hrw.org/sites/default/files/reports/indonesia0906webwcover.pdf, last accessed 25 October 2015.

Jong de, E. B.P. (2013). *Making a Living between Crises and Ceremonies in Tana Toraja. The Practice of Everyday Life of a South Sulawesi Highland Community in Indonesia*. Leiden: Brill.

Lumanauw, N. (2015, May 4). Jokowi: revoke licenses of private hospitals that refuse KIS patients. *The Jakarta Globe*. Retrieved from http://jakartaglobe.beritasatu.com/news/jokowi-revoke-licenses-of-private-hospitals-that-refuse-to-treat-kis-patients, last accessed 25 October 2015.

Mariani, E. (2003, November 29). Govt to evict hundreds to build shopping mall. *The Jakarta Post*. Retrieved from http://groups.yahoo.com/neo/groups/beritabhinneka/conversations/topics/73819, last accessed 15 September 2015.

McCarthy, P. (n.d.). Urban slums reports: the case of Jakarta. *Understanding Slums: Case Studies for the Global Report on Human Settlements*. Retrieved from www.ucl.ac.uk/dpu-projects/Global_Report/pdfs/Jakarta.pdf, last accessed 24 October 2015.

Muhammadi, F. Z. (2013, August 24). Relocation continues at Pluit Dam. *The Jakarta Post*. Retrieved from www.thejakartapost.com/news/2013/08/24/relocation-continues-pluit-dam.html, last accessed 25 October 2015.

Nooteboom, G. (2015). *Forgotten People: Poverty, Risk and Social Security in Indonesia: The Case of the Madurese*. Leiden: Brill.

Reerink, G. O. (2006). The price of uncertainty: Kampung land politics in post-Suharto Bandung. *IIAS Newsletter*, 40(14), 1.

Vaessen, S. (2014, January 10). Indonesia's health comes at a cost. *Al Jazeera*. Retrieved from http://blogs.aljazeera.com/blog/asia/indonesias-health-comes-cost, last accessed 25 October 2015.

2   Orang antisipasi

An autonomous, illegal but licit business

In standard speech and writing, the Indonesian term '*antisipasi*' or the English term 'anticipating' usually means something like 'acting or responding in advance', or 'to forestall and expect'. However, in Bantaran Kali, the notion has a rather different meaning. There, the nickname *orang antisipasi* and the verb *antisipasi* refer to those riverbank settlers who typically handle risks by exhibiting risk practices (1) that are autonomous rather than dependent or related to well-known aid institutions; (2) that offer short-term solutions to acute problems or stress experiences; and (3) that are 'illegal but licit' in the neighbourhood – strictly speaking illegal but permitted in kampong society nevertheless.

These practices set *orang antisipasi* aside from fellow residents, many of whom, as we will see in later chapters, try to exhibit what is considered 'good' or pious behaviour in order not to draw disapproval from more powerful or economically resourceful actors, exhibit long-term risk strategies, evacuate to government safe shelters, and invest in social relations with external aid institutions or other useful institutions involved in Bantaran Kali's flood management.

The first sections of this chapter will describe in more detail the risk practices that characterize the behaviour of *orang antisipasi* in Bantaran Kali. Next, I explore the factors underlying this risk style, arguing that it is shaped by a combination of circumstantial and psychological factors. In order to develop this argument, I borrow from Bourdieu's notion of habitus and propose that the *antisipasi* risk style is both shaped by a 'habitus of poverty' as well as a reproducer of it. Next, I discuss this argument in relation to alternative theories of poverty and risk, showing that popular theories such as the 'culture of poverty' are too limited to explain the *antisipasi* risk style in Bantaran Kali. In the final part of this chapter I compare the *antisipasi* style as observed by me in Bantaran Kali with human risk behaviour as observed by other scholars in different contexts of risk and uncertainty.

Orang antisipasi

Orang antisipasi do not accept help in evacuating after a flood-risk warning message has been circulated in their kampong, they do not reside in evacuation shelters of the *kelurahan* during floods, and they do not accept support from external aid institutions in the recovery phase. Instead, they find ways to handle flood risks more or less autonomously from the actors and institutions that are involved in Bantaran Kali's flood management. For example, *orang antisipasi* generally ignore safety warnings to evacuate early and hence evacuate late or not at all (instead seeking shelter on their rooftop or in a self-built shelter in their house). In order to survive within or atop their own houses rather than in an external shelter, most *orang antisipasi* prepare 'flood-food', *makanan banjir*, and store basic foods in their houses.[1] Many of them also prepare batteries and flashlights that can be used in times of need. During the recovery phase, instead of accepting financial aid from external institutions, *orang antisipasi* typically borrow money from money lenders against high interest rates to afford their recovery. For the same goal, they cut off consumption much more often than people exhibiting other risk styles, or sell their household's goods after a flood.

This latter practice points to the second characteristic that typifies the *antisipasi* risk style, which concerns the fact that *orang antisipasi* typically do not pursue long-term prevention strategies that might mitigate flood risk. Instead, they usually exploit short-term risk practices in order to protect their well-being during the time a disaster takes place, or after it has already struck. Examples of long-term risk practices that are typically exhibited by other inhabitants of Bantaran Kali are setting aside money beforehand to be used during evacuation; participating in communal saving institutions specifically for the aim of buffering 'disaster money' (*uang bencana*); and participating in subsidized government programs for the poor, such as cheap rice (Beras untuk Orang Miskin, RASKIN) and health (Surat Keterangan Tidak Mampu, SKTM).[2] I call these risk practices long-term strategies because they can be – and often are – used by riverbank settlers to accumulate money for a longer period of time and then invest it into the pre-set goal of a flood-mitigating measure. These long-term risk strategies are very common in Bantaran Kali, but consistently not among *orang antisipasi*. Instead, as remarked above, *orang antisipasi* are often forced to fall back on short-term coping and recovery strategies. That may be the case because the English proverb 'counting one's chickens before they hatch' applies neatly to the way *orang antisipasi* organize their livelihood. They are known to wheel and deal; to take financial risks; and to sell what they do not own yet. If this behaviour generally provides *orang antisipasi* with enough money to make daily ends meet, they never hold on to it long enough to accumulate and actually decrease the risks that are part of normal uncertainty in the long run.

A third characteristic that typifies the *orang antisipasi* is the fact that they are generally involved in businesses that are considered 'illegal but licit' in kampong society. They are involved in moneylending and shady trade, they work as middlemen or local strongman, or they offer services in the areas of security or prostitution. While these professions are considered useful by fellow residents of kampong society, they are also perceived as forbidden (*haram*). As a result of these social norms, *orang antisipasi* are generally spoken of disparagingly in public discourse, and they occupy a rather low position in the neighbourhood hierarchy; at the same time, their practices and services are needed and often used by fellow residents. I will explain more about the status of *orang antisipasi* in the social hierarchy later in this chapter, but first it is important to consider for a moment the risks other than flooding that characterize the normal uncertainty in this riverbank settlement, namely poverty-related risks and eviction.

From my interviews and surveys with *orang antisipasi*, it became clear that, when it concerns those risks, *orang antisipasi* again make use of autonomous and short-term strategies. To give some examples of the short-term practices that are commonly used by *orang antisipasi* when dealing with poverty-related risks: if a person from their household turns ill, *orang antisipasi* will generally borrow money at high interest rates from money lenders to pay for medical treatment in a (government-subsidized and therefore relatively affordable) health clinic, or try and sell goods from their household, as they have not saved money as a buffer beforehand, and as they generally make no use of the support provided by external aid institutions. This means that potential disease or a sudden drop in income generally causes severe economic stress in the lives of *orang antisipasi*. Often, they also try to solve these economic problems by engaging in illegal (but licit) practices.

A similar behavioural pattern is exhibited in relation to the hazard of eviction. *Orang antisipasi* do not seem to prepare themselves for a potential eviction, for example by accumulating money that can be used for moving house, or by socializing politicians or employees of aid institutions in the hope that these people may stand up for them and hence prevent eviction or at least support the evictees. In later chapters, it will become clear that many other riverbank settlers use such strategies to deal with these risks – here I want to emphasize that *orang antisipasi* do not. This means that, if Bantaran Kali is evicted in the near future, *orang antisipasi* will most likely fall back on their short-term, autonomous and illegal practices to cope with the problem.

In order to offer a more concrete idea of what defines an *antisipasi* risk style, the next sections introduce two respondents whom are widely known in the kampong as *orang antisipasi*: Edi and Ida.

Edi's antisipasi practices

Edi (47) is a former thug (*preman*) who was famous for his ruthless robberies of truck drivers in Jakarta. He lost most of his money after he was put to jail in the late 1990s. Since he came back to the kampong, only the blurred tattoos on Edi's arms remind of the criminal successes that he enjoyed in his young days. He has never been able to make up his financial losses. He wears torn clothing and walks around on bare feet. His wife and children left him during his time in prison, and besides his elderly sister Hannah (72 years old), Edi has no other family members living in Bantaran Kali. Ever since the large flood in 2007 demolished his house, Edi is homeless. Nowadays, all he possesses is a wooden closet with four drawers, in which he keeps some clothing and personal valuables: a black and white photo of himself in his younger years, a key-ring that he once found in the street, an incomplete chessboard, a wallet, a notebook, a pencil and a lock. Edi sleeps next to his closet in the street, and locks it whenever he leaves his stand.

Since he has turned away from criminal activities, Edi has become one of the few moneylenders (or, in local terms, *rentenir*) working in Bantaran Kali. Moneylenders live from the profits of their loans. And many of the loans that are arranged in this riverbank settlement are arranged during flood events. Edi's business thrives on the fact that most people in Bantaran Kali are in constant need of cash due to recurrent floods, because they are not considered eligible for formal safety-net funding in the public sector, such as a loan from the bank or insurance. The following narrative about Edi's current livelihood will serve to show that flood victims' high costs also offer advantages for inhabitants with an *antisipasi* risk style, like Edi. The events discussed in the narrative take place during the medium-sized 2010 flood that I experienced in Bantaran Kali, and that I began to describe in the Introduction to this book.

When Edi heard people screaming that a flood was on its way to the kampong, he threw off the blanket under which he slept on a side-road of Bantaran Kali, grabbed his cigarettes, wallet and notebook from a drawer in his closet, locked it and ran as fast as he could out into the kampong. 'Where are you going?' asked his older sister Hannah, sitting in the dark in front of her house to prepare the *lonton* that she was planning to sell on the night market. Edi took no time to answer her, but neighbours seemed to know exactly where he was heading. '*Nenek*, prepare! A flood comes this way!' they warned his sister, after which Hannah nodded understandingly. 'Then he will be busy in the neighbourhood', she concluded. 'If a flood comes, Edi must work all day and night. He is an *orang antisipasi* like that'.

And busy he was indeed during this flood. While Hannah prepared to evacuate, and while other residents were already walking away from the riverbanks of Bantaran Kali in the direction of the shelter that was being set up by the *kelurahan*, Edi ran in the opposite direction. He quickly went from door to door in the kampong. In one hand he held his notebook, in his other his pen. His small black wallet was attached to the belt around his hip. Most people shook their head as soon as they saw him to wave him off, but some gestured him to enter their house. With them, Edi exchanged few words, after which he took a small pile of banknotes from his bag, counted these, handed them over, recounted them together with the receiver of the money, and finally wrote something down in his notebook. After he had performed this ritual with ten people, Edi showed me his empty wallet. He said:

> Floods are good for my business. This is going to be a good flood! See, I have just started working and I am already out of cash to lend to people – now I only need to wait until I earn more [money]. But if you want to borrow cash yourself, Roanne, I can try and get some more? Floods are expensive, you know, you ought to have some money with you if you evacuate.

His neatly updated notebook showed that nine people already had a loan with him before the flood occurred; that three of them increased that loan during the flood; and that seven others set up a loan with Edi after the flood-warning message was spread by residential volunteers. As a *rentenir*, Edi makes use of people's financial problems, so he explained:

> If I know that we are going to have another flood, I must act fast. I know the situations of all neighbours and I can predict precisely who will have financial struggles. For example, if people have small children and they usually evacuate, then I know that they must buy food for all family members in the streets and that this will be expensive for them! Then I can offer them my loans and help them survive the flood. Afterwards, they must pay me back and I can make some profit myself. It is smart, right? But it is also handy for my neighbours that I do this. Without my business, people could not survive floods.

This quote shows how Edi emphasizes both his streetwise skills as well as the need for him to act in the way that he does: without his service, he suggests, residents would not have sufficient cash to handle flood risk. This suggests that he does them a favour by lending money to them.

What Edi does *not* highlight, in this and other narratives about the ways in which he makes a living, is the fact that he profits enormously from his neighbours' financial problems. Neither does he refer to the harsh ways in which he acts towards neighbours who are unable to repay the loan. In order to get a clearer view about these aspects of his livelihood, let me clarify how Edi makes his money.

Edi's moneylending business model is complex: first, if Edi expects that neighbours will be in need of cash, he borrows money from several Chinese-Indonesian merchants that live right outside the neighbourhood, to whom he pays an interest rate of 10 to 20 per cent for the loaned sum per week. Next, Edi lends out their money to his own neighbours in return for interest rates that fluctuate between 30 and 80 per cent per week, depending on what Edi believes that people can afford and what people are willing to pay. Edi keeps what profit is left for himself after he has paid back the debts that he has built up with the Chinese-Indonesian merchants.

Two examples of his deals give an insight into his business: in the week before the flood, Edi's neighbour Aty borrowed 50,000 Rupiah (Rp) (the equivalent of about 3,36 EUR) from him to pay for the extension of her Identity card. She agreed to pay him an interest rate of 30 per cent over this sum, which amounted to 65,000 Rupiah. Aty and Edi agreed that she would pay him back Rp 3,000 of this amount per day; hence, she would have paid her dues in 17 days. Neighbour Ida already had a loan of Rp 20,000 with Edi before the flood occurred, and when she heard that the river would overflow again, she decided that she needed more cash as she expected that she would earn less money with her business during the flood and yet needed money to feed her children and herself. Ida therefore borrowed another 80,000 Rupiah from Edi and agreed to pay him an interest rate of 40 per cent over the course of a week. Thus her total debt was Rp 140,000. They agreed that she would pay him back 4,000 Rupiah a day; hence, it would take her 35 days to pay back her dues. While Ida complained that this rental percentage was high, she agreed to it nevertheless as she felt that 'during floods I usually get so deep in trouble that I have no other choice than to accept Edi's offers'.

The business of Edi may appear lucrative, but in practice his incomes do not decrease Edi's vulnerability towards floods or other risks. First of all, the lack of shelter and the need to work during floods, often in strong currents and amidst potentially collapsing houses, strongly increase his vulnerability towards floods. Even if the kampong is declared unsafe terrain during very large floods, Edi typically refuses to evacuate from the kampong as he considers the floods a good chance to earn money. Running the risk of being hurt by flood debris, he puts himself in physical danger during floods. Indeed, after most floods, Edi turns ill from waterborne bacteria. He then frequently is forced to loan money from other moneylenders in order to pay for his own needed medicines.

Second, Edi's income flows through his hands. He immediately lends out everything he earns; the money never stays with him long enough to accumulate. As a result, Edi is not able to build himself a house that might offer him some protection against recurring floods.

A third reason for his vulnerability towards risks has to do with the fact that Edi continually runs an economic risk with his business, as people might not be able or willing to pay him back. This means that he himself might not always be able to pay back his creditors in time due to defaulting customers, and consequently might be physically abused by his creditors. Different residents to whom I spoke about Edi's money-lending business remembered days on which Edi returned from the market with a swollen and blue eye or a sore back. He himself said about this:

> If I don't earn enough from my neighbours, I get into deep problems myself. Sometimes I must hide away for a while so the [Chinese-Indonesian] merchants cannot try to kick their money out of me. They can be very aggressive if they think you betray them, and of course, they are always suspicious of me because they know I am homeless, and they understand that people like me would rather keep the money themselves. So, yes, they can behave harsh! But most of the time I can pay them back in time and sometimes I make a little profit.

Yet his creditors are not the only ones who threaten him. Members of the civil militia group Betawi Brotherhood Forum (Forum Betawi Rempug, FBR) living in the neighbourhood overtly threaten to 'beat them up' if they see *rentenir* like Edi working. To them, the moneylending business is *haram*. To avoid physical abuse, it is common for *rentenir* like Edi to preventively pay the leader of FBR a small amount of money. We might say that in this way, he is buying off the risk of being beaten up, or he trades running a physical risk for a financial risk. During my fieldwork, I learned that Edi did this by paying the leader of the FBR a daily amount of Rp 3,000. He furthermore paid Rp 2,000 per day to the kampong leader – called 'cigarette money' by both of them – in return for the kampong's leader assumed ignorance of Edi's illegal business. He also paid the same amount of Rupiahs – in those occasions called 'safety money' – to some inhabitants with high social status in the neighbourhood on an irregular basis.[3] Finally, Edi also regularly paid 'safety money' to several police officers who worked close to the market, allowing him to work in the neighbourhood without them interfering.

I explained earlier that Edi tries to decrease his own economic risk by allowing his lenders to pay him back in small, daily instalments. However, this does not yet solve the problem that most of his clients try actively to avoid meeting with him as long as they owe him money. As a result, Edi spends most of his days in the kampong searching for his debtors, who, as soon as they see him coming, hastily leave the house in order to avoid paying their instalment for the day. Edi is thus forced to chase after them, even if this sometimes takes him a full day, to demand the daily instalment. This 'demanding' can be done with an informal talk on the street between moneylender and debtor, but it can also be a euphemism for extortion, threatening, or putting up a fight. I learned from residents that Edi was often engaged in fights and it was widely known in the kampong that he usually carries a knife with him; some neighbours told me that he owns guns as well. I myself observed that, if people claimed that they did not have money, Edi took an asset from the household in exchange for their debt or threatened them with harsher punishments.

It has now become clear that Edi is stuck in a cycle of threatening and being threatened. It also became clear that he constantly balances between being in debt and having a small income that enables him to survive, but never makes enough to decrease his vulnerability towards risk, which again increases the need to continue his risky livelihood. In order to show that this situation is not unique for Edi, but is instead characteristic for the *orang antisipasi* in Bantaran Kali, I will now introduce Ida, whom we already briefly met in the Introduction to this book as well as in this chapter, and who is also known as an *orang antisipasi* in the kampong.

Ida's antisipasi practices

Edi is able to earn money from a flood; by contrast Ida only loses whenever the river overflows. Ida is a widow who lives in Bantaran Kali with her four children (the youngest is 8 years old, the eldest 13). She derives her main source of income from the different men with whom she has sex in her house on a regular basis in return for goods or, in rare cases, food or small amounts of pocket money. She calls their payments 'gifts', and her customers 'boyfriends'. Some of these men are male kampong residents, but Ida also has three customers who live elsewhere in Jakarta. These 'boyfriends' are immigrants who have moved to the capital to earn a livelihood, sending remittances to their families in rural Java. They each pass by twice a month at the least. Ida explains how her livelihood enables her to make ends meet:

> Whenever men become lonely they knock on my door. If they have an urge [for sex] but their spouses do not want to give it to them, they come to me. Thanks to this service that I offer to my boyfriends I can survive here in the slums of Jakarta. It is not a love relationship; it is a kind of a business relationship.

Because we do not love one another. No, we just help one another. Therefore I am not jealous of their spouses. They are just boyfriends to me, so they do not care for me like a husband would. I only offer them the mattress in return for some [material] help.

If Ida's house is flooded, she refuses to evacuate because she wants her boyfriends to be able to find her if they 'have the urge'. And this 'urge', says Ida, may become more pressing during long-term floods, as then residents have sought refuge in the *kelurahan* safety shelter:

We have so many floods here. I cannot let floods prevent me from working. What will my boyfriends think if I am gone every time we have a flood? No, they must always know where to find me, so this is why I always stay in my house even though it is flooded. Everyone knows that even if this neighbourhood is flooded, one can still find me on the roof. While, in a shelter, you can't have sex there! There are hundreds of people in that shelter! So, I stay here, and the men come to me when they get the urge.

All in all, Ida usually has enough customers each month for her to survive. When I once visited her in her house, she summed up the goods that she had received from 'boyfriends' over the past three months: five boxes of cigarettes, a fake Gucci watch, a dress, a purse and a football for her 11-year-old son. She also received 5,000 Rupiah in cash, which, as she emphasized, was not a direct payment for her sexual services but instead 'just some cigarette money' (*uang rokok*) or 'pocket money' (*uang jajan*). Ida sold most of her 'gifts' in return for cash, but calculated that she made hardly enough to accumulate any of her earnings. Not only because the 'gifts' lost part of their value as they became second-hand after Ida received them and she was forced to sell them back to market merchants for a relatively low price, but also because she reinvested almost all of her income immediately in her service business. According to Ida, these investments were generally higher than her income and she lived in deep debt consequently. For this reason she had not been able to afford to send her eldest children (aged 11, 12, and 13) to junior school over the past few years. Instead, they usually played football or cards in the streets of Bantaran Kali and sometimes took odd jobs such as collecting water for neighbours in return for pocket money. During my stay in Bantaran Kali, only Ida's youngest daughter (eight years old) attended a state-run primary school. In the months following floods, however, Ida usually took her daughter out of school because she felt she must prioritize financial investments in her business.

In order for me to get an insight into her financial situation, Ida agreed to note down all of her income and expenditure for a total time period of three months. The analysis of her budget showed that Ida's livelihood earnings were not sufficient to decrease her vulnerability to flood risk. In an average month, Ida made about Rp 730,000 from her boyfriends (after selling their gifts on the market). She used most of this income to buy food for herself and her children (Rp 200,000), to pay the monthly rent (Rp 150,000) and to invest in clothing (Rp 100,000) that Ida believes will impress her current boyfriends, as she explained:

> I have to buy nice dresses, even though they cost me too much. If I look like an average kampong woman, then my boyfriends will become tired of me and look for another woman. Only when I look pretty all the time, always offering them my service, then they will think of me each time they want sex. This is just how I survive in this slum.

Her other money was spent on her beloved cigarettes (Rp 18,000), transport for her youngest to go to school (Rp 10,000), the electricity bill (Rp 40,000), a refill of her perfume bottle (Rp 10,000), spices (called *jamu* or *kunjit*) from a Madurese *ibu jamu* who sells her spice mixtures in the neighbourhood (Rp 20,000), and special dishes that Ida bought on the market 'to increase lust' (Rp 20,000 in the first month, Rp 60,000 in the second and Rp 35,000 in the third – each time orderly labelled as 'other expenses' (*biaya lain-lain*) in her notebook). Ida explained what these expenses precisely were during one of our visits to the morning market:

> I need to buy many natural spices and other ingredients because I do not feel any lust for my boyfriends… But men get angry if I turn them down, because they always have an urge for sex. They do not understand that women need to eat special foods in order to want sex. We need ginger to heat ourselves up, and eggs, and sweet milk and fruits. Especially mango. Did you know that, Roanne? Only if you eat enough of these things, your body will be healthy and you will like to have sex. If my boyfriends approach me I must first eat that [the spices and ingredients]. Even if I am out of money I will still go to the market and buy it, even though I must make an expensive loan for it. Only then I can offer them the service, you understand?

The above analysis of her monthly expenditures shows that Ida could, in theory, set aside some of her money after she has paid for basic needs for the aim of decreasing her vulnerability to floods or other risks in the long run. Yet in practice, Ida typically prioritizes (re)investments in her livelihood, which make it impossible for her to accumulate her income. Consequently, her household remains extremely vulnerable to financial stressors caused by floods. She has never accumulated a financial buffer to be used during flood events; nor has she invested in ceramic tiles, which are easier to clean from flood mud than a floor made from wood or cement and therefore are believed to prevent flood victims from contracting typical waterborne illnesses. As she consistently refuses to evacuate during floods, each large flood damages Ida's goods severely, and she and her children often become ill after floods. In those times of need, she buys many of her basic needs on credit, by paying a small time creditor (*tukang kredit*) in daily instalments – which includes an interest rate of 5 to 10 per cent per day. For medical treatment and other payments that she needs to make after floods, Ida borrows money from more expensive *rentenir* like Edi. Moreover, because Ida believes that investments in her appearance are important for her profession, after floods she prioritizes the rebuying of sexy clothing, perfume and supposedly lust-increasing ingredients over other damaged household goods, and also over the educational fees of her children.

Due to these financial decisions, Ida always owes money to different creditors at the same time, with a total debt that fluctuates between a hundred thousand Rupiah up to a million Rupiah. 'And they all demand high interest rates, so I am only making it worse if I don't pay them off', she more than once complained to me. Ida often worried about her financial situation and told me several times that she felt she was stuck in a hazardous situation. 'Sometimes I earn some money but I always have to pay back other people even more money. Especially after floods – they are so expensive! After floods I must start all over again. It is hopeless. This is why I will always be stuck in this slum', she said. Several times a 'boyfriend' had supported Ida by offering her extra 'gifts' after floods, but according to Ida, these needed to be returned later 'on the mattress'. In other words, she was then in a physical debt with her 'boyfriends' – promising these men more of her sexual service as a way of repaying her debts to them.

The above portrait of Ida shows that, as was the case with Edi, this *orang anti-sipasi* exhibits short-term practices to overcome daily financial problems, but at the same time these practices do not enable her to decrease her vulnerability to floods. The same can be said for Ida's ways of handling poverty-related risks or the risk of eviction. Unlike many of her other neighbours, I learned that Ida had not saved 'disaster money' which could be used when one of her children would fall ill. Neither had she invested in social relations with resourceful actors that may be able to help her in future times of need. This means that if disaster strikes, Ida will have to fall back on her *antisipasi* risk style.

Ida's vulnerability to risk is worsened because, like Edi, she is extorted by different actors. Members of the civil militia group FBR overtly threaten prostitutes; the local FBR leader says that they are 'not allowed' in Bantaran Kali and that they should be 'chased out' of the neighbourhood if they are ever discovered. During my stay in Bantaran Kali, Ida did not pay FBR to be left in peace, but instead paid the kampong leader a small amount of money in return for his protection. Unlike Edi, Ida did not pay policemen or average neighbours, but instead she sometimes 'offered the mattress' to local powerful men, because otherwise she feared being expelled.

The situation in which Ida and Edi find themselves was common among the other *orang antisipasi* that I got to know in Bantaran Kali. While they used different strategies to protect their safety and well-being in a context of normal uncertainty, *orang antisipasi* all had in common that they exhibited short-term and autonomous risk practices that were typically 'illegal but licit' in the neighbourhood. They also had in common that they did not seem able or willing to accumulate a financial buffer that could help to mitigate hazard or effectively handle financial stressors caused by floods or other risk. Finally, they consistently refused to evacuate and instead tried to survive floods in their houses. For all of the reasons above, they generally remain relatively vulnerable to both flood hazards and other types of hazards, as a flood may force them into deeper debts, or vice versa: an economic stressor may increase their vulnerability to floods.

The above presented narratives of Edi and Ida furthermore suggest that they feel stuck in a way of life that they themselves experience as problematic and insecure. Edi indicated that he dreads losing the money he earns, and Ida described her situation as 'hopeless' and expected to be 'always stuck on the flood-prone riverbanks'. Again, this also was the case for other *orang antisipasi* in Bantaran Kali, and we will read of their concerns later in this chapter. Yet first I wish to explore the underlying factors of an *antisipasi* risk style.

For this aim it is useful to describe the problematic situation of *orang antisipasi* as what poverty scholars may recognize as a poverty trap or, as I prefer to call it throughout this book, a trap of risk and uncertainty. The next sections of this chapter explore what hampers an escape from this trap, or, put differently, what underlies an *antisipasi* risk style. Showing that the *antisipasi* risk style is shaped by a combination of structural and agentic factors, I start my analysis by discussing the low hierarchy that *orang antisipasi* take in in society and argue that this lack of power impacts their risk style. Next, I introduce the notion of a 'habitus of poverty' to show that *orang antisipasi* have developed over their course of life a habitual tendency to act and perceive the world in a way that reinforces their vulnerability to risk.

Haram but needed

As is the case with most other inhabitants of Bantaran Kali, the practices of *orang antisipasi* are strongly limited and determined by unequal social structures in Indonesian society. Slum dwellers are limited in their options to make a livelihood or to choose a place of residence (and hence, eventually, to protect themselves against flood risk) by power inequalities in wider society. Faced with a scarcity of options, for many uneducated people in the crowded urban slums of Jakarta, involvement in petty criminality, extortion or organized gangs and vigilante groups remains one of a limited set of options for making ends meet (Wilson 2012: 1). Take Edi, who, without any education and with a track record as a thug, would probably not be able to find a well-paid and lawful livelihood in an environment of a higher socioeconomic class. This is part of the reason why he finds himself dependent on more resourceful Chinese-Indonesian merchants that he does business with as a small middleman. Likewise, Ida made the decision to become a prostitute within a relatively small amount of room to manoeuvre.

However, the fact that *orang antisipasi* are marginalized in Indonesian society tells us little about the factors underlying their particular risk style. After all, *orang antisipasi* have in common with their neighbours their relatively powerless position in Jakartan society, so why would *orang antisipasi* behave differently in relation to risk than other riverbank settlers?

This, I believe, has to do with the fact that *orang antisipasi* are also subject to more powerful actors *within* kampong society. For instance, we have seen that Edi is forced to share his income with the FBR and other more powerful actors in kampong society in order to remain tolerated in Bantaran Kali despite his *haram* profession. As a result, he is unable to accumulate money that can be used as a financial buffer in future times of need, or even for a house that would offer shelter from floods. Due to his livelihood, Edi is not only part of a chain of threatening, extortion, debts and credit; he is also trapped in a situation of risk and uncertainty. For Ida, we have already seen that similar pressing forces are at play. Not only does she pay different actors in return for 'protection', she also feels forced to accept payments in 'gifts' – which are less valuable than cash – in order to remain tolerated in the kampong. Consequently, she survives day by day – but there is no outlook on an escape from her living environment, which is characterized by normal uncertainty.

So, why, one may wonder, do *orang antisipasi* take up such a low social position in Bantaran Kali? What makes them feel forced to pay fellow residents, or to be subject to the will of others? In order to answer these questions, it is useful to know a bit more about the ways in which *orang antisipasi* are perceived by fellow residents.

Throughout interviews and informal conversations with the inhabitants of Bantaran Kali, it struck me that *orang antisipasi* were consistently characterized by fellow residents in negative ways. They were often described to me as 'tough' (*keras*) and 'untrustworthy' (*yang tidak dapat dipercaya*) kinds of people. Most importantly, they were overtly despised for their *haram* livelihoods. For example, the kampong leader said that:

> In order to overcome their problems, they [*orang antisipasi*] always do things that are forbidden by Allah. And you know what? They could not care less that they behave as bad Muslims! They do not think about life after death, no, they only *antisipasi* for their current lives.

Another example is offered by Rio – the young street musician who introduced me to Bantaran Kali. When I once sat with Rio on my doorstep, Edi walked by and stopped for small talk. After Edi left, Rio warned me that 'people like Edi do very bad things. We call them *orang antisipasi*. They never help other people or behave socially in any other ways. They are only busy with helping themselves'. A young female inhabitant that overheard our conversation agreed with this description of *orang antisipasi*:

> *Orang antisipasi* use weak people like myself to improve their own situation. If they hear that a flood is coming, they might for example try to make money from flood victims. Because they have tough characters, they don't care what other people think of them. They just always save themselves before all others.

Hannah, the sister of Edi, once warned me by grabbing my wrist hard when we came to speak about her brother:

> Don't you ever get involved with people like him. There are many alike in Jakarta, especially in poor slums like this, and they like to betray you for their own good. They can be dangerous for good people like you and me because they usually act in tough ways.

From these quotations we can take that *orang antisipasi* in Bantaran Kali are overtly despised for their 'bad' behaviour and are in a very low position in the social hierarchy. Such negative perceptions about *orang antisipasi* were not only reflected in public discourse, but also in the ways in which residents interacted with *orang antisipasi*, or rather, in the ways in which they mostly tried to avoid interaction with them. During my stay in the field, none of the 29 *orang antisipasi* that participated in my study was ever invited for otherwise popular social events in the kampong such as weddings, circumcisions, religious meetings or saving groups (*arisan*). Just like Hannah and Rio warned me to stay away from Edi, it was common for residents to openly discuss their aim to avoid meeting with *orang antisipasi*. They are people one should not be seen with, neighbours typically said to one another, and they are people one shall not mingle with, parents frequently warned their children.

However, despite these apparent negative perceptions of residents towards *orang antisipasi*, there are two main reasons why I believe that these public discourses have to be nuanced. First, if people generally disagree with the type of practices that *orang antisipasi* engage in, they also regard them as 'strong' and streetwise kind of people. Inhabitants described the ways in which *orang antisipasi* like Ida and Edi handle risks as 'tough', but also as rather effective to the extent that they suffice to overcome recurring problems such as floods or financial struggles. Hence, we might say that *orang antisipasi* are admired in a sense by their fellow residents for their survivor skills.

Second, even if riverbank settlers publically disapproved of the *antisipasi* practices of their fellow residents, I found that in daily practice, many of them made use of their services. That is the case because *orang antisipasi* fulfil important societal demands in Bantaran Kali that would have remained otherwise hard to access for slum dwellers.

For instance, *rentenir* like Edi offer households the financial relief that formal safety-net institutions currently do not offer slum dwellers. Despite the fact that over the last decade, Indonesia has experienced a proliferation of social welfare programmes, local and informal safety nets are still the primary networks on which the Indonesian poor rely in times of need (Koning & Hüsken 2006; Aspinall 2014; Kwon & Kim 2015). Times of need can for example arise in cases where someone turns ill, or when a flood damages people's assets, or when one is put out of work. As the majority of the riverbank settlers has not accumulated sufficient financial buffer for such stresses, informal financial arrangements must be sought. The poor in Jakarta may turn first to illegal pawnshops to sell their assets in return for some cash or they may try to borrow small amounts from family members and acquaintances. Yet if more money is needed, and especially when it is needed immediately, moneylenders offer an instant – and very expensive – solution. In the words of the kampong leader:

> We are all poor, and we always have more expenditure than we can afford. So if a child is born, or if that child needs uniforms and books to go to school, we need even more money than normal, and we have to borrow it. And if there is a flood, things get worse: then we are all in sudden need of cash. To whom else could we turn, than to people like Edi?

Indeed, while publically disapproving of their practices, at the same time, many riverbank settlers acknowledge that moneylenders like Edi perform a valuable role in their society in times of financial difficulties. Rio explained this as follows:

> Edi is a bad Muslim for asking high interest rates of poor people like me. That is not even allowed by Allah, that is *haram*. But I am actually also happy that Edi lives here because he always has money while I never have enough to survive. So at least my family can borrow money from someone.

Somewhat similarly, we might argue that Ida offers a sexual service in the kampong which fulfils male demands for (extramarital) sex. Just like Edi, she offers an illegal and *haram* yet licit service in the kampong that serves the societal system.

In sum, I have claimed in the past section that the repertoire of risk practices of *orang antisipasi*, as well as their vulnerability to risk, are produced by unequal power structures both within Bantaran Kali and wider society. While many people make use of their services, *orang antisipasi* are also despised, extorted and marginalized, which leaves them a relatively small amount of room to manoeuvre. That having been said, we must certainly not regard the *orang antisipasi* as nothing more than victims of the circumstances. In the next section, I highlight the agency of *orang antisipasi*, showing that *orang antisipasi* themselves contribute to the reproduction of their vulnerability to risk, by deliberately using the risky environment of a flood-prone kampong to pursue their illegal but licit activities.

Reproduction of vulnerability

Orang antisipasi are able to make a living not just despite of their marginalized position in society, but also exactly because of the fact that people in a riverbank settlement such as Bantaran Kali hardly have access to formal safety nets or other services that are needed in society. For that reason, *orang antisipasi* can and do make use of the needy situation of their neighbours.

Abdoumaliq Simone concluded from his study of Jakarta that poor people in the city are often able to handle daily hazard, but only as long as they remain located in the shadow-like existence 'in-between the governments, corporations and institutions that run cities' (Simone 2010: 1). This observation certainly seems to describe well the situation that *orang antisipasi* find themselves in. I have explained earlier that *orang antisipasi* in Bantaran Kali typically make fast money with occupations that are formally considered illegal, and that they are tolerated and needed in kampong society because of the gaps in Indonesia's formal social safety institutions. Therefore, *orang antisipasi* are aware that it is in their interest to maintain their livelihoods in a flood-prone, poor and illegal neighbourhood, as this might well be the best of a range of options in their reach.

For example, Edi would probably not be able to find as many people in need of a loan in a wealthy and less flood-prone neighbourhood in Jakarta. In Bantaran Kali, however, he is able to exploit the many flood victims for his business to thrive. Similarly, *orang antisipasi* Ida is well aware that while her service is still tolerated in Bantaran Kali, her business may run a larger risk elsewhere in the city as it is formally considered 'criminal'. While we saw above that others extort payment from her in Bantaran Kali and she makes too little a living to actually break away from the trap of risk and uncertainty, we might also consider that she uses the familiar environment of the kampong to remain tolerated and hence protected by fellow residents, while she is able to earn a living with a *haram* profession that allows her to buy clothing, perfumes and food for her children. Hence, if the unequal structures in Indonesian and kampong society have a huge impact on the *antisipasi* risk style, the agency of *orang antisipasi*, or their own actions and decisions, certainly plays a part in their risk style as well.

Another reason why I claim that we should not overlook the agency of *orang antisipasi* when interpreting their risk style has to do with Pierre Bourdieu's notion of habitus. Habitus can be defined as the system of dispositions and ways of thinking about and acting in the world that is constituted early on in life. This system consists of dispositions that are shaped by past events and structures, and these dispositions, in turn, shape current practices and structures; also, importantly, they condition our very perceptions of these (Bourdieu 1984: 170; Bourdieu 1990; Desmond 2006: 391). In other words, the notion of habitus emphasizes not only that circumstances and structures impact people's perceptions and behaviour, but also that the opposite is true – an actor's decisions and practices impact circumstances. I take over this idea of Bourdieu and propose that the *antisipasi* risk style in Bantaran Kali is partly shaped by what I call a habitus of poverty: a subjective, intermediary force between structure and agency, or an internalization of social norms in which *orang antisipasi* have learned to perceive themselves as 'bad' and 'poor' types of persons. Consequently, they are unable to perceive themselves in any other situation than the problematic one they find themselves in nowadays and therefore they feel forced to maintain an *antisipasi* risk style.

The strong impact of habitus becomes clearer if we consider that, even if *orang antisipasi* are offered a chance to decrease their vulnerability (and improve their personal situation), they tend to reject such offers, instead sticking to an *antisipasi* risk style. Below I offer examples from the biographies of Ida and Edi in which they rejected a chance to decrease their objective material vulnerability to risk, after which I present a more general analysis of the way in which a habitus of poverty underlies an *antisipasi* risk style.

Ida's habitus of poverty

When Ida was selected by a civil servant to join a newly set-up saving system (*simpan pinjam*) that would be run by the *kelurahan* to allow poor slum residents to save and borrow larger amounts of money without taking financial risks, in order to finally move out of the kampong, Ida immediately rejected the offer. That bold decision still enrages the female official that selected her:

> I granted that woman this enormous chance for a better life because I had heard she was a widow with four children who is always in debt. So I ordered her to come here and told her that this was her one and only chance to get out of this slum! Can you believe that she refused? She must like it to be poor.

Ida, however, reflected otherwise on her refusal when I asked her about it:

> The woman wanted me to accumulate my money and invest it in her *simpan pinjam*, but I cannot save my money for long periods! I tried to explain to her what I have also explained to you: that I need all of it for my business! My business would end if I offended my boyfriends, so the arrangement was impossible for me. Oh, I'm already over it. What could a woman like me do with that money anyhow? Set up a brothel along the riverbanks? [laughs out loud].

The answer of Ida offers three reasons why she might have deemed it more pragmatic to refuse this long-term saving option, and stick instead with her autonomous, short-term risk strategies. First, Ida prioritized her financial expenditures in a different way than the civil servant did and therefore prioritized reinvestments in sexy clothing and 'lust-food' over long-term savings.

The second reason exposes distrustful perceptions of the institution of a saving group. It must be emphasized here that riverbank settlers, based on their direct and indirect experiences with *simpan pinjam*, indeed have plenty of realistic reasons to distrust such institutional saving systems. The *kelurahan* had set up a *simpan pinjam* two years earlier in Bantaran Kali which ended in bankruptcy, and other former *simpan pinjam* that were run by kampong leaders in society have also been unsuccessful. Several riverbank settlers never got back any of their investments in such saving groups, and the financial struggles that they faced after their participation were widely known in the kampong, including by Ida. She once admitted to me:

> I don't like politicians (*orang politik*) to decide when I can have my money. What if they corrupt the money? That happens a lot in Indonesia. I know many such stories. And of course it would happen again. Why would people like

that, want to help people like me? They know I am only a woman from the slums, and they can always betray me if they please… I can better manage my money myself like I do it now, because even though I always have debts, at least I never betray myself.

Hence, Ida's reason to refuse the offer of the civil servant seems the result of a pragmatic and experience-based risk assessment – in which the institution was distrusted, with good reason.

The third reason is, however, not explainable with a practical risk-assessment analysis, but has to do with the less-tangible notions of self-efficacy and habitus. The above-presented quotes of Ida indicate that she does not have high expectations of her future possibilities; therefore she has taken no action to radically improve it. Following psychological risk literature we could also say that Ida has low self-efficacy: she does not believe that she is capable of producing desired effects by her own actions. In Ida's case, the result of this belief has been that she has not even tried to save money to move to a safer neighbourhood, even though she indicated many times to me that she would like to move. In her mind, there's no point in saving – things will never work out for her anyway.

But even if she were able to accumulate some money, she believes that her situation would not improve. While the civil servant considered her offer a fair chance for Ida 'to get out of this slum', Ida at most fantasized that the money could eventually make it possible for a woman 'like her' to 'set up a brothel along the riverbanks'. In other words, she did not regard herself as able to live a successful life outside of Bantaran Kali, nor did she perceive herself in any other job than one that is *haram*. Moreover, Ida indicated that she is well aware of her marginalized position in society and expected that a chance to improve that situation might turn into a disappointment as 'they know I am only a woman from the slums and they can always betray me if they please'. Hence, Ida's decision to refuse a potential chance to accumulate money was influenced not only by an internalization of ideas about her 'type of woman', but also reflected negative expectations of the ways in which more powerful, political institutions in society would treat 'her type of person'.

The way in which a habitus of poverty – and especially people's learned perceptions of their own position and chances in society – can influence their risk practices became most clear to me during an informal conversation that I had with Ida that touched on these topics. In this conversation, I questioned Ida about what her ideal life would look like, or what could be the best that could ever happen to her in this life. Initially she was confused by the question that I posed. Clearly puzzled, she first started laughing and then asked me in return:

What do you mean? The *best* in my life? My life is just…this is my life! It will always be as difficult as it is now! How could it ever be different? I am a slum woman, only surviving here […] I learned from an early age that our lives are difficult because we are poor and we cannot afford to buy a registered piece of land, so we must live along the riverbanks and we are always flooded.

But even if we have many problems, I can survive because I always find smart ways to stay safe. This is just how my life is and I must accept it, even though it is shameful to live like this.

Below, Edi's biography offers yet another example of how the acquired perceptions of *orang antisipasi*, particularly their low self-efficacy and their mistrust of other actors, make it so difficult for them to escape from the trap of risk and uncertainty.

Edi's habitus of poverty

In 2007, when Edi was selected by a local foundation to receive financial support after a flood, he rejected this offer for similar reasons as Ida did. After employees of this foundation coincidently ran into Edi on the street and heard that he had become homeless after a flood, one of them offered for him to live in a house in a different, less flood-prone neighbourhood of Jakarta. Edi would only have to pay a very small amount of rent, as the house was owned by a rich family member of the employee who was eager to help poor people like Edi. As if this offer was not generous enough, Edi was also offered a job in the garage of the family member. But Edi said no to all these offers. His explanation for his refusal, just as with Ida, points towards a mixture of pragmatic risk assessment and the impact of habitus. His pragmatic risk assessment is reflected in the following narrative:

> What do you think would happen if I left the riverbanks? I would be like a baby again in another neighbourhood: I would have to start up again and learn everything from scratch…While here, I am an adult! I already know how to live here, I can survive here whatever happens.

Rather than moving away to a floodless, legal, yet economically risky environment that has little use for his moneylending business, Edi preferred to stay where he was. In that shadow-like existence in between more powerful actors, he could continue to make use of his detailed knowledge of kampong structures and neighbours' needs. Be reminded that Edi does not have many family members in the kampong and hence no fallback in his direct social environment. This pragmatic consideration is another part of the reason why he did not dare to take a chance and trust the employee of the foundation, but instead chose to stick to his habitual livelihood strategies. Besides these risk assessments, Edi's subjective perceptions of his personality and role in society also influenced his decision to reject the offer. He explained this in the following way:

> If they [the employees of the foundation] get to know me better, they will fire me again or chase me away, because rich people like that do not like tough (*keras*) people like me. So there is no way that this could have worked out well.

Here, Edi indicated that he regards himself as a certain 'type' of person, and he deemed it logical that wealthier people would no longer tolerate him in their environment after they had recognized what 'type' of person he actually is. Such habitus echoes normative ideas in Indonesian society about what is considered 'good' or 'bad' behaviour. Asked to describe his own 'type', Edi answered as follows:

> Don't think that I don't know that I do things that are bad. Acting harsh towards good Muslims, being tough to people who are just as poor as I am. But this is just the way I am. If you ask me what I would like to be if I was not myself, well, I would have liked to be a successful merchant, like the men on the market whom I see earning fair money with their businesses. Of course! Everybody would like to live in that way, right? But that is just fantasy for me…Anyone here will be able to tell you that I am not good like that. I am only good at fighting and being tough, that is all I learned in this slum-life.

In yet another conversation, Edi explained how he believes that he became as 'bad' as he is now:

> If you have learned how to stay safe even though life is very difficult, we call it *antisipasi*. That is what I do, right? While many of my neighbours cannot survive a flood or another problem autonomously. That is because they are good people, they are better Muslims than I am. So, they are too weak to stay safe in cases of emergency. If a flood comes, they keep hoping that life will become better or that Allah or the government will finally help them. While I already know that this is a naïve expectation. Nobody helps people like me in this country. I only survive because I can act tough and I have a tough heart. I have learned the hard way how to survive.

The interplay between agency and structure

Other people who are nicknamed *orang antisipasi* in Bantaran Kali generally expressed comparable views of their own positions and future chances in society as did Ida and Edi. The following quotations of *orang antisipasi* indicate that their future hopes barely reach beyond their current poor life in the kampong:

> I don't like living here. The floods give me headaches and I am always worrying about my money. But nothing much will ever change for me…I am too stupid to earn enough money to rent a safer house, and you know I have never followed education! So all I can do is survive here. But at least I survive always, because I can be tough and smart with money if needed. Even if I need to do things that are *haram*! So I don't need anyone else to survive here.

> My future? Just a slum dweller, I guess. What else could I become? I would like to be a business man and live in a luxury flat in some rich neighbourhood [laughs out loud], but that cannot happen. No way. People like me can never reach anything like that! That is for good Muslims, not for stupid people like me from the slums. We just *antisipasi*, doing *haram* things…

The main point that I am trying to make is not whether the above expressed convictions of *orang antisipasi* accurately reflect their capacities and opportunities in life. Rather, the point most relevant here is that their pessimistic views and representations of themselves are experienced by them as natural and taken for granted. This is in line with what Bourdieu described as habitus. Habitus, even though it can be orally expressed, is mostly pre-discursive, felt and experienced by people without them even thinking about it. Accordingly, the above quotations from *orang antisipasi* show features of a habitus in which it is considered impossible that one lives a life beyond the current circumstances of an urban squatter. We can thus conclude that *orang antisipasi* believe that they are well able to handle risk and overcome daily problems in Bantaran Kali, but only as long as they continue to exhibit the *antisipasi* risk practices that they have become familiar with in the course of their lives. Here, they feel confident that they can survive by acting *keras* or *haram*. Their expectations of the future become more pessimistic, however, as soon as it concerns an unfamiliar environment, or a radically different way of making a livelihood. Hence, I propose that a habitus of poverty, in an interplay with structural factors, shapes an *antisipasi* risk style.

In sum, then, although I agree with Small et al., who wrote that 'ultimately, the greatest barrier to middle-class status among the poor is sustained material deprivation itself' (Small et al. 2010); on the base of my experiences in the field I would add that the marginal position of Edi and Ida offers only a partial explanation for their current uncertain situation. An overly structural explanation overlooks the agency of *orang antisipasi* and the role that their own decisions and perceptions play. More specifically, it overlooks the fact that *antisipasi* risk practices are a product of a habitus in which the current marginalized position of *orang antisipasi* is experienced by them as logical and inevitable and, therefore, not challenged.

I deem it crucial, however, to underline that I carefully distinguish my position – that the vulnerability of *orang antisipasi* to floods and other hazard is partly reproduced by their own habitual perceptions and practices – from the position of scholars who tend to treat mental constructs as fixed and the main creators of poverty. I refer here specifically to the widely known 'Culture of Poverty' theory, which in basis holds that poverty traps are maintained over generations because of an intergenerational 'subculture' that arises among the poor as a response to economic adversity.

Although cultural explanations of poverty have been severely criticized in the past, they have been echoed again recently. In the last two decades there has been a revival of interest in the relation between culture and poverty (Cohen 2010; Kumar 2010; Small et al. 2010). Regarding this resurgence of cultural explanations of poverty in social sciences, I deem it relevant to compare below the main assumptions of modern cultural explanations with my view on the habitus of poverty and the mechanisms behind the trap of risk and uncertainty that I observed in Bantaran Kali.

After briefly discussing the main hypothesis of the Culture of Poverty, in the final sections of this chapter I will argue that it is not some type of fixated 'culture' of poor people that keeps them trapped in risky situations; instead, a habitus of poverty is the result of pragmatic considerations in the face of everyday life in an extremely uncertain and unequal environment. This also means that the situation is more open to change than the Culture of Poverty theory suggests. Although a habitus of poverty produces risk perceptions and practices that are habitual rather than innovative, my findings indicate that these mental constructs can and do change if circumstances radically alter.

Pragmatism versus a 'culture of poverty'

According to the Culture of Poverty theory, common characteristics of a culture of poverty include a high present-time orientation with little future orientation; a sense of resignation or fatalism; an inability to defer gratification; feelings of pow-erlessness, of inferiority and of personal unworthiness; and low educational moti-vation (Lewis 1961, 1997, 1988; Payne 2005). Although this culture rose initially as a response by the poor to their marginal position in a class-stratified society, it may well continue even if the circumstances that gave birth to it were to disappear. That is because once established, the patterned practices strongly predispose poor people towards reproduction of the same or similar tendencies and behaviours. For example, low education of the parents may lead to an inadequate prepara-tion for their children's education, which may again perpetuate unemployment, poverty and despair (Burke Leacock 1971: 11). It may also lead to a sociocultur-ally rooted psychological vulnerability, which reinforces behaviours that are asso-ciated with poverty, as well as very humble aspirations for one's personal future (Chakravarti 2006; Appadurai 2004).

To some extent, it seems that the Culture of Poverty theory resembles my view on the ways in which the habitus of *orang antisipasi* reproduces vulnerabil-ity to risk. In line with cultural explanations, I suggest that people only aspire to those things that they believe suited to their specific position in the social environment. Furthermore, I have argued that because *orang antisipasi* do not believe that an actual improvement of their position is possible for their 'type' of people, they often reject aid and act in a way that reproduces societal inequality. However, there are two main reasons why I disagree with purely cultural expla-nations of poverty. First, in Bantaran Kali, we cannot necessarily speak of an intergenerational culture of poverty. *Orang antisipasi* have quite different percep-tions of their own chances compared to those of their children. This becomes clear by the fact that they generally believe that their children should get an education, as this might offer them a better life. For example, when I started giving English classes to children in Bantaran Kali free of charge, Ida made sure that none of her four children ever missed any of them, because she believed that knowledge of the English language would help her children in their later careers. This indicates that her decision not to let her eldest children follow *for-mal* education is based on economic considerations rather than on subcultural ideas about their capacities and possibilities in life. Ida often said that she con-sidered English a useful skill for youngsters in the kampong to learn, because she believed it to be 'the language of the future'. If her children could succeed in improving their English skills, Ida believed that they might find a highly valued job and a related income. However, when I once offered to teach her English as well, she refused and said:

> For me, it is too late to change my life. I am an old and uneducated slum-woman, it is unrealistic to think that I will ever find a decent job in an office or so. And where else would I need to speak English? None of my boyfriends speak it! [laughs] But my children still have the option to escape from the riverbanks. I always tell them that they can become rich people if they work hard and diligent. Even though their mother has always remained stupid and dependent on men, I tell my children that they have the opportunity to move away from this area and get a better life, a safe life.

Similar views about their children's opportunities were expressed by many other *orang antisipasi* in the kampong. While they seem to have accepted their own low socioeconomic position in society and thus see an *antisipasi* risk style as their best option, they hold higher hopes for their children. One informant, who is also known as *orang antisipasi*, once said:

> Sometimes I make some money, but then I always have many debts as well. That is just how my life is. But for my children it can be different. This is why you can always hear me telling them that I am a low person only, uneducated and good for nothing […] But they might become high people! If they work hard, they can become doctors or civil servants. Presidents of the country, maybe even. Why not?

This quotation indicates nothing like a 'learned helplessness' that sustains an intergenerational 'Culture of Poverty'; rather, it seems to me that *orang antisipasi* have a realistic attitude towards their future, rather than an overly negative or hopeless one. Edi and Ida, as well as the other *orang antisipasi* that were introduced in this chapter, appeared perfectly aware of the marginalized position that they occupy in wider society and the direct social environment of Bantaran Kali. I here agree with Abdoumaliq Simone, who argued that '[m]any of the poor recognize that they operate in a "game" where they have limited power to set the rules or agenda, or to guarantee a stable place from which to operate' (Simone 2010: 17). Put that way, it seems highly pragmatic that their future dreams remain located within a rather small and familiar environment with little room to manoeuvre.

In Bantaran Kali, the dreams of *orang antisipasi* were always located in the riverbank settlement where they live now, as marginalized members of the poorest class in society. They aspired to a life with fewer financial stressors or a house that protects their valuable goods somewhat from flooding, but no life in an elite neighbourhood, or one in which they would have earn a high salary with a 'good' job. Acknowledging that Indonesia now is progressing towards a more democratic and perhaps more equal society, *orang antisipasi*, at the same time, considered that their children might have better chances in life and hence stimulated them to get an education and look for a decent salary, leading to a safe life.

Another problem of cultural explanations such as the Culture of Poverty theory that I want to discuss here is that they tend to depict people's future expectations as a mental capability that is somehow outside and beyond the reality of their daily lives. By contrast, Bourdieu's concept of habitus puts more stress on the indirect impact of an unequal social environment and unequal power dimensions on human practices (Swartz 1997: 115). The cultural hypothesis implicitly holds that poverty is largely maintained by people's pessimistic future expectations. In its extreme form, this would mean that poor people's own actions could enable them to escape the poverty trap *if only people learned how to aspire to the right things.* Yet such a view undermines the reality of structural social, economic and political inequality that riverbank settlers in Jakarta face in their everyday lives. It became clear throughout this chapter that the risk practices of *orang antisipasi* are strongly interwoven with and impacted by power relations in the social order. Their financial struggles, their illegal status and their vulnerability to flood hazards will not automatically be solved by more hopeful or ambitious future expectations. If, for instance, Ida would indeed aspire to accumulate large shares of her money instead of directly reinvesting it in her business, she would still not have a formal bank account and would therefore still risk bankruptcy by trusting her money to a rather untrustworthy savings institution. And if Edi would aspire to set up a more profitable business or to move to an area with fewer floods, he would still be an uneducated and poor ex-gangster with little chance of economic success outside his familiar social environment. Hence, I wish to make clear that it is not just their psychological vulnerability that determines their risk behaviour; instead, their habitual actions and perceptions are organized to mitigate the very realistic structural problems that they face in their daily lives.

As Swidler (1986) already wrote in an early critique on the Culture of Poverty theory, one can hardly pursue success in a world where the accepted skills, style and informal know-how are unfamiliar. One does better to look for a line of action for which one already has the experience-based equipment. In line with this view, this chapter has shown that people's habitual and sceptical attitudes serve them rather well in the uncertain environment in which they live, as it helps them to overcome sudden problems inherent to their marginalized position. *Orang antisipasi* feel well acquainted with the ways of wheeling and dealing in their current situation to such extent that they consider themselves always able to survive or overcome daily problems even though they know that they are among the most marginalized. This also implies that Ida and Edi do not necessarily want to leave the normal uncertainty that characterizes the kampong, because they have become fluent in the current *antisipasi* risk strategies that are so useful for a life on the riverbanks; at the same time they have developed fewer of the skills and manners that might help them manage the hazards in another, unfamiliar environment. That is, their developed habitus of poverty helps them to maintain a rather effective risk style in a context of normal uncertainty – while it is less useful in a different context. This style may reinforce poverty and risk, but at least it offers a practical repertoire that works in the reality of daily life in Bantaran Kali.

Afterword: Antisipasi risk practices in and outside of Bantaran Kali

This chapter showed that the *antisipasi* risk style is largely affected by unequal power structures both within kampong society and in wider society. Operating at the margins of society, *orang antisipasi* have little other choice than to exhibit risk practices that are focused on short-term solutions for risks and problems, that are 'illegal but licit', and that are autonomous – or rather mistrustful of the help that authorities involved in Bantaran Kali offer. These patterns of behaviour that other scholars associate with a Culture of Poverty appear here instead as the result of human actors acting pragmatically, in their efforts to mitigate persistent societal inequality.

At the same time, it became clear that the social norms that justify unequal power structures are internalized by *orang antisipasi* through what I call a habitus of poverty: an intermediate force between structure and agency. Put differently, the habitus of *orang antisipasi* reflects their marginalized position, their low self-efficacy and their mistrust of the intentions of elite actors. This makes it extremely difficult for *orang antisipasi* to escape from risk and uncertainty. It can therefore be concluded that the *antisipasi* risk style is produced not only by unequal power structures but also in turn reproduces such structures.

Because one of the goals of this book is to introduce an analytical framework to define and interpret heterogeneous risk behaviour within communities facing natural hazards, one starting point is to compare my findings of the *antisipasi* risk style with observations of scholars working on risk behaviour in other areas of the world.

My interpretation of the behaviour and perceptions of *orang antisipasi* resembles a specific way of life that Abdoumaliq Simone recognized among increasing numbers of poor people in different megacities, including Jakarta and Dhakar. Simone describes how an increasing number of marginalized actors in urban society secure a viable place in the city by living according to a sceptical or what he labels 'ironic' worldview: they expect little good from the future, and have learned to react defensively in advance. This means that they typically deal with problems autonomously, and that their practices often go against wider social norms of what is 'good' behaviour. Moreover, Simone notes that such an ironic worldview of the marginalized in urban societies manifests itself 'in the frequent reluctance of the poor to work towards changes or improvements in their living environment even when they are plausible' (2010: 18). Clearly, this seems the case with the *orang antisipasi*.

Analysing the livelihoods and social security of peasants and migrant Madurese in East Kalimantan, Gerben Nooteboom also describes a pattern of behaviour that is somewhat reminiscent of the *antisipasi* risk style. With regard to a group of people that he gets to know as the *orang duit* ('money people'), he writes that they rely primarily on cash for survival and livelihood (instead of making long-term investments or being dependent on social institutions) and are generally reluctant to contribute to village arrangements and institutions of social security. As a consequence, they do not expect (nor receive) much help in times of social need. They 'hope to be able to earn money until their children are old enough to support them. They try to be, and remain, independent and self-prepared' (2015: 164). As long as their cash incomes are relatively stable, regular and reliable, the *orang duit* are able to overcome daily problems. However, if suddenly income falls, they mostly solve their urgent cash shortages by taking out loans, or selling or pawning assets (ibid.).

The *orang duit* seem to have in common with the *orang antisipasi* that they handle problems relatively autonomously. For the *orang duit*, this has to do with their migrant status: many *orang duit* are poor wage labourers, whose cash incomes, untied labour relationships and existing social relations with people in their place of origin make them flexible and relatively independent of village institutions. For the *orang antisipasi*, their status cannot account for their risk style. About half of the *orang antisipasi* were born and raised in Jakarta, while the other half were newcomers to Bantaran Kali. Hence, the *antisipasi* style cannot be explained by status, but instead by circumstantial and psychological factors highlighted in this chapter.

Notes

1 In the Introduction to this book it was explained that fermented eggs are considered useful 'flood foods' as these are nutrients and can be stored for a relatively long period without decaying. Other examples of 'flood foods' are salted fish, cooked rice and *petai* (stink beans).
2 RASKIN is a subsidized rice program for poor families which provides 10 kg of rice per poor households at the price of Rp 1,000 per kg (for more information and evaluations of the program's effectivity, see SMERU 2008; Arif et al.2010). SKTM used to be a health card that offered the desperate poor subsidized or free treatment at state hospitals and clinics throughout the country. In theory, the resulting medical claims had to be met by a combination of local taxes and central government revenues. In practice, however, the SKTM system proved to be rather ineffective. Not only was it very difficult for residents to obtain a card, but it was also not guaranteed that they would get free medical care if they possessed a card (Gale 2011). In 2014, the card was replaced by Indonesia's Health Card (Kartu Indonesia Sehatan or KIS) as part of a new healthcare plan for Indonesia, which should guarantee affordable healthcare for all 240 million Indonesians by 2019.
3 These actors are known as '*orang ajar*' in Bantaran Kali. I introduce some of them in Chapter 3.

References

Appadurai, A. (2004). The capacity to aspire: culture and terms of recognition. In V. Rao & M. Walton (Eds.), *Culture and Public Action* (pp. 59–84). New Delhi: Permanent Black.
Arif, S., Syukri, M., Holmes, R., & Febriani, V. (2010, October). *Gendered Risks, Poverty and Vulnerability. Case Study of the Raskin Food Subsidy Programme In Indonesia.* Retrieved from www.odi.org.uk/sites/odi.org.uk/files/odi-assets/publications-opinion-files/6256. pdf, last accessed 25 October 2015.
Aspinall, E. (2014). Health care and democratization in Indonesia. *Democratization*, 21(5), 803–823.

Bourdieu, P. (1984). *Distinction: A Social Critique of the Judgment of Taste*. Harvard: Harvard University Press.

Bourdieu, P. (1990). *The Logic of Practice*. Stanford, California: Stanford University Press.

Burke Leacock, E. (1971). *'The Culture of Poverty': A Critique*. New York: Simon and Schuster.

Chakravarti, D. (2006). Voices unheard: the psychology of consumption in poverty and development. *Journal of Consumer Psychology*, 16(4), 363–376.

Cohen, P. (2010, October 17). Culture of poverty makes a comeback. *The New York Times*. Retrieved from www.nytimes.com/2010/10/18/us/18poverty.html?pagewanted=all&_r=0, last accessed 25 October 2015.

Desmond, M. (2006). Becoming a firefighter. *Ethnography*, 7(4), 387–421.

Gale, B. (2011, July 15). Healthcare sector fails many Indonesians. *Straits Times Indonesia*. Retrieved from www.thejakartaglobe.com/archive/healthcare-sector-fails-many-indonesians, last accessed 25 October 2015.

Koning, J. & Hüsken, F. (Eds.) (2006). *Ropewalking and Safety Nets: Local Ways of Managing Insecurity in Indonesia*. Leiden, Boston: Brill.

Kumar, M. (2010). Poverty and culture of daily life. *Psychology and Developing Societies*, 22(2), 331–359.

Kwon, H. & Kim, W. (2015). The evolution of cash transfers in Indonesia: policy transfer and national adaptation. *Asia & the Pacific Policy Studies*, 2(2), 425–440.

Lewis, O. (1961). *The Children of Sanchez. Autobiography of a Mexican Family*. New York: Random House.

Lewis, O. (1988). The culture of poverty. In G. Gmelch & W.P. Zenner (Eds.), *Urban Life: Readings in Urban Anthropology* (pp. 269–278). Illinois: Waveland Press.

Lewis, O. (1997). The culture of poverty. *Society*, 35(2), 7–9.

Nooteboom, G. (2015). *Forgotten People: Poverty, Risk and Social Security in Indonesia: The Case of the Madurese*. Leiden: Brill.

Payne, R. K. (2005). *Framework for Understanding Poverty*. Highlands, Tex: Aha! Process.

Simone, A. (2010). *Movements at the Crossroads: Urbanization from Jakarta to Dakar*. New York: Routledge.

Small, M. L., Harding, D., & Lamont, M. (2010). Reconsidering culture and poverty. *Annals of the American Academy of Political and Social Science*, 629(1), 6–27.

SMERU Research Institute (2008, February). *Research Report: The Effectiveness of the Raskin Program*. Retrieved from www.smeru.or.id/en/content/effectiveness-raskin-program, last accessed 25 October 2015.

Swartz, D. (1997). *Culture and Power: The Sociology of Pierre Bourdieu*. Chicago: The University of Chicago Press.

Swidler, A. (1986, April). Culture in action: symbols and strategies. *American Sociological Review*, 51, 273–286.

Wilson, I. (2012, April 7). War against thugs or war against the poor? *The Jakarta Post*. Retrieved from www.thejakartapost.com/news/2012/04/07/war-against-thugs-or-a-war-against-poor.html, last accessed 25 October 2015.

3 Orang ajar

Cooperation with the government

The previous chapter examined the range of ways in which unequal power structures can affect people's behaviour in the face of floods and other risks that shape the 'normal uncertainty' in Bantaran Kali. This chapter investigates in more depth the complex topic of power in relation to risk behaviour. For this aim it analyses the risk style of people with a much higher social status in kampong society than the *orang antisipasi* from Chapter 2. Here I introduce a group of residents who are nicknamed the *orang mengajar keamanan* in the neighbourhood, or, shorter, the *orang ajar*. *Mengajar* is the Indonesian verb for 'teaching' or 'lecturing' and is abbreviated to *ajar; keamanan* means 'safety'. Hence, an *orang ajar* might be described as a person who lectures fellow resident about the topic of safety.

It will become clear in this chapter that these lectures reflect the opinions of the Jakarta elite about what constitutes a threat to the social order in the city. In contrast with the *orang antisipasi*, who handle risks in relative autonomous ways, the practices that *orang ajar* exhibit in relation to flood risk most often involve others, particularly political actors. After describing these practices, I explore the effects of the *ajar* risk style for social dynamics and power hierarchies both within and beyond the borders of the kampong. In the final sections I compare the *ajar* style as observed by me in Bantaran Kali with human risk behaviour as observed by other scholars in different contexts.

To become familiar with the *orang ajar* in Bantaran Kali, I begin this chapter with picking up again the story of the flood that already started in the Introduction to this book and continued in Chapter 2, this time describing the risk practices and perceptions associated with an *ajar* risk style.

An ajar risk style

At about five o'clock in the morning, Yusuf, the man who alarmed me and many other residents of Bantaran Kali for the flood, was helping people to evacuate to the government shelter. It was no coincidence that Yusuf offered his neighbours a hand during this flood: Yusuf's risk style typically circles around the assistance of – and interference with – fellow residents. Yusuf is regarded, by himself and by his neighbours, as one of the inhabitants who helps fellow residents to stay safe. Yusuf feels obliged to do so, because he is widely known as an *orang ajar*.

After he had helped a family to install in the *kelurahan* evacuation shelter, Yusuf left the flood victims behind again and ran back towards the kampong to help yet others evacuate. The water splashed around him when he entered the inundated streets of Bantaran Kali and he quickly disappeared in the labyrinth of narrow hallways. Only four hours later Yusuf returned to the evacuation shelter. Finally, he could sit down to rest. He rubbed his sore muscles and hastily ate two full plates of rice, as he took no time to eat during the previous hours of the flood.

I noticed that, while eating, Yusuf was continually praised by fellow residents for his hard work. Several evacuees in the shelter told him that they were thankful for his assistance, while others indicated their gratefulness by bowing their heads towards him, their hands in prayer position in front of their hearts. One of the evacuees explained to me that he and his neighbours must 'show respect' for people such as Yusuf: 'He is a good man, an *orang ajar*. He always helps weaker people like us during floods'. 'He always does that', added another, 'because *orang ajar* know what to do'.

These quotes indicate that, as was the case with the nickname *orang antisipasi*, the informal title *orang ajar* is widely recognized in Bantaran Kali. I discuss its main characteristics below.

As soon as he finished his meal, Yusuf joined in the conversation. Passionate in tone, he underlined again and again that helping others during floods was not some arbitrary choice for him; instead, it was his moral and semi-official 'duty' (*tugas*) in Bantaran Kali:

> All residents of this kampong can tell you that I have a duty to keep things safe on the riverbanks. That is because I devote all my time and energy to our safety. My money, even! Everything that I once possessed I have used to buy an HT so that now, I can help my neighbours to survive floods.

HT is the popular abbreviation in the kampong for a 'Handie Talkie': a handheld two-way radio receiver. It can be used by ordinary citizens to receive information from the sluice-gate keepers about the water level in the sluices in and nearby Jakarta. In the case of a large flood, it can also be used to alarm KORAMIL (Komando Rayon Militair), the sub-district military command involved in Jakarta's flood management and the city's security unit.[1]

Orang ajar in Bantaran Kali

Including Yusuf, eight people in Bantaran Kali possessed an HT during the time I lived in Bantaran Kali. Together these people participated in a self-supported flood-warning system. The nickname '*orang ajar*' referred to the eight owners of an HT, as well as to the many other inhabitants of the kampong who regularly assisted these people in carrying out their duties. Before I further introduce the residents who participate in the flood-warning system and who are all known as *orang ajar*, let me explain briefly how the flood-warning system works.

If residents want to gain access to the valuable flood information that can be received via an HT, they must themselves invest in the device, which costs on average 2.5 million Rupiah or the equivalent of approximately 165 Euro. Despite the fact that this is a very large financial investment for most inhabitants of the riverbanks, later in this chapter I show that even the poorest among them are sometimes able and willing to make it. According to riverbank settlers, the first HT entered the kampong in 2002, after a large flood had inundated Bantaran Kali. This first radio device was provided to a kampong leader by the *kecamatan* (administrative sub-district), to serve as a kind of flood-warning mechanism. That plan, however, did not work out: the device was lost in the next flood that inundated the kampong, in 2003. The *kecamatan* never replaced this HT, but residents themselves did. In past years, different people have personally invested in the radio equipment, thereby functionally expanding the flood-warning system in Bantaran Kali.

The *kecamatan* is still involved in the flood-warning system, albeit from the sidelines. The institution provides users with a private radio frequency which can be used to communicate with KORAMIL. The *kecamatan* also facilitates the radio contact between the sluice-gate keepers in Jakarta and the riverbank settlers who possess an HT. When users of an HT hear sluice-gate keepers speak of 'phase 3' over the radio, they know the implications for their neighbourhood: the water in the sluice uptown has risen to 110 centimetres, which means that the water in the nearby sluice in Jakarta will soon rise to 750 centimetres at least; thus, within hours, the river in Bantaran Kali has a fair chance of flooding. In the words of Yusuf's wife: 'then, my husband needs to get everyone out of here'. Whenever owners of an HT expect that such immediate action is needed, on the basis of their information, they feel responsible to 'contact the [kampong] leaders, bang on doors, shout out loudly spreading the news, ask the military for assistance, order people to evacuate, tell them what to do and where to go...'

During floods, *orang ajar* maintain contact with external flood-management institutions of the Jakarta government and offer assistance to potential flood victims, often ordering them to follow their instructions. Furthermore, they help neighbours to evacuate.

The nickname '*orang ajar*' refers not only to the actions that are taken during a flood, however, but also to 'duties' that are performed throughout the year – be there floods or not. One important characteristic of the risk style of *orang ajar* concerns their long-term strategies. Here we touch upon a big difference between the risk practices of *orang antisipasi* and those of the *orang ajar*. The former exhibit short-term risk practices during and after floods, mostly based on survival and recovery; *orang ajar* put considerable energy into prevention and mitigation of flood risk. For instance, they actively gather up-to-date information about flood risks throughout the year through the use of their HT (or, if they do not possess one themselves, through their contacts with *orang ajar* who own an HT), and they put much time and energy into the development and maintenance of reciprocal relationships with *kecamatan* bureaucrats or employees of KORAMIL involved in the flood management of Bantaran Kali. Most importantly, *orang ajar* feel that they have the permanent task of 'teaching' or 'lecturing' (*mengajar*) residents who they consider to have less knowledge about issues of risk and safety than they do.

Lecturing residents

In their 'lectures', *orang ajar* tell fellow residents, in accordance with the safety instructions of the *kecamatan*, that they should not remain in or atop their houses after a flood-risk message has been spread, but evacuate to *kelurahan* shelters; that they should not return to their houses before the water has receded and one of the *orang ajar* has declared it safe to do so; and that after floods they should get themselves medically checked, wash themselves and clean their houses with clean water to prevent disease. According to *orang ajar* Memen (63), an enthusiastic organizer of such 'lectures' in Bantaran Kali:

> Our knowledge must be continually repeated to all of our neighbours. Otherwise people do not understand how dangerous floods are. They don't know what to do when a flood comes, and they cannot survive the large floods that we nowadays experience in this kampong. So we need to give lectures about that.

These 'lectures' do not take a formal nor a fixed shape, but instead are organized in different ways by different *orang ajar*. For example, during my fieldwork I observed that Memen gave his lectures almost daily in a local *warung*. While sipping from a mug of caramel-flavoured coffee, he would share romanticized memories with customers about past times when the river was still wide and clean and the sluices in Jakarta were not yet obstructed with garbage as they had become later:

> I was born and raised here. When I was a young man, me and my friends used to swim in the river, and bamboo was transported over water by large boats…Then more and more [people] settled in and started living on the riverbanks. Like you! [points his index finger at one of the customers] You have only been here…what? Fifteen years? Yeah, that's relatively short. Since you started building new houses, the river has become very shallow and narrow. It is because of people like you that this community suffers from floods nowadays. Therefore it is important to learn from us [the people who have radio contact with the sluices], so that we can still stay safe on the riverbanks.

Orang ajar Yusuf told fellow residents again and again during informal conversations in the street that *they* cause floods in the neighbourhood by 'taking up space that is meant for the water' and by 'polluting the river'. *Orang ajar* Lestari, a woman from rural Java who came to live in the neighbourhood 13 years ago, shouted her 'lecture' loudly for all in the street to hear, as she pointed to a man who crouched down to defecate in the river: 'If you continue to pollute the river like that, your house will be inundated by another flood some time soon!'

It needs be stressed that the content of these lectures is largely inaccurate. Besides the fact that the inhabitants on the riverbanks form only one aspect of the complex flood problem in Jakarta, the blaming narratives of *orang ajar* obscure the fact that they themselves bear no less 'guilt' in the flood problem than the people who are openly blamed by them. While blaming others for their residence of the riverbanks, *orang ajar* Yusuf himself lives in a house that was built directly on the riverbanks. Moreover, just as nearly all inhabitants of the kampong do, *orang ajar* dispose of their garbage in the river. Nevertheless, in Bantaran Kali, *orang ajar* teach their neighbours over and over again that *they* are to blame for the floods.

These narratives of cause and blame echo the ideas that circulate in the political institutions that carry formal responsibility for Jakarta's flood management. A bureaucrat of the *kecamatan* put it like this: 'They built their houses on flood plains! Of course they are flooded all the time! That is what flood plains are supposed to be for! We have floods because of those stupid *people*, not because of the river!' Another official in the *kecamatan* said in an interview that 'They are not just flood victims. They are actually more the *creators* of floods'. A final example of the 'blaming of the victim' is offered by the quotes of a policymaker in the Department of Public Works, the institution which formally manages Jakarta's flood problem:

> The real victim of floods is the Jakarta government. That is because we are forced to spend a large part of our budget on those stupid riverbank settlers, preventing them from drowning, trying to convince them to move away from the riverbanks. Without them, we wouldn't even *have* floods, and we could concern us instead with other priorities in our city.

As I claimed before, however, floods in Jakarta are created by a complex range of factors – encroachment of the riverbanks is only one of them. But that is not the main point here. What I find most important to point out at this stage of the book is that whatever the precise form or content of their 'lectures', all *orang ajar* have in common that they share their insights on risk with children as well as with elderly; with looked down upon drug addicts as well as with highly respected kampong leaders; with locals as well as with newcomers.[2] For them, active involvement in fellow residents' perceptions and practices is an important aspect of the way in which they handle risk. For this aim, after they return home from work, or early in the morning while buying a plate of *nasi goreng*, day in, day out, *orang ajar* 'lecture' neighbours on the risk of floods and the best ways to handle it.

All of these 'duties' are regarded by *orang ajar* as preventive practices that decrease flood risk for the whole community, thereby also decreasing the personal risk that *orang ajar* themselves run by living on flood-prone riverbanks. At the same time, their practices are a way for them to prove their support for the Jakarta government. This is particularly important because, as I will explain later in this chapter, *orang ajar* expect that they will be helped by the *kecamatan* or KORAMIL in times of disaster in return for their support. Hence, their current *ajar* practices are seen as an investment: one that will be earned back in the form of safety at some point in the future. Before elaborating on this and other (expected) benefits of this risk style for the *orang ajar*, allow me to discuss one final important characteristic of the *ajar* risk style.

Until now we have seen that their practices are long-term and usually involve political actors. Below I add that the risk 'duties' that *orang ajar* have taken up in kampong society do not concern only *flood* risk, but a much broader array of safety issues – most notably those associated with a potential threat to social order.

Managing floods, managing safety

Although the *orang ajar* generally underline only the usefulness of their HT during flood hazard events, observations of actual usage of the radio system in Bantaran Kali show that there are many different situations in which the HT is used. In fact, during my fieldwork, *orang ajar* hardly ever reported to KORAMIL on potential floods. Instead, *orang ajar* regularly reported about people or situations that they considered a threat to the social order and safety in the kampong. Interviews with *orang ajar* indicate that this was not only the case during the time I happened to live in Bantaran Kali, but that it has been like that ever since *orang ajar* cooperated with the *kecamatan*. *Orang ajar* Lestari, Yusuf and Memen described these aspects of their 'duties' as follows in a group interview with me:

> Yusuf: In Jakarta, public order is taken care of by the police, but safety issues are the responsibility of the military. Now, I already told you that this radio system belongs to the military. So together with the military, we are responsible for safety here…That can concern floods or other problems with safety (*masalah keamanan*) in the kampong.

> Lestari: We are actually like the intelligence, you know, like spies. So, if there is a problem with safety in this neighbourhood, we report about that. We call in every evening and we speak to the operator at the military.

> Memen: We can always contact KORAMIL because we have so many floods here, right…So now, because we already have the HTs anyway, if there is another safety problem here, we can share information about that with the military, and then the army can stand by to help us solve it.

These quotes suggest that the 'flood-warning' system that the HTs supposedly support in Bantaran Kali is in reality used for a broader range of safety issues, with *orang ajar* helping the elite to maintain social order in Bantaran Kali.

Different government actors also referred to the use of HTs for a wide range of 'problems with safety' in interviews with me: 'People along the riverbanks told you that they report on floods with an HT? Well, yeah, but maybe sometimes there is something else at hand…if they see something dangerous, then why not use the HT to report on that, right?' said one policymaker involved in flood management. The exclamation of a highly positioned civil servant in the army underscored in rather direct terms the actual value of the reports of *orang ajar* for the

Jakarta government: 'Why would we be interested in information about the river? We can monitor the river in much more detailed ways from our own radar! The people at the riverbanks know nothing about the river that we don't know. If they talk to us, they are like the newspaper, bringing us the news, you know'.

The 'news' can also be reported on through more informal channels, such as government-run *arisan* (saving) groups, of which nearly all *orang ajar* were members. (In contrast, even though residents with other risk styles were often engaged in local *arisan* groups, none of them was ever member of a government-run *arisan* group. That membership seemed reserved for 'close contacts' of the government only.) Below I explain that the 'news' reported on typically concerns potential social unrest, or people challenging or protesting against the government, and discuss several examples of such safety issues.

Memen felt that he was especially well able to recognize potential 'problems', as he was the only *orang ajar* in Bantaran Kali who was once personally instructed by a military officer living outside the neighbourhood. This informal training made such an impression on Memen that he scribbled the advice down in a pink notebook of his granddaughter which he has kept with him ever since. Every now and then he reads them over. His notes remind Memen that he, as the owner of an HT, has several duties that go far beyond flood management, such as 'protecting the community', 'functioning as a source of information', 'avoiding lawlessness' and 'functioning as the eyes and ears of those who know and understand the law'.

As did the other *orang ajar*, Memen regularly visited fellow residents in their houses to question them about seemingly relevant 'safety' issues, or he sat down at a street where other inhabitants group or joined in (uninvited) during an *arisan* gathering, to overhear the latest gossip that he might later report on. Other times he autonomously searched for situations to report on during what *orang ajar* call their 'patrols' (*patroli*). Late at night, I frequently saw them walking around the neighbourhood at a slow pace, looking around carefully as they zigzagged their ways through the riverbank's alleys.

These observations already shed some light on the many advantages that authorities enjoy from their cooperation with *orang ajar*: Political actors receive information about perceived 'problems' from an urban slum which would have otherwise remained hard to access. It is hard for political actors to derive insider information from poor and 'illegal' citizens, but *orang ajar* clearly have less difficulty in finding out what they deem relevant enough to report about.

Which 'safety problems' in Bantaran Kali can possibly be so dangerous that they need to be reported about by slum residents to Indonesia's politicians and army officials? The narrative description of *orang ajar* on their 'duties' is illuminative here. The following quotes of *orang ajar* were derived from the group interview mentioned above:

Lestari: If I hear gossip about a possible gang fight, I report. If I see someone walking around with weapons, I report. If I suspect someone wants to make trouble for the government, I report. Of course! It is the only way to keep our neighbourhood safe. If this would happen in all neighbourhoods in Indonesia, I tell you, our country would be the safest in the world.

Yusuf: When I first made use of an HT, the man who gave me the membership card of KORAMIL explained to me that the *kecamatan* and the military like to cooperate with us because they do not want troubles in this neighbourhood. No anarchy (*anarki*)! It must remain peaceful and safe…And we have the responsibility to maintain that [social order].

Asked for an example of potential social unrest, *orang ajar* consistently referred to former instances of public protest where citizens overtly challenged dominant classes in society. Most of the concrete examples provided by them referred to the political protests that took place in 1998, after which then-President Suharto resigned. According to the *orang ajar*, the social order has remained unstable ever since. Memen said about this:

If a city governor takes an action that people do not like, immediately, they want to protest! Especially the poor people in this city tend to be stupid like that.

And Lestari added:

Many poor people in Indonesia are stupid and hot-headed. They proved that already when they protested President Suharto. And there are still many poor people in this country because there is not much employment nowadays, while there are many floods that create financial problems for people. So that is why there can always be uprisings in slums like this. There are many hot-heads who like to make trouble against the government, because they think the government should provide them with food and jobs. Or because they are angry that our houses get flooded all the time.

These discourses about social order and stability resemble paternalistic ideas on the 'stupidity' of poor masses from the authoritarian regime of former president Suharto's New Order, when 'poor people' were looked down upon by elite classes and when patron–client relationships were characteristic of Indonesian society. The *orang ajar* seem to have internalized such ideas about their fellow residents from their political authorities. Consequently, they watch out for floods in their neighbourhood – but also, and especially, for 'stupid people' who are accused of being potential 'troublemakers' and 'hotheads'. Hence, in the name of the government, *orang ajar* hunt after any individuals that may protest against authorities.

Many of the ideas of *orang ajar* on the protesting tendencies of the poor masses pointed back to 1998, but they also frequently mentioned examples of more recent instances of protest. In 2002 and 2007, tens of riverbank settlers in Jakarta participated in protests that were focused against the flood-management policies of the Jakarta government. Among them were several inhabitants of Bantaran Kali.

Although these protests did not lead to a change in flood policies, they impacted the Jakarta government in another way. That is, they showed politicians that there (still) exists a potential for social unrest in the city. According to the *orang ajar*, it is their duty to prevent this potential from becoming reality.

> Yusuf: There have been protests at the sluice in Jakarta against floods. Some people from this neighbourhood participated in those…They were complaining that the government should stop flooding in our kampong, even though they have no knowledge about this complicated problem [of flooding]. Therefore we must keep an eye on them and keep things safe here.

> Memen: During past floods people here started making trouble. But now we have the task to maintain safety here, so I can predict that during the next flood, there will be no more problems in this neighbourhood.

> Lestari: If I find out that people try to organize a protest against the [city] government, for sure I report them to the military. And my neighbours know it – that is why nobody dares to do such thing.

I will shortly elaborate on the benefits that the political institutions in Jakarta enjoy through their cooperation with *orang ajar* in Bantaran Kali. But first, let me offer some concrete examples of the ways in which *orang ajar* have tried to maintain 'order and safety' during my stay in Bantaran Kali.

Reporting with the HT

A first and most relevant example for this study concerns the reports that were made against seven young riverbank settlers who organized a citizens forum to discuss the problem of flooding. During two meetings, both of which I attended, the members of this forum discussed possible solutions to floods: people could themselves clear away the garbage along the sides of the river, demand better flood management from the Jakarta government and demand financial compensation for flood victims from the Indonesian government. According to these riverbank settlers, flooding was 'unfair' (*tidak adil*) as poor riverbank settlers are much more disadvantaged by floods than are the people in the less flood-prone elite neighbourhoods. They suggested that it would be good for the many riverbank settlers to 'become unified' and 'form a strong group'. The possibility of yet another protest at the sluice was also mentioned several times, although no concrete plans were made for such an event. In the weeks after these meetings, two *orang ajar* independently told me that they had reported on the forum members because 'they make problems' and 'they can create anarchy'. Eventually the forum fell apart without forced intervention, as hardly any residents appeared interested in participating with the organizers. None of the residents explicitly expressed fear of joining in towards me, but several of them did mention that although the organization of a forum would 'actually be good because floods are a big problem', it was perhaps better to quit as it would also 'upset some people'. Therefore, they deemed it better for residents to 'just mind their own business', 'be neutral' and not to 'cause problems'. It seems likely that these 'problems' concerned a conflict with *orang ajar* or the authorities.

A second example was presented when a group of immigrant chicken butchers was reported on by *orang ajar*, and as a result they were expelled from the kampong. These chicken butchers had come to live in the kampong four years earlier, but did not intermingle much with their neighbours. Instead, they spent all their time working and ran a successful business in Bantaran Kali. However, after multiple complaints from *orang ajar* about these newcomers to KORAMIL and the *kecamatan*, the chicken butchers were expelled from the kampong by the kampong leader. The formal reason for their expulsion was that *orang ajar* said that these chicken butchers 'pollute the river' with meat residue, which, according to the *orang ajar*, caused an increase of flooding. In reality, however, several *orang ajar* independently told me that they wanted the chicken butchers to move away from the kampong because they had seen them gambling – a practice which is illegal in Indonesia. It thus seemed that this report had more to do with elite perceptions of (il)legality, and with *orang ajar*'s disapproval of these outsiders' behaviour. Hence, the report they made can be seen as a practice that serves, at least in the eyes of *orang ajar*, the maintenance of social order.

A third example concerns a fight between two men, one of them generally known to be a 'troublemaker' and a 'hothead'. He was reported on by *orang ajar* to KORAMIL, after which he was imprisoned for four months. According to *orang ajar* Lestari:

> I heard screaming and then I saw [name of this man] throwing a rock at his brother. [That man] is dangerous – he likes to protest and fight. I am not happy that he lives here. How can we ever feel safe with such people around us? So I asked my friend Memen what to do, and we decided to call up the military on his HT. A few days later, that man was sent to jail so we're safe again.[3]

Each of the three above examples of instances in which *orang ajar* have reported their fellow residents to political institutions exposes the powerful position that *orang ajar* have in kampong society. If, for some reason, they perceive a fellow inhabitant as a threat to social order or safety, they are able and willing to discipline or punish this person through the use of their HT and their contacts with elite actors in the *kecamatan* and the military. It seems unconvincing that a small group of gamblers, a sole 'hothead' or a tiny network of potential protesters would indeed form a serious threat to the safety of the social environment. Rather, it appears that *orang ajar* sometimes report on people for fear of protests against their collaborators in the Jakarta government. This explains why the *orang antisipasi*, many of whom as we saw in Chapter 2 are involved in illegal businesses, have never been reported by any of the *orang ajar*. The illegal practices of Edi and Ida may be *haram*, but they are apparently not perceived of as threatening enough towards authorities.

And there is another reason why it is unattractive for *orang ajar* to expel *orang antisipasi* from the kampong. While I already noted in Chapter 2 that some *orang antisipasi* pay 'safety money' to several powerful residents in the kampong, I can now add to this observation that I was referring to the *orang ajar* being paid. Hence, *orang antisipasi* form a source of income for the *orang ajar*. And besides being financially useful, we may remember that *orang antisipasi* also offer valuable services to riverbank settlers (including the *orang ajar*). Yusuf has borrowed money from *orang antisipasi* Edi more than once; at least two *orang ajar* whom I got to know have made use of Ida's 'mattress service'. We might therefore conclude that who is considered by *orang ajar* a 'troublemaker' has not so much to do with acting against the law, but more with the perceived potential of a person engaging in protest against the government, as well as with the 'usefulness' of an individual for other, more powerful actors in society. Similarly, it has become clear by now that the *orang ajar* are much more concerned with the fight against the risk of disturbance of the social order, and potential 'anarchy', than they are of the fear of floods and the fight against floods.

Clearly, perceptions of who poses such risk or who can be trusted are highly subjective and contested in the neighbourhood. Whether or not perceptions are translated into action is dependent on power hierarchies. While *orang ajar* have the power in Bantaran Kali to expel unpopular newcomers, to get a perceived 'hothead' imprisoned and to sabotage citizens' potential protest against the local government, the best that less powerful fellow residents can do is try *not* to be reported about, by obeying or at least not agitating *orang ajar*. It is therefore understandable that both Edi and Ida (Chapter 2) silently agree to pay 'safety money' to local, powerful inhabitants such as the *orang ajar* and that Ida sometimes feels forced to 'offer the mattress' to them 'for free'. I put the words 'for free' between inverted commas here, because even if it is true that Ida was never paid for her service by *orang ajar* in the form of 'presents' or 'cash', we might argue that she is 'paid' with favours by them: the 'favour' not to be reported about, and the 'favour' to remain tolerated and protected in kampong society despite one's illegal practices.

In the next section I elaborate on the powerful position that the *orang ajar* occupy in kampong society. I first discuss the personal benefits that *orang ajar* enjoy in return for their 'duties', after which I show how residents can acquire this powerful *ajar* position in Bantaran Kali.

The benefits of being an orang ajar

People in Bantaran Kali who have a socially recognized position as *orang ajar* enjoy various personal benefits. First of all, their risk style creates and maintains vertical bonds and linkages between them and more powerful actors in Jakarta society. The following interview extracts with *orang ajar* highlight that their risk style offers them access to a social network of elite actors that would otherwise remain out of reach for slum inhabitants.

Yusuf: It is funny…We live in a slum! We are the poorest in Indonesia's society! And still, we can be partners of the military.

Memen: I like to teach people about the safety here even though it costs me a lot of time….But I get to correspond with the army and the people in the [city] government…Yeah, even though they do not like people to live on the riverbanks, they approve of me anyhow. I know that because we chat over the radio like we are friends…

Second, their risk style offers *orang ajar* an increased sense of personal safety. *Orang ajar* expect that, during future flood emergencies, their family members will be advantaged because of their relations with elite actors. This belief is expressed in the following discourses from *orang ajar*:

Lestari: If my house gets flooded, the military will first search for me in this neighbourhood, because they know I assist them.

Yusuf: Normally the [Jakarta] government does nothing to help flood victims in slums. But for me, it has become different now because I have the HT. If there is a problem in my life, like a large flood […] for sure I will get help from my friends in the military and the *kecamatan*. Because they know I am cooperating with them, so I deserve their help.

Memen: I am never afraid during large floods because I know that I will be rescued by the military anyhow. They know I am loyal to them, so if there is a flood here, they will shout out my name and search for me.

The sense of safety described by *orang ajar* does not just concern floods, but also poverty-related risks and evictions. All *orang ajar* indicated in conversations with me that they believe that their cooperation with authorities may, in the longer run, help them to increase economic capital. Memen, for example, often expressed the hope that his grandson, who was at the time of fieldwork five years old, may later get a job with the military without having to pay the obligatory application cost. Memen deemed this a fair expectation because 'at KORAMIL they will clearly remember how this grandfather has always helped them during floods'. Likewise, *orang ajar* typically believed that their bureaucratic contacts would offer them support in times of acute need, for example when their household is threatened with the risk of illness or eviction. Yusuf, for example, once expressed his positive expectations of the future with me through these words: 'If my son becomes ill, the people in the army will pay for his treatment, because we have become friends now. It is the same with evictions: do you really think they will bulldozer away my house? Of course not. I am their friend. They will save my house'.

Whether these expectations are fulfilled, only the future will tell. To my knowledge no *orang ajar* has yet been financially rewarded for their duties by authorities, and none of their children has ever been offered a high-status job. Hence, the expectations must be considered only potential benefits and not guaranteed rewards.

A more acute benefit of exhibiting an *ajar* risk style has to do with the increasing social status of *orang ajar* within Bantaran Kali, both because of their possession of a radio device that is widely in demand, and also because of their access to elite contacts in wider society. The increase in social status that an acknowledged *orang ajar* earns became visible immediately after Yusuf bought his HT during my stay in the field, in October 2010. In my fieldwork diary, I jotted down the following observation:

> Today Yusuf came walking into the kampong with an HT. He grinned continuously while he showed off the black radio device to anyone who wanted to see it. And there were many! Visitors stood in front of the house and asked to hold the radio set or turn its switches, but nobody was allowed to do so. He carefully held the device in his own hands, protecting it from admiring hands. His father, watching the row of visitors in front of the house, was clearly proud: 'My son has become a leader', he told me. His mother agreed: 'Only powerful people can use an HT'.

The increase of the social status of *orang ajar* generally translates in the alteration of social norms and hierarchies in Bantaran Kali. For example, in the face of flooding, *orang ajar* can act autonomously from the kampong leader, or order around co-residents who might in other cases not have accepted this subordinate position. According to *orang ajar* Memen:

> Normally, citizens go to the kampong leader if they have a problem and he decides whether or not to contact the district authorities. But now that I have my HT, I can directly contact them myself. So during floods, me and my friends basically become the leaders of the kampong and we decide what needs be done.

This increased power of *orang ajar* during and right before flood events is widely acknowledged by fellow residents in Bantaran Kali. During floods, I observed that residents were instructed what to do and where to evacuate to by *orang ajar*, rather than by kampong leaders. In fact, kampong leaders were also instructed by *orang ajar* – and I have never seen them disobey their instructions. Kampong leader Hussen once explained to me that he is the only one who can give people legitimate orders during 'normal' times, but that the legitimate power shifts towards *orang ajar* during flood events. He once possessed an HT, but – how ironically – lost his in a flood and never managed to accumulate sufficient money to replace it. Therefore, he accepts *orang ajar* as his advisers:

> Nowadays my residents inform me about the floods, and instruct me to inform the others. It is the world upside-down…Normally I am in charge, but I must admit that during floods, they have better capabilities to manage safety here. They also have close friends in the *kecamatan*. So I can only obey them.

So, by becoming an *orang ajar*, one is able to rise in the social hierarchy to a respected and more powerful position in Bantaran Kali. As a consequence of this rise in status and hierarchy, *orang ajar* can adapt certain associated social norms, such as bypassing the formal kampong leaders. Let me underline here that while this is visible most clearly in the looming crisis of a flood, it also happens at other occasions. We may recall from the beginning of this chapter that *orang ajar* also give 'lectures' about flood risk to ordinary residents as well as to kampong leaders. These lectures are given at every opportunity and not just during flood events. Over and over again, kampong residents and kampong leaders are indoctrinated by these narratives of cause, blame and safety, and during my stay in the field, no one ever overtly disputed the 'lectures'. The same holds true for the topic of eviction. *Orang ajar* frequently raised this topic publically, and urged residents to 'move away peacefully and find another place to live, as you have no right to live here anyway. This is not your land but the government's land'.

Clearly, the *ajar* risk style offers its users many benefits. It is, however, not easy to reach the powerful position *orang ajar* occupy; nor is it easy to live up to the demands associated with the position. This becomes clear in the next section, where the personal situation of *orang ajar* Yusuf is described to identify the investments that residents must be able and willing to make in order to become recognized as an *orang ajar*.

What it takes to become an orang ajar

On a particular cloudy evening a week or so before the flood, as his spouse awaited her turn in line to fill a bucket with water from the public well, she loudly complained that Yusuf, ever since he bought his radio device few months ago, has 'become useless as a husband. He wants to have more children, but he is always too tired to have sex because he is continually busy with that radio. And he wants to earn money, but all he does is educate other people free of charge!'

Later that evening, I met Yusuf in front of his house, smoking. He acknowledged that his *ajar* 'duties' exhausted him. 'I am continually tired', he remarked, 'I work day and night and I am always occupied with my HT'. Yusuf was seated outside in a squatted position, his back leaning against his house, his elbows resting on his thighs. With his right arm, he firmly held his son who whined and struggled to get free. The radio device lay on the street next to his bare feet. It produced a loud rustling sound. Using only his left hand and his lips, Yusuf imperturbably rolled a new clove cigarette. He told me that ever since he bought the HT, he has carried it around in the pocket of his trousers during working hours, and that he has been sharing his mattress with his wife, their youngest son, and the HT. With every crack or beep that the device produced overnight, Yusuf woke up startled. During the day, he walked around the kampong with puffy eyes and in a grumpy mood. He had heard neighbours gossip that it was better to avoid him, as he was continually sleep-deprived and resultantly snapped at anyone for nothing.

To make things worse for Yusuf, his boss at the cleaning company had recently become dissatisfied with Yusuf's performance and threatened to fire him if Yusuf continued to prioritize his 'duties' as an *orang ajar* over his cleaning job. He had explicitly complained about the fact that Yusuf never shows up at work whenever there is a flood in his kampong. Yusuf had a ready answer:

> He wants me to come to the office anyhow during floods, but that is impossible for me. If my neighbourhood is inundated, I cannot just neglect my duties here and clean buildings in other parts of the city as if nothing is at hand! My friends at the military would be upset if I'd do that.

Yusuf's boss was however hardly impressed by such arguments. When Yusuf came to work a day after the flood that is described throughout this book, he received a final warning from his boss: one more instance of failing to work during a flood, and Yusuf would lose his job as a cleaner.

Losing his job would be problematic for Yusuf indeed. Even though both him and his wife had a job (she offered a laundry service to fellow residents), their salaries provided hardly enough for their family. With their wages, Yusuf and his spouse took care not only of their one-year-old son Rudi, who suffered from diabetes and was in need of expensive medicines, but also of Yusuf's old and unemployed parents, who came to live with the couple a few years ago. Yusuf and his wife paid for all their meals and other costs, such as clothing or medicines in times of illness. As a result of these high expenses, the young couple had little financial room to manoeuvre. After the rent for their house had been paid, there usually was about Rp 600,000 per month left – the equivalent of about 48 Euro – to be spent on the needs of all five family members. That is not much, but at least there always used to be enough for all of them to eat a hot meal two times a day, to pay for the medical needs of Rudi, and even to accumulate a little savings for future needs. But if Yusuf were fired, the economic situation would become more pressing. The possibility of getting fired therefore was a major concern to Yusuf:

> I was already constantly worrying about the floods in recent years, and also about my son's health. Now I have yet another problem in my life to worry about. If I lose my job, I cannot feed my family. But if I would give up my duties…my problems might get worse! Think of what would happen during the next flood. There would be too few people to help residents survive. These worries give me a headache.

How, one might ask, was this relatively poor inhabitant of Bantaran Kali ever able to acquire an expensive HT in the first place? He could not have been *that* poor if he was able to accumulate the 2.5 million Rupiah to buy an HT, could he? In fact, he *was* that poor, as are several of his fellow *orang ajar*. Nevertheless, they were determined enough to scratch together the money.

Yusuf managed to make the initial investment in his HT by borrowing money from three acquaintances in the neighbourhood and by selling the television that his parents liked to watch during the day. His wife was not exactly pleased when she discovered that he spent the savings that she had regularly put away underneath their mattress since the birth of their son for his later education – Rp 20,000 per week, adding up to about one million Rupiah after a full year of saving. 'That was meant for your son, not for you!' she was heard screaming out one morning in the kampong, to the amusement of neighbours.

This portrait of Yusuf shows that the social rise in status which *orang ajar* eventually enjoy does not necessarily accord with their economic status. Next to the fact that some of them make large financial investments in order to acquire an HT, it was also demonstrated earlier in this chapter that many of their expected returns for these investments are based on hope and trust rather than on guarantees or realistic expectations. If we consider the possibility that their positive expectations are not fulfilled in the future, we might posit that the economic risk that their household runs *increases* as a result of their risk style. Indeed, I suggest that people with an *ajar* risk style often become more, rather than less, vulnerable to floods.

For instance, if Yusuf's child were to become ill, there is no money left in his household to pay for medical treatment, because Yusuf has gone into debt (and used up the family savings) in order to buy the HT. Yusuf, therefore, can only hope that his acquaintances in the local government would offer financial support on such an occasion: 'Sometimes I worry because I have no cash left nowadays. What do I do if my child suddenly needs an operation? But I think it will be all right if I just go to a government health clinic and ask them to call my friends in the *kelurahan*. Maybe someone can help me. I help them as well, right?' Whether or not Yusuf's hope is realistic remains an unanswered question for now; however it needs be noted that if he continues his *ajar* practices, he risks losing his formal job and hence his fixed income, further increasing his family's financial struggles. Similar unstable financial situations are to be found among other *orang ajar*, many of whom spend their last Rupiahs on the HTs and most of their time and energy on their 'safety duties'. As a consequence, they tend to get deeper into financial struggles in the process of becoming an *orang ajar*.

Hence, as was the case with the *antisipasi* risk style described in Chapter 2, the *ajar* risk style is not sufficient to escape what I call normal uncertainty in this book: a living environment of covariate risks that are to some extent normalized, while they also threaten the safety and well-being of riverbank settlers. Such a conclusion, however, seems to suggest that 'moving away from the riverbanks' would be the ultimate goal of inhabitants of Bantaran Kali. Let me clarify that such a view would be both simplistic and normative. Departing from a bottom-up perspective, I try to show in this book precisely that a risk style is much more than just a way to handle flood risk. For *orang ajar*, it is a way to become part of the political elite, to gain power and contacts that may help in future times of need. This remark underscores the usefulness of this study's 'normal uncertainty' approach over the more commonly used 'disaster lens' perspective in studies of risk and its handling. If the latter would suggest that the practices of *orang ajar* can be seen as an isolated response to floods, this study's normal uncertainty approach shows that their risk style is a response to several hazards and problems that characterize the daily life of riverbank settlers: floods as well as political and economic marginalization.

Factors underlying the ajar risk style

Money, or the capacity and will to accumulate it, is one important factor underlying the *ajar* risk style, but it is certainly not all it takes to become an *orang ajar*. A talent in social skills seems to be of equal importance. This becomes clear if we consider how Memen became an *orang ajar*. Memen used to sell satay at a market that was located next to a military compound and decided to offer passing generals his dishes for free, in order to 'make friends'. He recalled what happened when he started doing this:

> Some of them were surprised with my kind offer in the beginning, and others laughed at me because they considered me too bold for a poor man, but they liked my satay and eventually they behaved kinder to me. Many greeted me by name when they got to work.

A few months later, when Memen wanted to invest in an HT, he asked these acquaintances to say a good word for him in the *kecamatan*: 'I asked them: "pity me, I am a poor flood victim and I have been sharing my food for months with you to pay you my respect. You know that I am a good man, that you can trust me as a friend."' Two months later, he received the code for the radio frequency from a bureaucrat at the *kecamatan*.

This example underscores that a potential *orang ajar* must not only be able to gather sufficient capital to invest in an HT, but that one must first and foremost have sufficient social skills to establish and maintain vertical reciprocal relationships with elite actors. For a marginalized group of residents, it is not usual to establish trustful relationships with political elite, but Memen's example shows that kampong residents who are creative or skilled enough are able to do so.

Not only should potential *orang ajar* establish vertical relationships with elite actors in Jakarta society, but they must also make sure to become part of the inner circle of *orang ajar* who are already acknowledged in Bantaran Kali. That is because bureaucrats working for the *kecamatan* base their eventual decision about who may participate in radio communication mainly on information that they receive from other *orang ajar*. Yusuf, for example, managed to get access to the radio frequency via his social contacts with existing *orang ajar* who had already established social networks with KORAMIL employees, and who recommended him again to these elite contacts as a new 'friend'.

A civil servant once explained to me how this system of check and control works:

> We don't just give the radio frequency to everyone who asks for it. If someone wishes to get access to it, our friends from the riverbanks first tell us what kind of person he is, where his family comes from, how he earns his income. Then we check with the military whether they have ever had troubles with the person. So we monitor them to be sure that only trustworthy people use an HT.

Hence, the *kecamatan* decides on the trustworthiness of potential *orang ajar*, based on and tested through social circulation of detailed information about him or her. In the words of a high official of the *kecamatan*: 'only our friends and *their* friends can use the HT'. It is clear then that the *orang antisipasi* from Chapter 2, in their social designation as the 'bad' people in kampong society, have little chance to become included in such a strictly monitored, closed social network. In contrast, Yusuf and Memen were apparently regarded as good candidates.

Next to their ability to accumulate money and the required talent in social skills, wannabe *orang ajar* must live up to yet another demand of this specific risk style. Namely, they have to be willing and able to invest a lot of time and energy in developing an *ajar* risk style, before they can be recognized fully as *orang ajar*. Yusuf had assisted other *orang ajar* for the previous four years with their 'duties' before he was finally able to able to obtain an HT himself. He would, for example, help people to evacuate after *orang ajar* had spread the news about an upcoming flood. Other inhabitants who have no access yet to elite actors from the *kecamatan*, or who cannot yet afford an HT, must in turn assist Yusuf and his fellow *orang ajar* while they await their chance to rise in the social ranks:

> When I was younger, I saw other people with the HT and they were helping me and my neighbours during floods. I was jealous of them at first, I can tell you this honestly. The first time I saw a HT, I thought 'wow, I would like to have one of those', because I realized that with a HT I could predict when a flood comes, and I could talk to the people from the military…It seemed interesting to me.

We already know where this interest led him. Over the following years, Yusuf collected relevant information about what was needed to acquire the radio device. He established social relationships with relevant elite actors, collected enough money to buy an HT, started giving *ajar* lectures, and began monitoring the practices of his neighbours – all practices he had never done before in his life, but to which he would soon grow accustomed. And by the time I met him, Yusuf had gained high social status in Bantaran Kali. Memen and Lestari also had invested similarly to Yusuf, as did the other *orang ajar* I came to know along the riverbanks.

Next to social skills, and the ability and willingness to invest time, money and energy into the developing of this style, there is one final underlying factor of the *ajar* risk style that I deem relevant to discuss, namely a habitus of poverty. In Chapter 2 it was claimed that a habitus of poverty is the main underlying factor of an *antisipasi* risk style. It might therefore be somewhat surprising that I deem this notion equally relevant for the analysis of an *ajar* risk style, since the differences between this and the *antisipasi* risk style appear enormous. For *orang antisipasi*, it was explained that their habitual ironic future expectations (in combination with unequal structures of economy and power) keep them trapped in a situation of risk and uncertainty. In contrast, this chapter showed that *orang ajar* seem to have rather positive and hopeful expectations for the future, perhaps even in a some-what naïve way. Moreover, unlike the *orang antisipasi*, who take in a low rank in social hierarchy, we have seen that *orang ajar* enjoy a relatively high social status within kampong society, and are able to establish potentially useful contacts with elite actors in wider society. Regarding these differences, to what extent can we maintain that a habitus of poverty impact these actors' practices? If the theory of habitus seems to offer a rather convincing explanation for the tendency of the *antisipasi* risk style to reproduce social inequality and vulnerability to risk, is the risk style of *orang ajar* not a perfect and contrasting example of the ways in which actors can reflect upon and alter structures?

It is my contention that it is not. While the risk styles of the *orang antisipasi* and *orang ajar* differ in many ways, they have in common that they are largely determined by what I call a habitus of poverty, which is again influenced by power inequality in wider Jakarta society. In the next and final sections of this chapter, I provide three reasons that underlie this claim: First, *orang ajar* have internal-ized and reproduce elite narratives of cause and blame. Second, while the risk style of *orang ajar* is not sufficient for them to escape the trap of risk and uncer-tainty, it serves the interests of the Jakarta government. Third, the risk style of *orang ajar* does not lead to less humble future expectations with regard to the future as soon as it regards a life outside of the riverbanks, and neither does it lead to high self-efficacy. And as Chapter 2 showed, hopeful future expectations and high self-efficacy are crucial conditions that are required to break out of a habitus of poverty.

Serving elite interests

One way in which the practices of *orang ajar* advantage the local government is by their reproduction of elite narratives of cause, blame and safety in Bantaran Kali. Likewise, they reproduce the government discourse on the stupid masses of the poor and the poor's presumed tendency of disturbing social order and threatening safety in wider society. By 'blaming the victim' in their lectures, responsibility for finding a solution for the structural problem of flooding remains not with bureaucrats, but is shifted towards the inhabitants of the city's riverbanks.

This shift in responsibilities is further legitimized and institutionalized by the pre-warning system that is managed by *orang ajar* in Bantaran Kali. In an interview, an official at the *kecamatan* applauded the advantage of the risk-management practices of *orang ajar* for the Jakarta government:

> They serve like a pre-warning system. Free of charge! [laughs] We, as a government, cannot stop the enormous problem of flooding in Jakarta. Due to the people who use the radios, riverbank settlers can nevertheless survive floods. It is not really a problem for us anymore. We just assist the people with the radios, so that they can help their neighbours.

While it can be argued that the informal pre-warning system (the usage of HTs) in Bantaran Kali advantages the riverbank community in the sense that it provides residents with flood-risk warning messages, the facilitation of the radio communication system also appears a cost-effective way for the Jakarta government to decrease the negative consequences of flooding. Instead of demanding from the Jakarta government an effective and costly pre-warning system, the flood victims along the riverbanks now invest in radio devices. As a result, political actors who are formally responsible for Jakarta's flood management can simply wait until they are alarmed by riverbank settlers in potential times of emergency. As a result of this institutionalized shift in responsibilities, if a flood alarm in Bantaran Kali is false or too late, it is not considered the fault of the Jakarta government or the *kecamatan* but of the *orang ajar*, who apparently did not perform their duties well.

Hence, I argue that the facilitation by the *kecamatan* of the HTs of *orang ajar* does not necessarily aim to decrease the objective risk of flooding for riverbank settlers, but rather, it serves to institutionalize the shift in *responsibility* for flood management from political institutions towards flood victims.

As noted earlier, there exists yet another way in which the Jakarta government benefits from the risk style of the *orang ajar*, and that concerns the assistance that they get from *orang ajar* in the monitoring and controlling of social order along the riverbanks. A policymaker in the *kecamatan* expressed his satisfaction with the *orang ajar* reporting potential protestors as follows:

> The people on the riverbanks, they have nothing, they are very poor. So when they become angry about a flood, they are ready to sacrifice their lives! They are stupid enough to bleed and die when they are angry! Therefore it is good that some of our acquaintances live there and monitor them. We cooperate with them so things remain calm.

A manager at Public Works had a similar opinion about the riverbank settlers in Bantaran Kali: 'They have already tried to create protests at the sluice, they were ready to fight because they were dissatisfied with the floods...But nowadays we cooperate with people in the neighbourhood so that we can avoid such anarchy'.

I wish to stress that the word 'cooperation' is misleading in this situation, as it suggests a symmetric relationship of power and exchange. The relationship of *orang ajar* with bureaucrats or actors in KORAMIL is, however, not at all symmetric. Whenever I observed *orang ajar* interacting with these elite actors (most often over the radio and a few times in personal meetings), their behaviour indicated inferiority to the bureaucrats: in their gestures which indicated respect, for example, by bowing their heads and being silent as long as the other was talking; in the way they followed up their instructions without questioning or commenting; and in the language in which they addressed these people – always indicating that the other took up a highly respected position. Hence, while *orang ajar* may have acquired a high social status within kampong society, the same cannot be said for their position in wider society. Despite their 'cooperation' with elite contacts, in reality they remain subordinate to more powerful actors in society. Therefore, it is more appropriate to speak of a situation of clientelism, or asymmetric but mutually beneficial relationships of power and exchange (Van Klinken & Barker 2009; Scott & Kerkvliet 1977). I discuss this issue later in this chapter – for now, it suffices to realize that *orang ajar* carry out tasks that benefit their patrons, in return for increased social status and an increased sense of personal safety.

The word 'cooperation' is also misleading for another reason, namely that the local government seems to get much more tangible benefits out of this 'cooperation' then do the *orang ajar* themselves. Not only are the *orang ajar* overwhelmed by their 'duties' in Bantaran Kali's flood management while the Jakarta government accepts little or no responsibility, the practices of *orang ajar* also make it harder for fellow riverbank settlers to alter the unequal structures in which they live. As soon as they express dissatisfaction with their marginalized position, they run a risk of being reported upon by *orang ajar*. Hence, we might say that *orang ajar* help to reproduce unequal power structures in Jakarta society, by making it extremely complex for fellow residents to challenge them. Taking this argument further, we could consider the idea that the risk style of *orang ajar* is counterproductive for their own situation. Instead of challenging their marginalized position, *orang ajar* take satisfaction in small incentives. This means that what may have appeared to be *orang ajar*'s autonomously created and deviating interpretations of risk and safety are actually heavily impacted by the hegemonic structures surrounding these actors. Here, the intermediate force of a habitus of poverty becomes clear.

Habitus of poverty

If *orang ajar*'s future perceptions appear hopeful at first sight, closer examination reveals that their aspirations remain located in the risky environment of Bantaran Kali. Admittedly, I demonstrated earlier that, once inhabitants of Bantaran Kali have acquired a higher social position in kampong society by becoming an *orang ajar*, they commonly establish future expectations that no longer objectively reflect their present circumstances. We saw, for example, that Yusuf and several other *orang ajar* expect future loyalty from elite actors who would probably have remained outside their social network if there had been no floods to connect their interests. Nevertheless, a closer examination of the perceptions of *orang ajar* makes clear that the present future expectations of *orang ajar* hardly reach beyond their current, risky kampong life. Yusuf, Memen and Lestari expect future loyalty from their 'friends' in the sense that they expect help during floods in their current flood-prone neighbourhood, but they certainly do not expect an actual improvement of their social position in wider society. While all of them expressed the opinion that moving away to a flood-free neighbourhood would solve most of their problems, none of them considered this event a realistic one for their 'types of people'. This became evident, for example, from the narratives of *orang ajar* Lestari. In an interview, she explained that she must train her children how to handle floods, as she felt sure that her family would always remain living in a flood-prone area:

> I hope that they can use this radio when I get old. In that way, they can hopefully stay safe even though we live here. Otherwise their future will be difficult, as the number of floods will increase here.

Somewhat surprised by this remark of Lestari, I asked her why she believed that using the radio would still be necessary in the future. Perhaps, I proposed, her children would soon live in a neighbourhood without floods. Lestari shook her head and replied:

> No, that is impossible for my family. That is only for high people (*orang tinggi*), like politicians (*orang politik*). We will just stay here. Even though we do not like this muddy neighbourhood, we are stuck here! [laughs] We have no education and no money, so where else would we go? I do not have enough money to move house to a better neighbourhood, right. Nor can I get that in the future.

I wondered out loud why she felt so sure that her life would hardly improve, regarding her many 'friends' in KORAMIL and the *kecamatan*. Could they not help her to find a safer place, I insisted?

> [laughs] No, it is not like that. They are not concerned for me like that! I just help them and they will help me to survive a flood, but why would they pay for me to move house? We are not family or good friends! No, people like that are very different from people like us. They live in elite areas, while you know I am only an ordinary person, living in a slum. So we can only be thankful that they at least help us to survive here. They do little to help us; but without them I would be lost.

This quote indicated to me that Lestari does not believe that she herself is capable of producing desired effects by her own actions. We might also say that her self-efficacy is low, and that, while she trusts that authorities are able and willing to help her in cases of emergency – they will only do so under specific circumstances.

Similar sceptical ideas about his future options were expressed by *orang ajar* Memen. If I wrote earlier in this chapter that he hopes that his grandson might one day be offered a job in the army in return for his *ajar* 'duties', a closer examination of his future expectations exhibits that Memen has no hopes for an radical economic or social improvement of his family's situation. This became clear to me after I once asked Memen what he thought the life of his grandson would look like, in the case the boy got a job in the army, as Memen hoped he would. He immediately replied that it would be 'the same like mine. Just as it is now'. He then explained:

> Even if he can work there, he will never become a general or an officer. No, he might become a cleaner or work as an assistant. Perhaps he can become an average soldier. In any case his salary will remain very low. Maybe his parents can improve our house a little if he has the job. Maybe they can pay for a cement wall rather than the wood one they have now, that would be nice. But then there will be no salary left to buy any furniture! [laughs] So his life might be a little bit different, but he will still have the same concerns about floods and money. I already told my grandson that, if he must clean a general's office, then he shall do that with a smile on his face. We can only be thankful for anything high people like that want to give him.

A final example is provided from an interview extract with Yusuf. When I asked him in which other neighbourhood he would like to live, at first he politely laughed away my question. When I insisted, he bluntly refused to think about the option of moving house.

> Why would I tire myself with thinking about neighbourhoods where I can never live? I am a man from the slum. My wife is just as poor as I am. We have no education. So why even bother about moving house? Perhaps one day we can find a better house in this neighbourhood. Or improve this house. A second floor would be nice so that our valuables can be protected for floods. But for sure we will continue to live right where we are now. And amidst floods – let us hope that the people in the government will keep helping us, because without them, we might drown.

These discourses about the future expectations of *orang ajar* indicate that, even though the risk practices of *orang ajar* have altered after they picked up certain 'duties', their perceptions about their own opportunities in society have remained rather constant. Their self-efficacy has been and still is low; their trust in acquaintances in the government might have grown – but still their future expectations do not entail a radically improved situation. At most, they perceive positively their own high social status and options to handle risk as compared to other residents in Bantaran Kali, but they are at the same time well aware that their social position in wider society has not radically changed and will not do so either.

Hence, as was the case with the *orang antisipasi*, the perceptions of *orang ajar* continue to reflect a marginalized position in wider society and therefore are still associated with what I have called a habitus of poverty. Consequently, *orang ajar* expect to remain living in a flood-prone slum and do not portray their future lives in any way that is radically different from the way it is now. Only within Bantaran Kali have they found pragmatic ways to receive small incentives from elite actors *despite* their objectively unchanged low position.

Similar to the *orang antisipasi*, we might even note that *orang ajar need* the risky environment of the kampong to maintain their relatively high status in Bantaran Kali. Were they to leave the riverbanks, they would be no longer able to participate in a flood-warning system that is facilitated by the *kecamatan*, and consequently they would lose their elite contacts and related high social status within the kampong. Moreover, since much of the hopes of *orang ajar* for the future are based on fragile trust rather than on guaranteed returns, *orang ajar* are basically forced to wait and see whether these hopes are ever fulfilled. Meanwhile, they continue to carry out the 'duties' or practices that reproduce the unequal structures which underlie riverbank settlers vulnerability to flood risk. We can therefore conclude that the risk style of *orang ajar* is impacted by an internalization of elite perceptions and interests, as well as by a habitus of poverty.

In the final sections of this chapter, I connect the above empirical arguments about the habitual ways in which *orang ajar* reproduce power structures to relevant theories of power and subordination. How should we understand these complex power structures in Bantaran Kali in relation to theories of dominance and resistance? Why do *orang ajar* cooperate in their own oppression, while most of their incentives are based on hope, rather than on an objective improvement in their current situation? To explore these topics, I will discuss the theoretical notion of hegemony.

Hegemony

Antonio Gramsci famously used the concept of hegemony to describe a situation where the values of the dominant elite in a society have also become the 'common sense' values of all people in that society. For Gramsci, the elite is the dominant class (or an alliance of classes) in a given society that succeeds in bringing into being a hegemonic culture that appears to represent the interests of society as a whole, but in fact embodies its own elite interests. In other words, people believe that what is good for the elite is actually good for them (Gramsci 1977/1980: 139–140; Crehan 2002: 71).

This theoretical idea is helpful in the analysis of the *ajar* risk style because it helps us to think about the complicated way consent and coercion are intertwined. It shows that the risk style of *orang ajar* by no means reflects simple coercion of the government over poor riverbank settlers. Instead, if we consider that *orang ajar* operate within a framework of government (elite) cultural hegemony, then we recognize that selected riverbank settlers cooperate in the reproduction of unequal power structures – not because they are forced, but because they truly believe that they act in their own interest. Hence, in accordance with Gramsci's notion of hegemony, I propose that the *orang ajar* in Bantaran Kali are not simply forced to enact specific behaviour by their authorities. Instead, they participate in a system of surveillance and discipline, which, though cultivated by the state, is also actively maintained by the *orang ajar*.

However helpful Gramsci's theoretical analysis of cultural hegemony for a better understanding of what underlies an *ajar* risk style, it does not explain the observed heterogeneity in risk styles in Bantaran Kali. If we accept that the practices and perceptions of *orang ajar* are, at least partly, influenced by unequal power structures and cultural hegemony, then how do we account for the differences in risk practices between them and other inhabitants of Bantaran Kali?

This is a particularly relevant question to ask because during fieldwork I learned that many riverbank settlers do not obey the formal safety instructions that *orang ajar* communicate. In Chapter 2 it was already stated that *orang antisipasi* do not evacuate to the government shelter, instead seeking their own ways of survival. In Chapter 5, I will demonstrate that this also occurs for a group of people known as the *orang siap*, who consistently disobey formal safety instructions and instead exhibit alternative practices. Are these people then *not* subject to a cultural hegemony, and if not, why not? Or might there be something else that explains this difference between the practices of people obeying and resisting cultural hegemony in Bantaran Kali?

I propose that the differences between people's risk styles are influenced by differentiated life experiences. Trying to analyse what brings about the risk style of *orang ajar*, we should consider that these actors have slowly but gradually internalized elite ideologies due to encounters and experiences with political actors. In the years in which they assisted other *orang ajar* and established contacts with actors from KORAMIL and the *kecamatan*, they have been socialized to adopt perceptions of risk that largely benefit the interests of the elite. *Orang ajar* have gradually internalized governmental ideologies to such an extent that they are nowadays reflected in their perceptions of risk and safety, and in their perceptions of their identity even.

At the same time, their habitus of poverty shaped a worldview in which the *ajar* risk style appeared as the most attractive option for their 'type of people'. This habitus reflects not only government ideologies and risk constructs that are the product of cultural hegemony, but also perceptions of the social position, abilities and future possibilities of *orang ajar*.

In contrast, fellow residents who lacked the will or capability to invest accumulated money and time into the process of becoming an *orang ajar*, or who lacked the social skills to become acknowledged as an *orang ajar*, or who were mistrusted for whatever reason by 'friends' of elite actors and could for that reason not develop an *ajar* risk style, have had no alternative than to stick to other perceptions and practices of risk. These people have no interest in blaming themselves for the causing of floods and instead blame external factors. Likewise, these people do not perceive their own actions as a threat to social order, and instead they fear other risks that may threaten their well-being. Consequently, they developed an alternative risk style.

Afterword: Ajar risk practices in and outside of Bantaran Kali

This chapter has shown that the looming hazard of flooding offers a critical conjuncture in which powerful and subordinate actors in wider Jakarta society interact. Floods offer selected people within kampong society a chance to establish potentially useful contacts with the elite, thus altering social norms and conventions.

In order to develop an *ajar* risk style, inhabitants have to be able and willing to invest much time, energy and money into the practices and means associated with this style – thereby increasing their vulnerability to flood risk. Moreover, they have to show their loyalty to authorities by reproducing government narratives of cause and blame, and by performing duties related to safety and social order in the kampong. People with an *ajar* risk style cooperate with government institutions involved in the flood management of Bantaran Kali before and during floods. They also collaborate with political actors in the maintenance of social order in the neighbourhood (for example by informing against potential opposition to the government, or by the lecturing, monitoring and disciplining of their fellow residents).

In return for these investments, the risk style that is exhibited by *orang ajar* offers several incentives. Most importantly, cooperation with authorities offers *orang ajar* a sense of safety in an environment characterized by uncertainty. It also allows them to rise in the kampong social hierarchy, which might offer financial rewards in the long run. At the same time it was demonstrated in this chapter that the risk style of *orang ajar* does not enable them to escape the trap of risk and uncertainty: an *ajar* risk style can only exist in a flood-prone, poor and illegal neighbourhood such as Bantaran Kali.

That is not to say that characteristics of an *ajar* risk style are unique for Jakarta, or Bantaran Kali even. Let me end this chapter by comparing my observations of the *ajar* risk style with relevant findings of scholars working on risk behaviour in other contexts.

For this aim it is important to emphasize, first, that the practices of *orang ajar* take place within widely unequal structures in which surveillance and suppression by the Indonesian government are commonplace. It is absolutely not uncommon for members of Indonesian society to cooperate with elite actors in maintaining the social order. Clientelism has long been an important theme in Indonesian studies. In these writings, it is often claimed that asymmetric but mutually beneficial relationships of power and exchange produce corrupt and particularistic politics in Indonesia (Van Klinken & Barker 2009: 21–22). That is because while clientelism is an enduring feature of all politics, it is especially active in contexts in which there are 'marked inequalities, and where there is a lack of government support, or state provision or welfare or other institutions that promote the security of the poor and the weak' (Scott & Kerkvliet 1977: 442). Clearly, the social environment of Bantaran Kali fits this description, and the same can obviously be said for many other places around the world. For example, Joshua Barker (2009) has described clientelist relations between the state and local actors in other Indonesian slum areas; Bankoff (2015) and Walch (2013) discuss the impact of political patronage in disaster-stricken areas in the Philippines; and Gallego (2012) does so for clientelism in the context of floods and landslides in Colombia. In these as well as in many other writings, scholars describe how citizens seek protection and safety, as well as the economic improvement of their situation, largely through instrumental relationships with patrons.

Notes

1 Flood management in Jakarta is coordinated by the Provincial Agency for Disaster Management (BPBD). During floods, BPBD cooperates with KORAMIL, as well as with the National Agency for Disaster Management Rapid Response Team, the police, Social Ministry, and government agencies in conducting evacuations and providing relief assistance to displaced families.
2 It is important to realize that the lectures of *orang ajar* are not specifically focused on immigrants. In fact, some of the *orang ajar* are newcomers to Jakarta themselves and have only lived in the neighbourhood for several years. As will become clear throughout this chapter, their disapproval and mistrust is focused on people who they feel cannot be trusted because they hold themselves aloof from kampong society.
3 He returned after my fieldwork ended. Respondents told me that there have been no further conflicts between this man and his neighbours, but that the man's health severely weakened in prison and that his family has struggled to pay for medical costs ever since. Even if this man and his family are aware who reported on them, to my best knowledge no reprimands were given.

References

Bankoff, G. (2015). 'Lahat para sa lahat' (everything to everybody): consensual leadership, social capital and disaster risk reduction in a Filipino community. *Disaster Prevention and Management: An International Journal*, 24(4), 430–447.
Barker, J. (2009). Negara Beling: street-level authority in an Indonesian slum. In G. van Klinken, & J. Barker (Eds.), *State of Authority: The State in Society in Indonesia* (pp. 47–72). Ithaca, New York: SEAP.
Crehan, K. (2002). *Gramsci, Culture and Anthropology*. London: Pluto Press.
Gallego, J. A. (2012). Natural disasters and clientelism: the case of floods and landslides in Colombia. *APSA 2012 Annual Meeting Paper*. Retrieved from http://ssrn.com/abstract=2106312, last accessed 25 October 2015.
Gramsci, A. (1980). Gramsci e Noi 1937–1977 (M. Jorn, trans.). In V. Gerratana, & G. Matteoli (Eds.), *Grondbegrippen van de Politiek. Hegemonie, Staat, Partij* [*Fundamental Notions of Politics. Hegemony, State, Party*]. Nijmegen: Socialistiese Uitgeverij Nijmegen (original work published 1977).
Scott, J. C. & Kerkvliet, B. J. (1977). How traditional rural patrons lose legitimacy: a theory with special reference to Southeast Asia. In S. Schmidt, L. Guasti, C.H. Landé & J.C. Scott (Eds.), *Friends, Followers, and Factions* (pp. 147–161). Berkeley: University of California Press.
Van Klinken, G. & Barker, J. (2009). *State of Authority: The State in Society in Indonesia*. Ithaca, New York: SEAP.
Walch, C. (2013). Disaster risk reduction and local ownership: the effect of political competition, patronage and armed conflict on the local ownership of disaster risk reduction in the Philippines. Input Paper, prepared for the *UNISDR Global Assessment Report on Disaster Risk Reduction 2015*. Retrieved from www.preventionweb.net/english/hyogo/gar/2015/en/bgdocs/inputs/Walch,%202013.%20Disaster%20risk%20reduction%20and%20local%20ownership.pdf, last accessed 25 October 2015.

4 Orang susah
Dependent on aid

The first two empirical chapters exposed that unequal structures of power and economy, in combination with a habitus of poverty, can have a huge impact on people's risk practices. However important these structures may be for our analysis of heterogeneous risk styles, King warns that studies of political and economic structures should never overlook individual interests and strategies. In every study, these should be addressed as embedded in structural relations (2008: 176).

In line with this view, in this and the next chapter I emphasize the role that human agency can play in the development of risk styles, or the room to manoeuvre that people have within social structures. The most important claim I will make is that people are no slaves of the circumstances in which they were born and raised. Instead, under certain conditions that may occur at any point in people's lives, they are able to critically reflect upon their own habitual risk behaviour and consciously change it. In other words, people can and do reinvent their acquired risk style, and this process is often triggered by traumatic or otherwise critical life experiences. In this chapter I provide a clear example of such a transformative process. I demonstrate that the increasing number of floods in Bantaran Kali brings excellent opportunities for some inhabitants to reject their former, habitual risk strategies in return for more lucrative ones.

To analyse this process of behavioural change, this chapter introduces a group of people whom I got to know in Bantaran Kali as the *orang susah*. These people used to exhibit autonomous and preventive risk practices during floods in earlier years, but more recently they have developed an alternative risk style that centres mainly around dependency relationships with patrons working in external aid institutions that support them with economic resources after floods. The shift in style for *orang susah* became possible due to the fact that floods have increased in severity and quantity over the years, which was paralleled with an increase in aid and assistance opportunities offered by external institutions to flood victims.

The chapter starts with an examination of the practices that *orang susah* nowadays typically exhibit in relation to floods, thus characterizing the *susah* risk style. Next, I trace back how this risk style has come into being over the years, or how people have shifted from rather autonomous practices towards dependency strategies. After exposing the relevant factors underlying this style, I discuss whether or not a *susah* risk style allows people to escape from the risks that characterize a context of normal uncertainty. In the final section of the chapter I relate my empirical findings of the *susah* risk style in Bantaran Kali to relevant literature about risk behaviour from other contexts.

Orang susah

In Indonesian, the term *susah* means 'difficult' or 'hard'. In Bantaran Kali, *orang susah* is a self-chosen nickname for people who perceive and experience life as full of hardships and/or difficulties. Life is *susah* and they lead a *susah* life.

According to riverbank settlers who refer to themselves as '*orang susah*', they are more vulnerable towards floods than other people are. They maintain that they have a more '*susah*' life and face more problems (*masalah*) in life than their co-residents. In many of their accounts, their *susah* life is persistently used to justify the fact that *orang susah* hardly ever take any autonomous or preventive measures to decrease the risk related to flooding when compared to other inhabitants of Bantaran Kali. Concretizing their claimed *susah* circumstances, many of the people with this risk style underscore their low and unstable incomes, their low educational background or particular problems their households face. Yati – a 34-year-old woman who we will get to know better later in this chapter – describes her own *susah* circumstances as follows:

> I never followed education as I had to help my mother in the house. I married a man who was addicted to alcohol and who abused me, then I divorced and now I do not even have a husband to support me; yet I have a son to take care of. And I am constantly flooded. Everyone can see that I have an extremely *susah* life, so what could I possibly do myself to stay safe from floods? It is only logical that I get some help from people with more money.

Like Yati, Kurdi (male, 48 years old) is also widely known as an *orang susah* in Bantaran Kali. Kurdi gives a similar description of his *susah* situation:

> I definitely have a more *susah* life than other people in this kampong. Many other people here are smart or strong, so they know what to do when a flood inundates their house, while I am dependent on people who can help me [...] I need them to survive floods.

Such reasoning of *orang susah*, however, contradicts their objective circumstances. Although for a few *orang susah* it is true that they are relatively vulnerable to floods due to deprived material conditions, *orang susah* are generally not in more material need than other inhabitants of Bantaran Kali. For example, Yati not only owns a shop that provides her with regular income, but also shares in the monthly salary of her teenage son. She owns four grams of gold, relatively expensive clothing, five bottles of perfume, a television, a stereo set and a DVD player. Compared to her neighbours, she could be categorized as middle class. Her fellow resident Kurdi is actually rather wealthy by kampong standards: both he and his wife have a regular income as market merchants selling vegetables, and his daughter, who lives with them, supplements their monthly incomes with her own monthly salary from her work in a clothing store. The family furthermore owns a motorcycle and seven grams of gold in jewellery.

Nevertheless, *orang susah* such as Yati and Kurdi generally take no autonomous and preventive actions in the face of floods and other risks, but instead invest in reciprocal relationships with institutions that support them with economic resources *after* disasters have struck. Such decisions typify the *susah* risk style.

A dependency risk style

It is clarifying to briefly compare the *susah* risk style with the two other risk styles that I have discussed so far: the *antisipasi* risk style and the *ajar* risk style. As became clear in Chapter 2, people with an *antisipasi* risk style exhibit autonomous and short-term risk practices in the face of risks. They typically do not accumulate savings to be used in times of need. Rather, whenever they are in need of cash (for example when a member of their household falls ill, when their house is flooded or when they are faced with eviction), they borrow money from moneylenders or sell goods from their household. During flood events, *orang antisipasi* do not make use of external aid: instead of evacuating to a government-run shelter, they use strategies that help them survive the floods in their houses, alone. While this risk style frequently creates financial stress among *orang antisipasi* and increases their vulnerability to risk, to them it has the advantage that it enables them to overcome problems more or less independently from the help of untrusted others.

If we compare this style to the risk behaviour of *orang susah*, big differences become clear. *Orang susah* could borrow money from local moneylenders during floods in order to make up for losses, hide atop the roof or on a self-built shelter in their houses if a flood-warning message is spread, stock foods to be eaten during floods, or prepare batteries and lights. But *orang susah* don't manage the hazard of floods via any such *antisipasi* practices.

They could also handle flood and other risk in a way that typifies the *orang ajar* (Chapter 3): acquiring useful information on floods from the sluice-gate keepers, reproducing government narratives of cause and blame and assisting neighbours (or interfering with them) during floods, and trying to socialize themselves into the inner circle of 'friends' of the political elite in return for expected financial aid or social protection in times of need. But people that consider themselves *orang susah* don't manage hazards via any such *ajar* practices.

Instead, *orang susah* invest all their assets, time and energy into social relations with patrons working in aid institutions, who, in return, help them overcome problems. For example, *orang susah* often carry out volunteer tasks whenever these institutions organize an event. They also spend much time socializing with their patrons or with relations of these patrons, in an effort to maintain a friendly relationship with them. In return, *orang susah* expect to be helped by their patrons during floods and other risks, such as illness or eviction. Hence, rather than saving 'disaster money', or borrowing money from a moneylender or trying to make fast money with illegal practices that may help to cope with risk or recover from it, *orang susah* turn to their patrons to ask for financial aid and social protection in such occasions.

Perhaps the clearest example of what typifies a *susah* risk style is provided by the issue of floods, and how *orang susah* respond to those. After a flood-risk warning message has been spread, *orang susah* do not independently evacuate their home and head towards a shelter, but instead they consciously show off their helplessness by awaiting their patron's assistance from their house. As became apparent in the Introduction to this book, this can create dangerous situations: Yati stayed put in a flooded house to await help even when water gushed in fast and people were advised to evacuate as soon as possible, taking the risk that she would not be helped in time. Nevertheless, we will later see that she will probably exhibit the same behaviour during the next flood.

Even if *orang susah* hardly take any autonomous preventive measures in the face of floods, they are generally able to recover well from floods. This is because during all large floods that have occurred in past years, these people have demanded and received assistance in recovery and coping from one of the two external aid institutions that regularly support flood victims in Bantaran Kali: (1) a Catholic foundation called 'Sanggar Ciliwung Merdeka', and (2) the kampong administration (*kelurahan*).

Aid institutions and patrons

The foundation Sanggar Ciliwung Merdeka was established in the year 2000 by an Indonesian activist, who wanted to help flood victims in slums. He nowadays runs the institution with the help of five employees and another handful of volunteers. The foundation is financially supported by international and local donors, such as the Ford Foundation and Indonesian individuals wanting to support. During floods in 2007 and 2013, the employees of the foundation sent rescue teams by boat into Bantaran Kali. Moreover, they have financed restorations after large floods of at least ten demolished houses in the neighbourhood, and have provided financial and material support for selected flood victims.

Some examples help to concretize the ways in which *orang susah* have received support from Ciliwung Merdeka. After a large flood in 2002 demolished the majority of the houses in Bantaran Kali, Yati's house was among those selected to be rebuilt by the foundation. As she points at the back wall that was re-erected, Yati explains that the building improved dramatically:

> My house used to be nothing but a shack. But now it looks really nice and it is much larger than before. The foundation even gave me a table and chairs. They also bought me a spring bed, while I was always used to sleeping on a thin mattress.

During the next large flood in 2007, the employees sent a boat to pick up Yati and her son, and they provided them with food, medicines and building materials to restore the house once more. During the medium-sized flood that is described earlier in this book, Yati again received money as well as food from the foundation. Of the 23 participants of this study who refer to themselves as '*orang susah*', 12 received similar regular help from the foundation.

Other *orang susah* who participated in this study are frequent beneficiaries of the *kelurahan*, the other institution in Bantaran Kali that regularly supports flood victims. In the Introduction to this book I already noted that during large floods, this government institution sets up an evacuation shelter with shared facilities for flood victims from Bantaran Kali. The *kelurahan* furthermore sends in rescue workers by boat during large floods, in order to help people evacuate.[1] Moreover, after large floods, the *kelurahan* regularly provides financial assistance to selected flood victims, so that they can replace lost household goods or repair their houses. Tens of households in the neighbourhood have received varying sums of money from the *kelurahan* after the three recent large floods that occurred in the neighbourhood (in 2002, 2007 and 2013). Formally, the amount of money they receive should depend on the extent to which the house was damaged, as well as on the ability of a household to recover without external support. After large floods, kampong leaders make a list of the houses in the neighbourhood which are most severely damaged, along with the names of the people most in need of external support (widows, for example), so that the *kelurahan* can divide financial assistance among these selected flood victims. In reality, however, *orang susah* receive a relatively large share of the aid money – even though, as I made clear before, they are not necessarily in more material or financial need than their neighbours.

Among the beneficiaries of the *kelurahan* is *orang susah* Kurdi. In 2002, Kurdi's house was rebuilt after a large flood at the cost of the *kelurahan*. In 2007, the building was again repaired and improved with money provided by this institution. During all large floods from 2002 onwards, Kurdi also received instant noodles, rice, eggs, milk and bread from the *kelurahan*. He laughs when he tells me about that:

> We have never eaten so much before in our lives…It was so much food that we got bored eating! Me and my wife sold half of the food to other neighbours, and we still gained weight! Life has become much easier since the *kelurahan* helps me after floods, but life is still very *susah*.

It needs be stressed here that the regular support that Kurdi receives from the *kelurahan* is not granted to all flood victims in Bantaran Kali. The same goes for the regular support that Yati receives from Ciliwung Merdeka. To contrast the specific situation of the *orang susah* with the situations of the riverbank settlers that we met in the former chapters, none of the *orang antisipasi* were ever supported by the *kelurahan* or Ciliwung Merdeka after floods, not even if they suffered equally large losses. Several *orang ajar* once received financial assistance from the *kelurahan* or Ciliwung Merdeka after a flood, but the amount of aid money that they received has always been much less than what *orang susah*, such as Kurdi and Yati, have received. Hence, it is important to distinguish the risk style of *orang susah* from those of flood victims in Bantaran Kali who have perhaps once or twice received financial support from an external aid institution.

As will be shown throughout this chapter, *orang susah* emphasize their neediness and claim that they have a *right* to be helped, while irregular beneficiates do not consider themselves as having a more *susah* life than others and thereby do not feel that they have the right to be supported. Instead, their narratives reveal that they perceive the support as an instance of good luck or a result of the incidental good-ness of well-doers. Therefore, irregular beneficiaries of external aid institutions make no effort to maintain a reciprocal relationship with external aid institutions after a once-off offer of help. In contrast, *orang susah* construct in words and sym-bols a sophisticated claim to lasting support from the resources of actors involved in flood management. As will be demonstrated throughout this chapter, the main risk strategies of *orang susah* center around keeping up a *susah* image towards aid institutions, which is accomplished via the careful maintenance of reciprocal rela-tionships with actors that represent these institutions. Moreover, in comparison with their neighbours, *orang susah* much more often demand (and receive) material or financial support from the aid institutions discussed in this chapter.

In sum, what *orang susah* have in common, and what distinguishes them from other flood victims who have irregularly received material or financial support after flood events, is their ability to *claim* and *maintain* a supportable social position in their flood-prone community. I will now present in more detail the innovative practices used by *orang susah* Yati and Kurdi to foster this image.[2] The first strategy deals with keeping up the image of 'having a life that is *susah*'; the second strategy deals with the active maintenance of social relations between the beneficiaries and the external aid institution.

Yati: A susah movie star

'Ssssssh! Quickly!' Yati whispered as she opened the door a crack. Evening prayer had just finished this Friday evening, and small groups of men made their way back from the mosque. Yati did not want them to see the ostentatious skirt that she was wearing. She locked her door carefully after I had come inside, then lay back on the floor where she had been busy painting her toenails in a bright purple colour.

I had gotten to know Yati as a pretty woman of about 1.5 meters in height, with short black hair and a charming smile that exposes her set of straight, white teeth. Since she divorced her abusive husband right after the birth of their only child, she lives with her teenage son in a house that she inherited from her parents. From a shutter in the wall of her living room she sells ice cream and cigarettes – per package or per piece – to other residents in the kampong. She is known in the riverbank settlement as a quiet and reserved woman who keeps her distance from most other neighbours. Although Yati was born and raised in Bantaran Kali, fellow inhabitants usually described her to me as an 'outsider' or as someone 'who is not interested in becoming friends with us'.

In none of these descriptions did people ever refer to what may be considered the most characteristic, and at the same time perhaps the most hidden, aspect of Yati's personality: her secret hobby of dressing up. Yet I soon found out during my meetings with her that she used to spend a considerable part of her spare time putting on colourful make-up and posing in front of a mirror. If no one other than her son or me could see her, Yati tried on clothes that did not look anything like the decent dresses that she wore in daily life. She once told me about this habit that she gets her 'inspiration from magazines that show photos of movie stars. They wear such beautiful clothing and make-up; they give me ideas to try to look like one myself'. Yati's version of a movie star wears elastic tiger-print skirts, push up bras and dazzling high heels.

She arched her back to show some more of her décolleté, smiling at her mirror image. Then her face grew gloomy. 'Time for reality again', she sighed, and she changed into her regular clothing before opening her shop.

When she was younger, Yati would not have changed clothes. Instead, she used to serve customers in what she calls her 'movie star' outfits, or – to put it subtly – in types of clothing that expose much of her skin and figure. If I had asked riverbank settlers back then to describe Yati, they would probably have mentioned her hobby of dressing up right away, as many of them still have vivid memories of her past appearance. In Ambran's words:

> My grandmother says that she looked like a prostitute before, and perhaps this is also the way in which she earned money. That is what people say at least, but I am not sure about that, because I was too young then to know. But nowadays, I can tell you that she looks decent, and I know for sure that she earns her money from her shop, not with *haram* things [like prostitution].[3]

Other neighbours confirmed this narrative of Ambran. According to them, Yati started to dress and act 'decent' after she became a regular beneficent of the foundation Sanggar Ciliwung Merdeka. Ever since, she has been concerned with the impression that the foundation's employees have of her, and she has strategically adapted her behaviour. She told me that being spotted by outsiders in her movie star outfit would harm her image:

> I am not supported by them because of my prettiness, I realize that well. Instead, they selected me to become their beneficiary because I have so many problems that cause me to have a *susah* life. So I must look poor and humble every time they see me. Why would they help a movie star? Movie stars don't have any problems; they only have fame and money. Even if the house of a movie star would be flooded up until the roof-ridge, she would not be worthy of help. Only *orang susah* are worthy of help.

Kurdi: Keeping up appearance

Kurdi, the beneficent of the *kelurahan*, exhibited comparable strategies to Yati in order to maintain the claim to his position with the *kelurahan*. In order to protect his *susah* image, Kurdi had ordered his wife and children not to flaunt any material possessions in the presence of people outside their nuclear family – what if civil servants would hear about their assets via neighbourhood gossip? Kurdi deemed it well possible that, in such a case, his patrons might stop helping his household cope with floods. Nevertheless, despite Kurdi's warnings, during my fieldwork, Kurdi's daughter bought a refrigerator on credit one day, which she proudly placed in front of their house to show to her neighbours. Ignoring Kurdi's agony, she enthusiastically told passers-by that she bought the device on doctor's advice – to keep milk and foods cool for her newborn baby. While residents admired the refrigerator, Kurdi paced up and down the street, nervously pulling his moustache. He expressed his concerns with me in the following words:

> Now what will they think of us when this story is heard at the *kelurahan*? I always keep my house empty because if we have too much furniture, others will think I am rich. But now my child buys a refrigerator! [That is] inconsiderate! There is no need to show off that thing [refrigerator] – people will only gossip about it. Maybe we should sell it again.

I posed that the *kelurahan* would probably recognize the usefulness of a refrigerator for the health of his grandchild, and, trying to cheer up Kurdi, I added that it seemed to me unlikely that they would think that 'Kurdi is rich' on the basis of one purchase. But Kurdi strongly disagreed:

> They will! This is really a very stupid act of my child. Due to my daughter's decision, probably now they [the civil servants from the *kelurahan*] will never help us again. For sure, when there is a flood they will just say: 'Kurdi, you can solve your own problems, you can just sell your refrigerator!'

Similarly, in fear of disturbing his *susah* image, Kurdi refused to take a loan that was offered to him at one point during my stay in Bantaran Kali. Even though he had himself asked for the loan from the company that his daughter worked for, he eventually turned down their offer of a loan of three million Rupiah (the equivalent of approximately 193 Euros) against a relatively low interest rate of 2 per cent. Kurdi explained his decision to me one morning while we sat on the porch of his house, where I watched him collect the eggs that his hens had laid a few hours ago:

> I always wanted to open a large shop, because that would raise our income. Presently, all we have is a cart from which we sell vegetables and eggs at the market, but that only offers us a little income. If I could get a loan, I could open a shop, then I could earn more, then I could save and move house to a flood-free area. So for that aim, I told my daughter a thousand times: ask your boss to give us a loan, tell him about my business plans…If he says no, ask him again! Suddenly, after many years of asking, the boss of my daughter said I could have a loan! It was a shock! But I had to refuse.

Apparently, I looked completely puzzled at this point of our conversation, therefore Kurdi laid aside two eggs that he held in his hands, sat down next to me, and started explaining his decision as slowly and clearly as he could:

> I could not accept the loan because if people from the *kelurahan* suspect that I receive money from others, they might think that my difficulties have disappeared and might start helping other neighbours instead of me [...] The *kelurahan* helps me only because they can see with their own eyes that all I possess are my chicken, and all I can sell are their eggs. So they know there is nothing I can do myself to stay safe from floods.

Still somewhat confused, I opted that if Kurdi would accept the loan, he might indeed be able to open a large shop, earn more money and thus become independent of external aid. What would the problem be, then? Kurdi answered that the trajectory I had proposed would most likely lead to a financial disaster:

> What if I use the loan to set up the business and then I make no profit? Then who helps me with paying back the loan? No one! Not the *kelurahan*, because they will think I have sufficient money to help myself! And if there is a flood, who will repair my house? No one! They will say that I can pay for that myself, from the income of my shop. Then it would have been better if I would have just stayed where I am now after all, right?

The above examples of how Yati and Kurdi tried to keep up a needy image help me to show that *orang susah* generally try to come across as poorer than they are – both towards their patrons and towards direct neighbours. Whatever profitable effects former support may have had on their material living standards, *orang susah*'s ways of life must never indicate that they can cope without aid from external institutions. These decisions may help *orang susah* to protect their needy image towards their patron, but they have the disadvantage that this behaviour helps to sustain the vulnerability of *orang susah* towards floods and other risks characteristic of the normal uncertainty in which they live. Because they are dependent on their patron and fear losing this patron's support, they cannot accept help from others, nor can they make too much money, as this would ruin their *susah* image and hence undermine their supportable position. Besides protecting their needy image, *orang susah* use another strategy to maintain their *susah* risk style, which is based on a patron–client relationship. I elaborate on the theoretical understandings of this notion below, after I have concretized Yati and Kurdi's risk practices.

Patronage and clientelism

Yati continually and actively invested in the maintenance of a reciprocal relationship with her patron (the founder of Ciliwung Merdeka) and with employees that work for his foundation. One way in which I observed her doing so was by regularly walking over to the office of the foundation to provide employees with homemade snacks. The office is located in a different neighbourhood in Jakarta, and it took Yati a few hours to reach her destination by foot. When I once met her on her way back home after such a visit, Yati explained to me why she made this effort, nevertheless:

> It is a hassle to go there, because I have to close down my shop on those days in order to walk there, and so I make no money on the days that I visit. Instead, I spend money: whenever I can afford to, I like to bake treats for the people working in the office. I go there at least once a week, but after large floods, I go each day. Of course I do that! I must show my gratefulness after they have helped me! This is a smart thing of me to do, because in this way they will always remember me, and when the next flood comes they will not have forgotten me.

Another example of the way in which Yati tries to maintain a reciprocal relationship with her patron concerns her volunteering activities for his foundation. Whenever the employees of the foundation organized an event, I noted that Yati shut down her shop immediately – again missing out on daily income that she actually needs to pay for her basic expenditures – and offered her services as a volunteer. For example, during my fieldwork period, the foundation organized a theatre play for street children that was staged for four days in a completely different part of the city. During each of these days, Yati volunteered indefatigably. She cleaned, distributed bottles of water to the young actors and cooked for all employees. After the play, when the actors and the employees went home, Yati and several other volunteers spent their nights on the porch in front of the theater to avoid expensive transport costs and in order to continue the work early the next morning.

When she returned home after nearly a week, Yati told me that she regretted her lack of income. Nevertheless, she still appeared satisfied with her social investments: she remarked several times that the employees had taken notice of her commitment and that she had thereby succeeded in strengthening their mutual relationship. In a later interview, she confirmed her prioritization of social investments with her patrons over investment in her own business, telling me that she considers socializing with employees of the foundation a lucrative activity: 'one time helping them equalizes a year of work in my shop'.

Kurdi also invested much time and energy in the maintenance of a reciprocal relationship with his patrons. In an interview, he explained which strategies he uses for this aim:

> You must know that I am very nice to the people at the *kelurahan*, very respectful. Yeah, I act exactly like this [Kurdi bows his head down and places the palms of his hands together in front of his chest, gesturing respectfulness]. If I meet them in the streets, I say 'hello Sir' to them. I also volunteer for them.

Every now and then I go there and I ask them when they have another special event. Or whether there are some other tasks that I can perform to help them. If they say yes, then I always help them out...without them paying me! Even though I am busy or ill, I volunteer and offer my help because I know that they appreciate it when one is committed like that.

Kurdi then described the variety of tasks that he performs as a volunteer: making sure there are enough chairs for the audience during meetings and that the microphones work, cleaning the office, serving water and coffee to employees, or 'whatever else they need'. He emphasized that he never demanded, nor received, money in return for his activities. To Kurdi, volunteering is a way to do something in return for the material support his family receives during and after floods:

> They often help me because they pity me and want to care for me. They help others [inhabitants of Bantaran Kali] as well – but they help me first because I am loyal to them. Others only beg them for money during floods, but in daily life, they never do anything in return for the *kelurahan*. That is why they do not get much help either after floods. They are hypocrites, only being nice if it suits them, while I always show my gratefulness and therefore I get more support from them. This is only fair, if you ask me.

The above quotations of Yati and Kurdi show that the effectiveness of the risk practices of *orang susah* is for a large part dependent on their ability and willingness to sustain reciprocal relations with actors with resources, working in aid institutions. If they succeed, we might consider that they have arranged for themselves some kind of informal flood-insurance policy – one that is paid for by their patron.

We can in the case of *orang susah* speak of a 'patron–client relationship' that characterizes their risk style: an unequal exchange relationship between 'an individual of higher socioeconomic status (patron) who uses his own influence or benefits, or both, for a person of lower status (client) who, for his part, reciprocates by offering general support and assistance, including personal services, to the patron' (Scott 1977: 124–125). In Chapter 3 I already noted that the importance of the themes of clientelism and patronage are widely recognized in research on Indonesian society (e.g. Aspinall 2013; Blunt et al 2012). The patron–client ties as described there as well as in this chapter offer empirical evidence of the continuing importance of patronage in Indonesian society.

The above section made apparent that the *susah* risk style demands *orang susah* continuously invest in the social bonds with their patrons. In the next section, I pay attention to one of the downsides of these investments. That is, many neighbours are jealous of the relatively large amount of aid and support that *orang susah* receive from their patrons. Consequently, they exclude *orang susah* from the local help networks that exist in the neighbourhood.

Local networks and social exclusion

While the patrons of *orang susah* generally trust the image that they are presented with by the beneficiary, their aid institutions are not located within the kampong and hence they have an incomplete perspective on the living circumstances of the inhabitants. The direct neighbours of *orang susah* are obviously in a better position to judge whether or not the constructed *susah* image of *orang susah* clashes with their actual situation. As noted, my study suggests that it often does: *orang susah* are not more poor than what is average in Bantaran Kali.

Due to the gap between the life of '*susah*' that *orang susah* themselves emphasize and the reality of the circumstances in which they live, the nickname by which *orang susah* describe themselves is rejected by others. Put differently, *orang susah* are the only ones in Bantaran Kali who call themselves '*orang susah*'. Fellow residents are aware of this self-appointed nickname and recognize it, but they usually do not use it to refer to these self-proclaimed '*orang susah*' neighbours. Instead, inhabitants describe *orang susah* as 'stingy' types of people (*pelit*), as 'beggars' (*pengamis*), or as people who are 'smart with money' (*pinter uang*). Hence, if *orang susah* seem to portray themselves as people with a need to be helped by others, their neighbours portray them as leeches or extortionists.

It follows, then, that the effectiveness of *orang susah*'s claim for support is not just dependent on to what extent they can convince their patrons of their 'right' to be helped, but also partly dependent on whether or not fellow residents will inform aid institutions about the actual situation of *orang susah*. This latter aspect is hard to control for *orang susah*, and they are, therefore, highly concerned about it. For example, the narratives of Yati and Kurdi indicate that they are well aware that they are always in competition with other potential beneficiaries who live in their kampong. What if a neighbour, jealous of the help that Kurdi receives, tells civil servants that their beneficiary is wealthier than most of his neighbours? Or what if someone tells the employees of the foundation that Yati spends all her money on luxury clothing and make-up? Such negative gossip could destroy their needy image and consequently also the safety net that *orang susah* have so neatly spun between themselves and their patrons.

To avoid this, *orang susah* publically trivialize the amount of help that they receive from external aid institutions. On occasions when people asked Yati about the building materials for her house that she had received from the foundation after the 2010 flood that I experienced in Bantaran Kali, she lied that her supporter paid for '(…) just a few things! I only got a small storage level on top of my house, while other households received a full second floor'. Likwise, Kurdi once interrupted a group of residents whom he overheard discussing the 'unfair' selections of the *kelurahan* support. Kurdi counterposed, repeatedly claiming that [the *kelurahan*] 'did not pay for my house! Only for some little things…'

Despite their efforts to hide away what they own, it comes as no surprise that the claim for support that *orang susah* try to maintain does not convince fellow residents, living as they do in this densely settled community with houses and people crammed together. In Bantaran Kali, one needs no Handie Talkie to hear who has bought a new refrigerator, or whose house was fully restored by a foundation. Jealousy and gossip about the relatively large amount of help that *orang susah* receive from external aid institutions are indeed widespread in the kampong and, as a result, *orang susah* take up one of the lowest ranks in the social hierarchy.

It is interesting to compare briefly, at this point of the book, the low social status of *orang susah* with the position of the riverbank settlers whom we met in earlier chapters. In Chapter 3, we saw that *orang ajar* take up such a powerful position in society that most residents dare not overtly disobey them, allowing these actors to even bypass formal kampong leaders at given times. In Chapter 2, we saw that many of the practices associated with an *antisipasi* risk style are considered illegal and disapproved of in public discourse, but it also became clear that *orang antisipasi* offer valuable services to the community, which explains why they remain tolerated and protected by fellow residents. By contrast, *orang susah* occupy a social position in kampong hierarchy at the bottom of the ranks. Not only do residents hold that the claims for support of *orang susah* are invalid, but they also consider the *orang susah* useless. *Orang susah* do not provide the community with the valued information or status that *orang ajar* have access to, nor do they offer the valued services of *orang antisipasi*. Instead, *orang susah* invest their energy, assets and skills on wealthy actors from outside the kampong, while neglecting social relations with fellow residents in Bantaran Kali.

Consequently, they take on a rather isolated position in the neighbourhood. During fieldwork, none of the *orang susah* were ever invited for social gatherings, such as funerals, weddings, or circumcision events. Neither were they welcome to participate in local support networks, such as religious meetings (offering mental support to residents through communal praying, as well as a social network offering financial support, see below) or saving groups such as *arisan*.

But even if *orang susah* would have been invited to join such social gatherings, it seems unlikely that they would have participated. That is because social gatherings in the neighbourhood are only able to solve the small financial problems of people – but they are never enough to improve one's situation. For example, if one needs money to buy a school uniform for one's children, it can be useful to participate in an *arisan* group. But if one needs money to repair a house – *arisan* will not be sufficient. Likewise, even though it was common for the women participating in the weekly religious gatherings in which I also attended to ask others for small financial loans if they needed to buy something but lacked cash, no large sums of money were ever exchanged there. Hence, attending a religious meeting is not going to help an *orang susah* coping with large problems in life, such as floods.

Clearly, such local support networks are not of interest to *orang susah*, who would rather direct their attention towards actors who are much wealthier than any of the riverbank settlers. Remember that a resident described Yati at the beginning of this chapter as a woman who is 'not interested in becoming friends with us'. It appears, here, that this is a rather accurate interpretation of Yati's behaviour, as she prioritizes social relations with actors from outside the kampong over friendly relationships with her less economically useful neighbours. We might also say that *orang susah* do not invest in horizontal reciprocity. The next stories of Kurdi and Yati expose what this social isolation of *orang susah* means for their safety and well-being.

A 'risky' risk style

Kurdi generally does not benefit from mutual help institutions in the kampong; nor do his family members. This became most visible when his daughter got married during my stay in Bantaran Kali. Kurdi, proud and excited, made an effort to organize the perfect wedding for his daughter. He printed tens of colourful invitations and distributed these among all neighbours; he rented a party tent and ordered cake and *nasi kuning* – a dish typically served at special events, and believed to bring good luck. In order to pay for all these expenses, Kurdi had taken loans with several family-in-law members, even though this put his daughter to shame. He planned to pay them back at once, the day after the wedding, with the help of financial gifts that he believed the guests would bring along. But hardly anyone showed up. Only some of his daughter's colleagues from outside Bantaran Kali attended the wedding and contributed a small donation to the costs. Their direct neighbours did not. Both Kurdi and his wife looked very sad and concerned throughout the wedding ceremony, and Kurdi's daughter told me she felt humiliated that she had to marry 'alone' and 'on the costs of my in-laws'. The next morning, Kurdi asked several of his contacts at the *kelurahan* to help him pay back the money and was shocked that they all refused. 'Now I am in deep debt', he told me, 'now my life has become even more *susah*'. It took him weeks to pay back his family members, who kept calling him and warning him that they needed their money back, soon.

Perhaps a more dramatic example of the social exclusion that a *susah* risk style can lead to is provided by the following story of Yati, which I jotted down in my fieldwork diary:

> It was late in the evening and I was interviewing the kampong leader and his wife at their place, when Yati's son knocked on the door to inform the kampong leader that Yati had turned ill. She had already been throwing up for two days and also suffered from severe diarrhea. She had attacks of fever and complained of severe headaches. 'There is no money to pay for the medicines', said the boy to his kampong leader, 'so please ask the people to help my mother'.

The demand that the son of Yati made to the kampong leader is not uncommon in Bantaran Kali. In cases of emergency, such as illness or death, it is usual for the community to offer financial support to fellow residents. In the year during which I stayed in Bantaran Kali, almost every week a collection was organized to pay for someone's medical treatment; five times people contributed to the costs of a funeral, and two times residents helped young mothers pay for the costs of the complicated birth of their babies in the public hospital. In such emergency cases, the wife of the kampong leader goes door to door to ask residents for a small amount of Rupiahs. On average, a household contributes Rp 3,000. It happens frequently that people do not have enough money left from their own costs to help the neighbour out, and on those days it is socially accepted to politely refuse one's share by stating that 'there is no money' (*tidak ada uang*). Nevertheless, there are usually enough people who can contribute a small amount; about Rp 130,000 on average is collected after a few hours.

During fieldwork, I kept track of these amounts and noted down how much money was collected, and for which residents. It appears that, if the money collection concerns an *orang ajar*, they generally receive a rather large amount of money, while fewer people are willing to spare some Rupiahs for *orang antisipasi*. To make this more concrete: of the three times that money was collected for an *orang ajar*, the average amount was Rp 175,000. Of the two times that money was collected for an *orang antisipasi*, the average amount was Rp 80,000. When Yati turned ill, however, *nobody* appeared willing to contribute to her medical treatment. The fact that Yati was not helped by anyone at all must thus be considered exceptional.

The wife of the kampong leader explained to me that she feels that it is justified that people do not support Yati financially, as 'she already has other people who can help her anyhow'. The kampong leader agreed, arguing that 'she will be helped by the foundation, so she does not need our money'. Later that evening I found that many residents used this reason to justify not helping Yati. Another reason that the riverbank settlers mentioned is that Yati herself hardly ever contributes to communal savings or collections. Admittedly, this reasoning is accurate. Never have I seen her participate in *arisan* or religious gatherings; she is hardly ever invited to weddings or funerals and as such does not support her neighbours during such costly events either. Moreover, it is publically known that whenever Yati is asked to contribute money for another ill person in the kampong, she mostly emphasizes her neediness and maintains that she has no money or too many of her own problems, her *susah* circumstances, to contribute.

This unsocial behaviour of Yati was punished when she fell ill. While fellow residents were unwilling to help her out, Yati herself appeared not to have money to pay for medical treatment, and, worst of all in her specific case, the expected backup of the foundation was disappointing as well. When Yati sent her son to the foundation's office to ask employees for some cash, he returned home empty-handed. In a later interview with me, the leader of the foundation explained his decision to turn down Yati's demand of help by emphasizing that he helps *flood victims*, not people suffering from disease or experiencing other types of hazard. Eventually, Yati felt forced to sell most of her jewellery. She also took an expensive loan with a local *rentenir*, after which she was able to pay for her medical treatments, but also ended up with a total debt of nearly one million Rupiah. After three weeks of illness (and lack of income), she recovered and got back to work. It took her two months to pay back the moneylender, and by the time fieldwork for this study ended, Yati was still struggling financially. She looked pale and skinny, and asked me to loan her the money for her electricity bill ('because none of the others here will help me anyhow'). Meanwhile, her son had started begging neighbours for food.[4]

Yati's situation exposes the fragility of the *susah* risk style. Instead of developing autonomous strategies by which one can decrease one's objective risk towards floods or other hazards, *orang susah* mainly trust patrons who offer them access to economic capital in times of need. But the relationship between patron and client is far from equal. Riverbank settlers are in much higher need of the patron's support than vice versa. This creates a potentially dangerous situation: what if the expectations of *orang susah* are rejected, like what happened with Yati during her illness, and with Kurdi when his daughter's wedding got him into debt? What if the employees of the foundation lose interest in supporting poor riverbank settlers, or if the *kelurahan* prioritizes other financial needs over those of flood victims in Bantaran Kali?

The above examples of the times in which Yati and Kurdi's trust in their patrons was unrealized show that what may appear a lucrative risk strategy should be regarded as a gamble. In the next section, I argue that the vulnerability of *orang susah* to economic hazards might have actually *increased* after they became dependent on a patron. I use the biographies of Yati and Kurdi to trace how this situation developed.

A flood of opportunities: The invention of a susah risk style

In 2002, Bantaran Kali was inundated by a large flood. Yati's house – as well as the houses of most other inhabitants – was covered by river water that rose to a height of three meters. As it kept raining for weeks, the water inundated Yati's house and her possessions for over ten days. When I met her nearly eight years later, she reflected on those days as follows:

> On the night the flood started, I woke up when I heard people screaming that we would be flooded. I took little time to pack my goods, because I was afraid that the water would rise higher. I could move fast because I was well prepared. I always kept my valuables on the highest shelves in my house, so now I only had to hang my high heels [shoes] to the ceiling with ropes. After that I took my wallet and our television and left our house with my son. I always kept some cash in my wallet, in case a flood would force me to evacuate. At the outskirts of the neighbourhood I told my son to wait by the television, and I ran back to pick up two bags with clothing. Also my son's school-uniform I took along. Thank Allah I could save all those goods! Thank Allah I had been smart enough to set them aside, as to always be prepared for disasters! We hurried and found a dry area near the neighbourhood. I was able to buy food and water because of the money that I had brought along, and some

other neighbours who had sought shelter in the same area also helped us. Back then, I still had many friends in the kampong, you know…They gave my son sweets and eggs, and all of us exchanged food and other goods such as soap and shampoo. Finally, after about a week or so, the water receded. Some other evacuees and I walked back to our houses, and all of us discussed how we would clean up our houses.

But when Yati and her son reached the place where their house used to stand, they saw 'only mud'. 'Everything that I had not taken from the house, had flooded', Yati recalled. 'The walls had collapsed and there were only some stacks of wood left. Our mattress had flooded as well. I had no idea what to do'.

At that moment a man approached Yati and introduced himself as the owner of a foundation. He said that he wanted to help flood victims, and while Yati could not believe it as first, the man kept his word. It appeared that Yati was selected as one of the ten people whose houses would be completely rebuilt through funds from the foundation. The fact that Yati was chosen to become a beneficiary of the foundation was a coincidence, as one of the employees explained to me in an interview:

> One has to be pragmatic if one wants to help flood victims. All inhabitants of the riverbanks were in need in that time, and they all demanded help fast. So there simply was no time for us to get to know each and every flood victim at first, and then calculate who needed our support most. No, we just had to be quick that time and we chose to help Yati even though we suspected there were poorer people than her, people who needed help as well. She was just one of the first people we met.

Hence, it appears to have been more good luck that Yati was selected by the aid institution than a result of any personal *susah* situation.

A similar coincidence seems to have benefitted Kurdi, who became a beneficiary of the *kelurahan* after the same flood in 2002. He described what happened as follows:

> After we heard that a flood would enter the neighbourhood, my wife and I and our daughter quickly evacuated to an acquaintance in another neighbourhood in Jakarta. We had taken our identity cards, most of our valuables, and we had parked our motor bike in a dry area in Jakarta. Just the things we always saved during floods. When we came back after the flood an official from the *kelurahan* came up to me. He and his colleagues walked around in the neighbourhood with notebooks to write down how bad each person's situation was. This man I knew, because he was a distant uncle of my wife. We talked about our losses. My house had not been completely demolished, but the back side had collapsed. I told the people from the *kelurahan* that I was worried about my daughter, who had become ill during the evacuation, and

who kept on coughing. I said to them: 'How can my child recover if there are no walls to protect her from rain and wind?' The man felt pity for me and he told me: 'It is no life to live without a wall. I will help you'. Then a week later the man came by again and he told me the *kelurahan* would restore the house for us. We told him how grateful we were and my wife even cried from joy.

Similar to what happened to Yati, it seems that the fact that Kurdi was selected for help was mostly a matter of good luck. In 2002, the *kelurahan* had received orders from the Jakarta government to provide financial support to flood victims. *Kelurahan* employees, in turn, instructed kampong leaders to help them define the most needy residents. I already explained at the beginning of this chapter that officially, the idea was that inhabitants would receive help on the basis of their losses: those whose houses were completely demolished would receive more help than those whose houses were only relatively lightly damaged. In practice, however, it seems the support was divided on rather arbitrary grounds. Kurdi had fewer losses than many of his direct neighbours; nevertheless, he received much more financial support than they did. Perhaps this was due to his family connection, or perhaps it was due to the fact that the *kelurahan* official was touched by Kurdi's personal story. Whatever may have been the precise reason for this first selection, it is a fact that ever since Kurdi has remained a regular beneficiary. In his own words: 'We were not only saved that time by this man! We have been saved by the *kelurahan* many more times'.

The above stories of how Yati and Kurdi first encountered their patrons offer two important indications of the way in which people can develop a *susah* risk style. First, the narratives show that the origin of the *susah* risk style is not the result of a strategic action of riverbank settlers, but that it is instead the outcome of a coincidental opportunity that was offered to *orang susah* due to the increase of floods in their neighbourhood and the related increased attention of external aid institutions. This does not only apply for Yati and Kurdi, but also for other *orang susah* who became regular beneficiaries of the *kelurahan* or the foundation after the 2002 flood. Even though the damage to their buildings was sometimes small compared to others in the neighbourhood, they were selected as a beneficiary. Ever since, they have consistently received the largest amounts of aid money in the kampong.

A second important overlap in the stories of *orang susah* exposes the ways in which their risk style has *altered* over the past years. Both Yati and Kurdi describe their former risk practices as rather autonomous and preventive, while we know that this can no longer be said for the present. We saw that Yati had built high shelves in her house where she put her valuables; that she used to set cash aside to be used as a buffer during floods; and that she was able to pack her goods fast because she had already taken preventive measures beforehand. She also evacuated during a rather early stage of the flood, and did so without the help of others. By contrast, during more recent floods, she has made it a habit to wait for the employees of the foundation to evacuate her.

She spoke to me about this change in her behaviour in a conversation which I had with her over the phone, after the period of fieldwork had already ended. I called Yati in 2013, after I learned that a large flood had inundated the kampong, and I wanted to know whether she was alright. To my great relief, Yati told me that she was in good health. She also told me that she had stayed in her house during the first hours of the flood, because she expected that the employees of the foundation would come by boat to evacuate her and her son. She added that she had done the same during large floods in 2003 and later years, and explained her decision as follows:

> I know that I will always be safe if I stay put, because the people of the foundation have a boat and they have told me that they will use it during large floods to search for me and my son. It is better for me to wait for that boat than to risk my life by trying to swim through the current, as I used to do when I was younger. In fact I *have* to wait – what if they would show up for nothing? For me to leave without their help, that would be ungrateful!

This interview section shows that ever since Yati was selected as a beneficiary of the foundation, she no longer evacuates autonomously during large floods, but instead waits to be evacuated. Yati also indicated in earlier interviews that, while she used to set cash aside to be used during flood evacuations, she no longer does so. Asked about the reason for her altered risk practices, she answered:

> I really do not know why. Maybe it is because I just do not think about it [floods] anymore as I used to do. I used to have nightmares all the time about floods, but now I feel more calm. Luckily, the foundation helps me nowadays after floods so I do not have as many concerns about money as I used to.

Again, this narrative indicates that Yati has altered her typical way of handling flood risk, from autonomous risk practices towards a more dependent risk style. Likewise, Kurdi's style developed from active and preventive towards a more reactive risk style. Just like Yati, he used to evacuate from his house autonomously after flood-risk messages were communicated. And just like Yati, he no longer does this but instead waits in his house for help to come. Furthermore, Kurdi became more nonchalant in his flood-prevention measures after he became a regular beneficiary of a patron. As is the case with Yati, it appears that Kurdi has become less concerned with floods, because he feels more secure that he will recover from a flood event due to the help of his patrons. Again, we may conclude that the risk practices of Kurdi have developed from a more autonomous style towards the *susah* risk style that he nowadays exhibits.

Before I discuss the most important factors underlying a *susah* risk style, let me point out that the alteration in the risk behaviour of *orang susah* resulted in a decrease in popularity in the neighbourhood. According to residents, Yati used to participate in different *arisan* groups before she got engaged with the foundation, and she also frequently attended weddings and other social events. In line with these stories, Yati told me that she 'used to have many friends here, and we did many things together, like going to weddings or discussing problems with our husbands during *arisan*. But now they hate me because I get helped by the foundation and they want that as well. They are just jealous'. This explains why Yati, during the flood in 2002, still shared food and other goods with befriended flood victims from her neighbourhood, while nowadays, she no longer participates in any such collective risk strategies during floods. Moreover, as became clear before, she has been excluded from the kampong's social safety systems. The same seems true for Kurdi:

> I used to be close to my neighbours but now we have become strangers. I used to join my neighbours for prayers and I participated in two *arisan* groups. Now, I say 'hello' to them, but we never actually talk or do things together. They share bad gossip about me; that is how people in this neighbourhood act if they do not like you. But I don't mind, because I like my other friends [in the *kelurahan*] better.

Underlying factors

Let me start by recalling the fact that *orang susah* are not poorer than their neighbours. I underline this fact because readers might intuitively associate a dependent risk style with low capacity and/or means to cope autonomously. Indeed, as mentioned in Chapter 1, much of the risk and vulnerability literature suggests that poverty determines risk behaviour. However, the heterogeneity in risk styles that I observed in Bantaran Kali cannot be explained by factors typically associated with vulnerability, such as gender, age, wealth, income or status. Instead, my study indicates that it is other, non-material factors that explain the differences between the risk styles: self-efficacy, trust in other actors and a habitus of poverty. In order to clarify the variation between the three risk styles discussed in this book so far, below I discuss the main factors underlying the *susah* style, while occasionally contrasting this with the *antisipasi* and the *ajar* risk style in order to point out relevant overlaps and differences.

Low self-efficacy

In Chapters 2 and 3 it became clear that both the *orang antisipasi* and the *orang ajar* feel that they have sufficient skills or opportunities to handle the risk of flooding – as long as this concerns the familiar environment of Bantaran Kali. These perceptions are reflected in the autonomous and short-term *antisipasi* risk style or in the *ajar* risk practices, respectively. By contrast, *orang susah* consistently indicated in interviews with me that they believed they were unable to protect themselves against the negative consequences of a flood in Bantaran Kali.

Interestingly, *orang susah* suggested in narratives that they agree with both the *orang antisipasi* and the *orang ajar* that these people – but not the *orang susah* themselves – are able to handle risk effectively. *Orang susah* described the *orang antisipasi* as either 'strong' or 'tough' and the *orang ajar* as 'knowledgeable' or 'socially skilled'. In the opinion of the *orang susah*, this helped to justify why these neighbours are not dependent on patrons and external aid institutions in their handling of floods. At the same time, as we may also remember from the above narratives of Yati and Kurdi, *orang susah* describe themselves as 'too stupid' or 'too weak' to handle risk autonomously. Consequently, they believe it is 'only logical' that they receive more help than others: 'I am not strong like some of my neighbours', *orang susah* would typically say, 'they can always recover from floods in one way or another, while I usually have no money or energy left and need help to survive', or 'What can I do myself to stay safe from floods? Nothing! I am too weak to swim through the currents. So of course I need to be helped, because otherwise I might drown'.

Even if it seems attractive to regard these narratives of *orang susah* solely as strategic aspects of their potentially lucrative risk style, we must also consider that this expressed low self-efficacy of *orang susah* is actually experienced and internalized by them. Such internalized views of themselves – people with a *susah* life, people lacking capacity to act effectively – are for example reflected in the ways in which they narrated to me their biographies and former life experiences. In these stories, *orang susah* frequently described themselves as 'weak' types of people, 'stupid' (*bodoh*) and 'not able to do things right'. Some would refer to themselves as 'low people' (*orang rendah*).

As a result of their perceived 'lowness' and 'stupidity', *orang susah* indicate that they feel that they have little control over the ways their life develops. It is impossible for me – and not my intention – to 'control' whether these people speak 'the truth' and hence truly feel unable to act autonomously, or whether they are just strategically narrating their experiences in a way that emphasizes their feelings of dependency and hence legitimates their claim to support. My experiences with these people push me towards believing that it is a combination of the two. By this I mean to say that even though *orang susah*'s perceptions of their own capacities do not match objective reality, they have internalized the belief that they need others to help them survive and overcome floods. This belief started to develop after they became beneficiaries of their patrons, and was strengthened each and every time *orang susah* received support from their patrons. For *orang susah*, the fact that they, and not others, are supported serves as proof that they must be in more need of support than others. In comparison with them, other residents are stronger and smarter; therefore their neighbours do not need help. The fact that *orang susah* are able to successfully claim support from external actors does not positively change the expectations that they have of their own abilities and capacities in relation to risk. On the contrary, we saw that along with the increase of aid came an increased conviction that they need this support because they cannot overcome flood risk by themselves. So, even if their biographies show us that they were able to handle floods autonomously earlier in their lives, *orang susah* have become convinced that, in their current situation, a dependency style is their best option to stay safe.

Trust in patrons

With the support of a patron, *orang susah* believe that they will remain safe and protected in their current flood-prone environment, but without that patron, they are sure that they would not be as well off. This indicates that *orang susah* have high trust in other actors involved in flood management (most notably their patrons). If asked whether *orang susah* believe they could, at any point in their lives, independently improve their current situation, they consistently and wholeheartedly rejected such ideas. For example, they would often say something similar to this: 'I would like to live a better life, but there is nothing I can do to change this. I am only a low person'. Or they might say: 'All my difficulties make me confused. I don't know where to start to get out of here, even though I would like to live in a neighbourhood where there are no floods'. However, when it comes to potential future improvements with the support of their beneficiaries, *orang susah* appear much more positive:

> The foundation has helped me many times. So I think that if I have more problems later on in my life, then I will receive aid again.

> I myself do not know what to do to make things better. But the people of the foundation might know how to help me. They are knowledgeable people – I am not like that.

> Maybe the people in the *kelurahan* will pity me if my daughter gets ill. They have helped us before during floods, so I hope that they will do so again. This helps me to stay calm even though I have so many things to worry about in my life.

Let me briefly compare the high level of trust reflected in the above narratives of *orang susah* with the attitudes of neighbours with other risk styles. We have seen that *orang antisipasi* (Chapter 2) tend to trust only themselves instead of other actors in society. In line with these perceptions, they exhibit largely autonomous practices in the face of floods. *Orang ajar* (Chapter 3), in contrast, trust their elite contacts to such an extent that they are willing to make risky investments in the present, in return for hopeful expectations with regard to their future. At the same time, *orang ajar* make sure to maintain a concrete powerful position in kampong society, which is based on a culture of fear and surveillance. So while 'trusting in other actors' is an important aspect of their risk style, they are not completely dependent on others for their recovery and coping, but also maintain control themselves. Finally, for *orang susah*, this chapter showed that trusting their patron forms the dominant aspect of their risk style.

Even if they cannot be sure that their social investments are paid back in the end, *orang susah* spend much of their time and energy in the establishment and maintenance of reciprocal relationships with actors with resources because they trust that they will be helped by them in future times of need. We could also say that *orang susah* have *exchanged* the risk of flooding for the risk of trusting a patron. Inherent in this exchange is a move from more self-efficacy towards less self-efficacy, and hence, an alteration of the way in which risk is constructed and perceived by these riverbank settlers.

But why, we must ask, do these *orang susah* trust so strongly that they will always be helped in time by their patrons during future times of need, even if present reality sometimes suggests that this may not be the case? If we remember that Yati's patron rejected her demand for support during the time she fell ill, then how can she still blindly trust that he will help her survive and recover from future disasters? And Kurdi, whose trust in the *kelurahan* was disappointed when he got into financial problems, why would he not simply revert to his former autonomous and preventive risk strategies instead of hoping that he won't be disappointed another time by his patron? I propose that the answer to these questions lies in what may be called the habitual or structured characteristic of the practice of trusting. In order to develop this argument, in the next and final sections of this chapter I discuss relevant theories of trust, which I then connect to my concept of the habitus of poverty.

Trusting in theory

From the sociological literature on trust and risk, we can learn that feelings of trust – or, as I prefer to call it, favourable expectations towards other people's actions – come about from a mixture of rational assessments and cognitively structured mechanisms (Simmel 1990/1900: 79; Luhmann 1968: 96; Luhmann 1993). That is, whether or not we trust a person in a situation of risk and contingency is partly a matter of cognitive knowledge and reasoning, and partly a matter of habit. Let me concretize this theoretical argument by applying it to the specific case of the *orang susah*.

The favourable expectations that *orang susah* have regarding their patron are partly based on rational risk assessment. These riverbank settlers have learned from their past, mainly positive, experiences with patrons that they have a fair chance of earning back their investments in the future. Both Yati and Kurdi have been supported by their patron before during floods, therefore it is not at all unthinkable that this might well happen again during the next flood. But they cannot be sure about that, as they have no direct control over actions of other actors. Nevertheless, they appear sure that they will continue to receive aid – and it is this apparent certainty that enables them to keep calm despite the many uncertainties and problems that characterize their daily lives. This apparent certainty proves that trusting is never just based on rational calculations. Instead, it always involves 'irrational' hope or what Möllering calls 'unaccountable faith' (Möllering 2001: 410). The unaccountable or irrational aspect of trusting is not based on a realistic idea of what is actually happening at this very moment, but more so on a habitual feeling that was shaped by what has happened before.

The fact that a part of trusting is based on habit, rather than on rationale, has to do with the function that trusting has for people in situations of uncertainty.

As I wrote in the Introduction to this book, trusting serves to calm our minds in cases of risk and contingency. If our perceptions of who we can trust in times of need shifted along with every new uncertain situation we faced, we would face high anxiety each and every time as well. Instead, our future expectations are neither arbitrary nor easily adapted, but rather lean on patterned logics. Hence, once we have established a favourable or trustful expectation of another actor's intentions and actions, we tend to stick to these even though realistic circumstances may disappoint us. Indeed, even if trustful expectations are at one point dashed, people tend to cling to these favourable expectations, nevertheless, because they have become habitual and as such provide people with a sense of calm.

Human actors can stick to these favourable or trustful expectations by considering the disappointment of our expectations as *an exception*. This mechanism allows people to maintain their normative, favourable expectations, while acknowledging that their trust has been disappointed in an incident. Yati's interpretation of why she was not helped during her illness by her patron offers a clear example of how people can deal with disappointments from a trusted person's actions, by considering these disappointments as exceptions to the norm. Reflect on the way in which Yati described to me what happened:

> I think it was because the foundation was low in money that time I asked them for help, so therefore they could not help me. But if I would turn ill again, they would help me for sure. They always like to help me. Just not that one time, because they could not do it.

That this explanation is inaccurate may be clear by now, but that is not the main point here. Rather, this quote serves to show that for Yati, by considering this disappointment as an exception instead of a warning that her trust in the foundation employees may be naïve, she can keep her sense of calm in a context of contingency. A similar mechanism can be recognized in the narrative that *orang susah* Kurdi presented to me when he reflected on the time he was not helped by people of the *kelurahan* when he was indebted to his family-in-law:

> That is just because it was still very early in the morning when I went to ask for help. So none of my close contacts had yet arrived at the office [of the *kelurahan*], and so nobody was able to arrange help for me. They would have done so eventually but by the time they found out, they must have thought I had already found another solution and help was no longer needed. Next time I'm in trouble, they will make it up to me.

Kurdi's interpretation of what happens is most probably not accurate. But his narrative does make clear that maintaining his favourable expectations of the *kelurahan* offers him a sense of calm in a context of normal uncertainty. It is important to realize that the value of trusting as a risk practice is not determined by the extent to which one's favourable expectations are – objectively seen – realistic and therefore fulfilled, but instead by one's *subjective* belief that these expectations will be fulfilled, which offers a sense of certainty, a feeling of calm, or what other sociologists may call ontological security (Giddens 1990; Harries 2008). Hence, trusting may be regarded as a rather 'risky' risk practice on an objective level, but for *orang susah* it seems to be an effective way to keep a sense of calm and safety in a highly precarious environment.

It follows, then, that it is not the objective environment that necessarily creates a human actor's sense of safety, but that it is at least partly the product of a cognitive coping mechanism that protects people's sense of safety *despite objective risk*. For *orang susah*, their dependent and 'trusting' risk style helps to decrease their perceived, subjective, risk towards floods. At the same time, we have seen that the more they became dependent on a patron, the less they believed they were able to autonomously cope with risks and problems. In a way, it thus seems that *orang susah* prioritize the protection of their sense of safety over their objective physical and material vulnerability.

In Chapter 5, I explore the limits of this function of 'trusting' as a risk practice, and consider what happens when people's expectations are disappointed to such an extent that they can no longer be considered 'exceptions' to the norm. Yet first, in the final sections of this chapter I will relate the notions of self-efficacy and trust to the notion of a habitus of poverty (introduced in Chapters 2 and 3).

Habitus of poverty

I have claimed several times that *orang susah's* low self-efficacy and high levels of trust play a rather *recent* role in their risk behaviour. How should we understand this recent development in relation to the notion of a habitus of poverty, which we know tends to be reproductive, rather than innovative? The answer, I propose, has to do with the difference between a general and a specific habitus.

As Bourdieu pointed out in *Pascalian Meditations* (1997/2000), a 'general habitus' is a system of dispositions and ways of thinking about and acting in the world that is constituted early on in life, while a 'specific habitus' is acquired later through education, training, socialization and discipline within particular institutions. We might then take from the theory of habitus that *orang susah's* limited expectations of a radical improvement of their situation in the future spring from their general habitus of poverty, which was constituted early on in their life. Through the more recent experiences with actors from aid institutions, *orang susah* acquired a specific habitus and came to believe that they need to be dependent on a patron in order to handle flood risk. Hence, while maintaining the idea that a radical improvement of their life is impossible (general habitus), more recently they also developed a new, habitual belief that they themselves are unable to act effectively in relation to flood risk, just as they acquired and developed the idea that their patrons are to be trusted (specific habitus). Accordingly, we have seen that their risk style has altered over the course of several years, from autonomous and preventive risk practices towards more dependent practices.

We might also consider that *orang susah* are not only dependent on their patron, but in some way also dependent on their marginal residence in a flood-prone neighbourhood. Were they to live in a safer area, or were they to take a loan and open a successful business, they could no longer claim aid from their current patron. Hence, as was the case with the risk styles discussed in Chapters 2 and 3, we see here how riverbank settlers remain trapped in a situation of risk and poverty.

Afterword: Susah risk practices in and outside of Bantaran Kali

A new opportunity (created by increased flooding and increased attention of external aid institutions for flood victims) enabled *orang susah* to invite an alternative risk style. They nowadays have access to a form of personal insurance and invest in trustful relations with a patron, but at the same time this risk style translates into decreasing self-efficacy and a lack of autonomous, preventive risk measures. In combination with their early-acquired habitus of poverty, these perceptions of high trust and low self-efficacy keep *orang susah* satisfied with dependency relationships with patrons, and they thus prefer the small benefits thereof over a more radical alteration of deeply unequal structures of power and economic distribution. In order to maintain these benefits, *orang susah* do not overtly protest unequal structures in or beyond kampong society, and instead try to avoid conflict with actors higher in the social hierarchy. For the same reasons, they do not dare to take autonomous actions that may carry the risk of disturbing the relationship with their patron.

The *susah* risk style recalls two behavioural styles that have been described in studies of risk and vulnerability that were conducted in other contexts. In a study on flood-risk responses in London, Tim Harries observed that trusting was used as a main strategy by certain people to maintain a sense of calm and safety despite an objectively increasing flood risk. Instead of taking action to prevent their houses from flooding, and instead of taking seriously recent government warnings of increased floods, these people trusted that their environment would remain safe enough without them doing anything about that (Harries 2008). Of course, the relatively wealthy informants of Harries have many more opportunities to cope with floods than do Jakartan riverbank settlers. In the case of acute emergency, they might still be able to repair their house by using their own financial resources, or they might be able to evacuate to an expensive hotel in a dry area. However, they have in common with the *orang susah* that they put what Giddens calls their 'ontological security' above their physical security. This may not come across as an effective risk strategy for outsiders, but, as I have shown in this chapter, it surely is an effective strategy to avoid anxiety in a highly contingent situation.

The *susah* risk style is also reminiscent of the social security style of *'orang pelit'* that Nooteboom distinguishes in his work on social security styles in rural Eastland

Java. He describes the *orang pelit* as 'those who try to benefit from the support given through the old mutual exchange economy, minimise investments, and ignore the claims of others in reciprocal relationships as far as possible' (2003: 213). He also writes that these people try to accumulate capital on the basis of local resources and that they make use of village institutions and arrangements, while trying to avoid the social pressures of sharing, redistribution, care, and mutual help, thereby keeping the costs of investing in social relationships as low as possible (ibid.). What the *orang susah* and the *orang pelit* have in common is that they do not want to invest much in social security arrangements because they have the opinion that not much can be expected from local institutions such as mutual help. However, a clear difference between the *orang pelit* and the *orang susah* is that the former benefit from village institutions and arrangements, while the latter do not. This is because *orang susah* are excluded by neighbours in the social network because people are jealous of the relatively large amount of aid they receive. Another difference between the *orang pelit* and the *orang susah* is that the former try to accumulate money as a means of self-insurance, while the *orang susah* are completely dependent on their patron for insurance.

On a final note for this chapter, I wish to stress that I am not suggesting that offering help to flood victims should be discontinued in order to avoid dependency relations. On the contrary, my experiences with the many different kinds of hazards that people in Bantaran Kali have to face in their daily lives leads me instead to believe that riverbank settlers need *much more* external support to decrease their objective vulnerability to floods and other risks. Ideally, that support needs to be focused on a radical alternation of the highly unequal power structures in wider society, instead of incidental recovery from large floods. This point is further discussed in the conclusion of this book.

Notes

1   As we know from Chapter 3, they are often assisted by *orang ajar* in carrying out these tasks.
2   The selection of the words 'strategies' and 'innovative practices' is conscious in this paragraph, indicating that I consider the practices of *orang susah* active and sometimes strategic. I emphasize this because some readers may intuitively associate the practices of *orang susah* with self-pity, fatalism, or even apathy. I disagree strongly with such views when it concerns the *orang susah*. Instead, in this chapter I aim to show that *orang susah* are in fact very active in ensuring their own safety – only that they do so via social investments, instead of by autonomous flood-risk measures.
3   Ambran's supposition is correct. From my interviews with Yati, I learned that she has had her shop for many years and has since made most of her income with it. However, after she divorced her husband and up until 2002, she also irregularly had sex with men in return for money or goods. She stopped doing that when she developed her *susah* risk style and became dependent on a patron.
4   Yati's question created an ethical dilemma for me. On the one hand, I wanted to help her, but on the other, I did not want to be seen as an aid giver, as this might affect my research. I eventually lent Yati an amount of money that was considered reasonable in the neighbourhood (Rp 50,000).

References

Aspinall, E. (2013). A nation in fragments: patronage and neoliberalism in contemporary Indonesia. *Critical Asian Studies*, 45 (1), 27–54.

Blunt, P., Turner, M., & Lindroth, H. (2012.) Patronage, service delivery, and social justice in Indonesia. *International Journal of Public Administration*, 35 (3), 214–220.

Bourdieu, P. (2000). *Pascalian Meditations*. (R. Nice, Trans.). Cambridge: Polity Press (original work published 1997).

Giddens, A. (1990). *The Consequences of Modernity*. Cambridge: Polity Press.

Harries, T. (2008). Feeling secure or being secure? Why it can seem better not to protect yourself against a natural hazard. *Health, Risk and Society*, 10(5), 479–490.

King, V. T. (2008). *The Sociology of Southeast Asia. Transformation in a Developing Region*. Copenhagen: NIAS Press.

Luhmann, N. (1968). *Vertrauen. Ein Mechanismus der Reduktion sozialer Komplexität* [*Trust. A Mechanism to Reduce Social Complexity*] (4th ed.). Stuttgart: Lucius & Lucius.

Luhmann, N. (1993). *Risk: A Sociological Theory*. New York: A. de Gruyter.

Möllering, G. (2001). The nature of trust: from Georg Simmel to a theory of expectation, interpretation and suspension. *Sociology*, 35(2), 403–420.

Nooteboom, G. (2003). *A Matter of Style. Social Security and Livelihood in Upland East Java* (unpublished doctoral dissertation). Nijmegen University, Nijmegen.

Scott, J. C. (1977). *The Moral Economy of the Peasant: Rebellion and Subsistence in Southeast Asia*. Yale: Yale University Press.

Simmel, G. (1990). *The Philosophy of Money* (2nd ed.). London: Routledge (original work published 1900).

5 Orang siap

Challenging the government, altering structures

In previous chapters I have shown that people's risk styles are often habitual and tend to reproduce unequal structures, rather than being innovative and challenging structures. This chapter, however, examines the clear exceptions to that observation. It considers instances where agents critically reflect upon their own habitual perceptions and practices and eventually develop a radically new risk style, thus creating a scope for change. Therefore, while in previous chapters it appeared most useful to trace how people develop a habitual practice and reproduce structures, this time, the focus of the analysis lies more explicitly with the process of change in behaviour, as well as on attempts to challenge structures.

I examine the precise moments in the lives of actors where older habits are critically reflected upon by them and strategically altered. Tracing back when and how a so-called 'siap' risk style has developed among some residents of the riverbank enables me to explain why and how people's habitual strategies became seriously undermined, and how they turned into *orang siap*. Furthermore, it enables me to pinpoint which factors underlie the alternatively developed *siap* risk style. Finally, it allows me to consider how and whether this style enables *orang siap* to challenge structured inequalities, or, to put that differently: whether a *siap* risk style helps them to escape their living situation of normal uncertainty.

A defensive risk style

Siap means 'ready' or 'prepared' in Indonesian, and *bersiap*, the verb from *siap*, means to prepare or to get ready. The *orang siap* in Bantaran Kali exhibit what might best be described as a defensive risk style. In social scientific jargon, defensive practices generally refer to aggressive behaviour towards the perceived threat, or to expressed feelings of anxiety about the threat (Baan 2008; Eagly & Chaiken 1993). The defensive risk practices that are associated with a *siap* risk style include (often loud and publically) worrying about floods and other perceived risk; crying; having nightmares; having feelings of anxiety, and readily expressing them to fellow residents; and overtly expressing feelings of fear about and anger towards the political institutions that are involved in Bantaran Kali's flood management (the *kelurahan* and the *kecamatan*) as well as to local residents associated with these institutions, such as the *orang ajar*. Also, *orang siap* consistently refuse aid or cooperation with these institutions. Hence, during floods, *orang siap* typically disobey governmental safety instructions and refuse to evacuate to a government shelter. After floods, they refuse financial aid from political institutions such as the *kelurahan*.

Not only do *orang siap* publically express their anger and frustration against the political institutions involved in flood management, they also overtly challenge the *orang ajar* (introduced in Chapter 3). It may have already become clear in this book that by challenging the orders of *orang ajar*, inhabitants of Bantaran Kali run the risk of being disciplined or punished by powerful actors in society. Nonetheless, *orang siap* sometimes overtly raise objections to *orang ajar*, for example, by refusing to follow their safety advice, by walking away as soon as an *orang ajar* wants to start a 'lecture' about floods, or by expressing different opinions about the causes of floods towards *orang ajar*. As I will explain in more detail later in this chapter, *orang siap* react in this way towards political institutions or people associated with those because they believe that the Jakarta government has a second agenda of slum clearance of the riverbanks, and that politicians therefore do little to prevent floods in Bantaran Kali.

While other residents describe such behaviour as 'crazy' and wonder 'what has come over them', the *orang siap* often refer to their neighbours as 'naïve' and portray themselves as the only ones who 'are prepared' (*siap*) for the risks to be encountered in the near future.

The *siap* risk style is not only exhibited during flood risk events, but also in the face of other hazards in which distrusted actors associated with the Jakarta government are involved. Let me offer a few examples to clarify this point. Regarding poverty-related risks, it is notable that, even though *orang siap* often engage in local self-help groups such as *arisan*, they do not participate in government-run *arisan* groups. In case of illness, none of the *orang siap* ever made use of the services of a (government-subsidized and therefore relatively affordable) health clinic during the period of fieldwork. Instead, they pay high costs to consult alternative medics who may have no formal medical background, but who are at least not associated with the government. According to different *orang siap*, these alternative medics 'treat poor people as best as they can', while the government doctors were consistently described as persons who 'hate poor people and [purposely] let us suffer'. This contrasts with the practices of people with any of the three other risk styles discussed in this book, who often made use of government health clinics whenever they were ill.

Regarding the risk of eviction, *orang siap* were actively trying to protect themselves from potential future evictions. From my interviews, we see that a large majority of them invest relatively large amounts of money in fake land documents that they believe useful to prove their 'right' to live along the riverbanks; they also hang plastic bags with their most important documents in strategic places in their houses where they can quickly take them 'any time a bulldozer approaches', and they carry all tax payment receipts with them as proof of their legitimate residence whenever they leave their houses. Also, *orang siap* make radical decisions in order to accumulate money and protect themselves against risk: some took their children out of school to save costs 'because we might have to move soon and therefore we need all the money we can save'; others started to sell their household assets for a similar reason – in this chapter we will come across several such scenarios and other examples. For now, it is most important to know that these defensive practices are not exhibited by people with any of the other three risk styles discussed in this book.

In the following sections I pick up once more on the narrative of the flood that I experienced in Bantaran Kali during fieldwork. In this part of the story we will get to know two people that represent the *siap* risk style: Tono and Ratna. What is striking in their biographies is that their current *siap* practices differ enormously from how they typically behaved towards risk during previous years. Tono was widely known as an *orang ajar* and cooperated with actors in the military and the government before he radically changed his behaviour and started to overtly protest the authorities instead. Ratna was widely known as an *orang susah* and largely depended on her patrons for coping with risks until she developed a *siap* risk style and started to refuse any further aid or interference from them in her life. While their former risk practices differed from person to person, Tono, Ratna and the other *orang siap* in Bantaran Kali have in common that they all went through a process of radical behavioural change and nowadays exhibit defensive practices in relation to perceived risk.

It is relevant to note that the *siap* risk style seems like a rather recently developed risk style in Bantaran Kali. During the time I lived in Bantaran Kali, the defensive practices of Ratna and Tono were still rather new and unfamiliar to fellow residents, and hence it is logical that fellow residents were not familiar with the self-chosen nickname '*orang siap*'. Most of them seemed to lag behind when describing the people who could nowadays be categorized as '*orang siap*', and still called them by former nicknames. For instance, Tono was still described to me by many as an *orang ajar*, and Ratna was still frequently described as someone who leans on a patron – even though we will soon learn that this was no longer the case during the time I met her in the field. The longer Tono and Ratna exhibited their initially unfamiliar *siap* behaviour, however, the more often their fellow residents overtly acknowledged that something about them was changing, for example by remarking that 'something had come over them'. Still, the nickname '*orang siap*' was hardly ever used by any of them. Instead, as I remarked above, they called the people who call themselves the *orang siap* 'crazy'. The nickname *orang siap* that I use to depict the risk style of people, such as Tono and Ratna, was thus derived from their own descriptions, rather than from a widely acknowledged nickname.

Evacuation during a flood

It had turned seven o'clock in the evening. Together with some other residents, I had found a dry spot inside the *kelurahan* shelter not far from the inundated houses and streets of Bantaran Kali. This shelter was made from strong materials to protect individuals from rain and sunshine, and it offered free public facilities: people could wash themselves with clean water and use the toilet. Blankets and medicines were provided, as were soap, water and rice meals, as well as sweet milk for small children. A team of eight civil servants, dressed in blue T-shirts with the emblem of the sub-district printed on the back, were instructed to care full-time for evacuees. In reality, however, there was hardly anything for them to do: the *kelurahan* shelter had remained largely empty.

The few flood victims who had settled in the shelter declared that there was 'so much food that we get bored with eating'. This evening, Kurdi – whom we got to know in Chapter 4 as an *orang susah* – had already received two full plates of *nasi telor*, and was told that he could come back for a third refill. He did not. Later that night, leftovers were thrown away. Clothes that were supposed to be freely distributed among all flood victims were now taken to be sold by the few evacuees present. The underemployed civil servants slept through most of their shifts, or played computer games on their mobile phones. Earlier, they still had some tasks to carry out: uniformed males tied up ropes and pulled up poles, while their female colleagues prepared hot meals for evacuees. One woman was in charge of the monitoring of evacuees in the shelter. She registered the name, age, gender and address of everyone who came in. These details would help kampong leaders to check who is safe in the evacuation shelter and who might be still in danger, or left behind in the kampong. 'Come in', she invited flood victims who were trickling in, 'are you in good health? We feel sorry for you, come in!' But it seemed that not as many flood victims wanted to make use of the *kelurahan* services as was expected by the civil servant. After hours of waiting, she put her notebook away. 'After a full day of waiting, I have only registered the names of about 30 people. And I don't think more people will be coming in. Wherever they are, waiting for them is a waste of my time', she said.

Where were the other inhabitants of Bantaran Kali? My analysis of the interviews I did with inhabitants during and after the flood shows that they were scattered in and around their neighbourhood. Approximately 26 per cent of the total research population (N = 130) remained in or atop their flooded house during the whole flood (as Ida did in the Introduction). Like Ida, most of these people have an '*antisipasi*' risk style. Another 24 per cent of the riverbank settlers sought safety in the *kelurahan* shelter, some known as '*orang ajar*', and most of them having a '*susah*' risk style (as the above paragraphs exposed, *orang susah* Kurdi was among them). Eight per cent fled to the office of the foundation Sanggar Ciliwung Merdeka (introduced in Chapter 4); most of them are '*orang susah*' – Yati from Chapter 4 was among them. Thirteen per cent of the respondents, including the kampong leader and *orang ajar* Yusuf, kept moving during the hours when flood waters were high, never settling down in one specific place, but instead running back and forth between the *kelurahan* shelter and the houses of inhabitants in order to help people evacuate. Another 6 per cent of my respondents evacuated to the houses of family members or acquaintances who live in dryer neighbourhoods of Jakarta or in rural Java. Finally, 23 per cent of this study's participants evacuated to a provisionary shelter located on the opposite side of the kampong outskirts, a few hundred meters from where civil servants set up the *kelurahan* shelter. It is this latter group of evacuees that we will get to know better in this chapter.

Evacuation: But where to go?

When evening fell and it turned dark, tens of flood victims shivered in their humid clothes. They were inhabitants from Bantaran Kali who had sought refuse in a poor-looking, self-built shelter. Compared to the relatively comfortable shelter of the *kelurahan*, the situation in the provisional shelter appeared more problematic for evacuees. One disadvantage concerned its location: the shelter had been built in a relatively low area just outside Bantaran Kali, where the soil was muddy from flood water. Its rooftop, made from pieces of thin plastic that were found in the river and along the streets, was full of holes, allowing the temperature to rise during the hot morning hours, while later, heavy afternoon showers poured in. Every morning after the flood, the place smelled strongly like urine. Hygienic circumstances deteriorated quickly. As there was no medical service in this provisional shelter, the wounds of flood victims were not taken care of. Though several neighbours had brought along cooking pots from their homes, and others had brought along rice and eggs, there was not enough food for everyone, nor was there enough drinking water. Within three days, lice, cockroaches and rats were everywhere and families moved to the streets surrounding the shelter because 'even though we cannot protect our heads from rain here, at least it does not smell as bad as over there [inside the provisional shelter]'. Many evacuees complained of hunger. Others worried out loud about the money that they felt forced to spend on food now that they could not cook, or on the costly medications they needed, now that they had become ill or wounded. All of them appeared distressed about their situation.

To recount, these flood victims had other options. They could have evacuated to the *kelurahan* shelter, yet they did not. Even though these evacuees could get free meals a few hundred meters down the road, they chose to buy expensive flood foods in the streets. Even though they could make use of a doctor's services free of charge in the *kelurahan* shelter, these people bandaged their own grazed arms and hoped that their coughing would not become worse.

The question of why they made such decisions when seemingly better alternatives were available occupied my mind during my fieldwork, and also the minds of the evacuees in the *kelurahan* shelter, who discussed it out loud in my presence. 'They used to stay with us during floods, now suddenly they no longer do. They must have gone crazy', speculated one evacuee in the *kelurahan* shelter. 'Yes', said another, 'the flood has caused a shock and now they cannot think clear anymore'.

Two names were often mentioned in these discussions: Tono and Ratna. 'Did you know that Tono is there as well?' people asked one another, and others typically replied with another rhetorical question, 'Why is he there and not here with us?' About the inhabitant named Ratna, people seemed equally surprised that she was staying in the provisional shelter. Both the civil servants and the evacuees declared 'I cannot believe Ratna stays there as well', and explained to me that 'Ratna always used to be with the *kelurahan* during floods'. For both Tono and Ratna, the evacuees in the *kelurahan* shelter wondered 'what has come over them' as they observed that these inhabitants of Bantaran Kali exhibited highly unusual behaviour.

On the third morning after the flood, some of the evacuees in the *kelurahan* shelter, including *orang ajar* Yusuf (Chapter 2), headed to the provisional shelter to find out what had changed their fellow residents' minds. Yusuf started talking to Ratna, whom he knows very well because she was his sister-in-law before her husband passed away: 'The *kelurahan* tent is much better than the dump where you sleep now. Let the people of the *kelurahan* care for you. They want to help you. They are close to you'. But Ratna stayed put. For a while, Yusuf looked in the direction of Tono, whom he knew well also, but he decided not to approach him when he saw the angry look on Tono's face.

After the visit, Yusuf reported to the evacuees in the *kelurahan* shelter that 'Ratna never acted like she does now! This is not her! She always used to be thankful if the *kelurahan* offered help during past floods, and she has often made use of their support; but now, to be honest, she acts hard-hearted'. Other people agreed: 'It is as if she has become another person', said Kurdi. And his wife added: 'Ratna used to be different'.

They were no less confused by Tono's recent decisions. 'Tono', said Yusuf in a serious tone, 'has changed personality, so it seems to me. He was always behaving friendly and respectful with me. Now, he acted crazy and stubborn – he did not even want to speak to me'. It became clear from listeners' responses that this announcement was shocking for residents in Bantaran Kali. The people who heard Yusuf talk shook their head in expressions of disbelief, speculating out loud 'What made them crazy?' or asking, again and again, for more details of the story.

Now that we have read so much about Tono and Ratna, it is time to finally meet them and see what 'has come over them'.

Tono: From orang ajar to orang siap

Tono is a man in his early thirties, extraordinarily skinny and tall, with pock-marked skin. For the past 17 years, Tono and his wife have been living in a self-built house made of cement and stone, located in the lowest part of the kampong, right beside the river. They share the house with their two children and Tono's old mother. Tono earns a living by cleaning or serving food in a nearby cafeteria; his wife takes care of the family and the household chores. Tono is typically described by residents as a hard-working man, a 'good' person, a pious Muslim. Moreover, he is widely known as a man with 'contacts' and 'friends' in the *kelurahan*, the political institution involved in flood management in Bantaran Kali. Because of his good relations with bureaucrats from this institution, different people consider him a potential upcoming *orang ajar* in the kampong.

During the large floods that inundated the kampong in 2002 and 2007, Tono had cooperated with rescue workers sent by the government to help fellow residents evacuate. He also regularly assisted with the lectures by *orang ajar* in past years, and he reported to *orang ajar* on anything that he believed to be a potential threat to safety in Bantaran Kali. For a long time, he seemed eager to maintain and further improve these social relations with powerful actors in Jakarta society. Tono was saving a share of his income for the goal of buying a Handie Talkie (HT), the radio set that is commonly used by *orang ajar*. According to his wife, from 2006 Tono set aside an average of Rp 10,000 per month for the HT, and planned to buy the device within two years. About a month before the large 2007 flood that occurred in Bantaran Kali, he applied with several civil servants from the *kecamatan* for a radio frequency to receive flood information in the future.

When his family's house was flooded in 2010, however, Tono responded in a way that did not remind of the *ajar* style by which fellow residents described him above. This time, he did not help any of the *orang ajar* spread the risk-warning message in Bantaran Kali, nor did he help people evacuate. Neither did he follow the formal safety instructions for evacuation that he himself repeatedly 'taught' to fellow residents. His family did not evacuate to the *kelurahan* shelter – as ordered to by *orang ajar* – but instead moved to the overcrowded provisional shelter a few meters from their house. In fact, Tono was one of the men who helped set up this provisional shelter. When, a day after evacuation, his son started coughing, Tono decided that it might be healthier for his family members to move out of the overcrowded shelter. Still, he did not go to the *kelurahan* shelter; instead, the family moved to the streets. They spent the following days in the open air on pieces of cardboard, their backs pressed against the houses along the side of the road with cars and motorbikes constantly passing by. During afternoon rains, they tried to protect themselves from water with scraps of plastic and canvas. Because their gas stove was severely damaged by the flood, the family was now forced to buy meals for all five members – something which they could hardly afford. Tono worked long days, but made far too little to pay for these meals. He therefore decided to spend a part of his savings on it – savings that were initially meant to be spent on the education of his children.

When asked why he would not reside in the dry *kelurahan* shelter further down the road, making use of its free services, Tono sighed and explained:

> I need to be prepared (*siap*)…I must protect my belongings from politicians (*orang politik*). They act as if they are poor people's friends, but as soon as I leave my house to seek shelter with them, they will demolish my belongings! We must not believe anything good that they promise! If the people from the *kelurahan* tell you that they aim to help us, then that is a lie for sure. They will evict us! The government hates poor people like us! If you come back to Jakarta in the nearby future and this neighbourhood has been bulldozed, do not tell me that I have not warned you.

Tono referred to an issue that has already been touched upon several times in this book: the risk of eviction by the Jakarta government. As mentioned earlier, legal housing in Jakarta is generally unaffordable for the poorest residents of the city. For that reason, many of them reside in unregistered, often flood-prone or otherwise risky areas. According to formal law, residence on unregistered land is forbidden. This means that the inhabitants of the riverbanks are formally considered illegal occupiers of government land, and therefore they run the risk of being evicted at any point. The possibility of eviction has existed for a long time, but the threat has only recently become more concrete to the inhabitants of Bantaran Kali, because the Jakarta government has started to carry out evictions further downstream. By clearing the riverbanks, the city government is able to widen the river, which is believed to lessen the problem of flooding. Riverbank settlers will thus have to be resettled and compensated financially for their loss. It remains a question whether they will. Studies of earlier evictions in Jakarta have shown that riverbank settlers generally receive insufficient compensation for their loss, or nothing at all, which is justified by the government by stating that these settlers do not hold the formal rights to their land or house (Human Rights Watch 2006: 10; Mariani 2003).

Three weeks after the flood, Tono and his family members still resided in the street, as it had become impossible for them to live in their severely damaged house. A huge truck entered and stopped right in front of the family. It was met by the residents with loud cheers. Many people in Bantaran Kali had already heard from the kampong leaders that the *kelurahan* was planning to support some of the flood victims, by offering the households living in the lowest areas of Bantaran Kali free wood, cement and stone to rebuild or repair their houses. Now that this huge truck was parked in the kampong, the residents realized that the promise of the *kelurahan* would be fulfilled. And so it was: the truck was opened, and piles of bags with building materials were offloaded by the truck driver and some local volunteers. One of them lay two bags in front of Tono's family. But unlike his neighbours, Tono did not look at all happy with the gift. Instead, he looked at the bags in disgust. While other beneficiaries in the neighbourhood quickly started rebuilding and repairing their houses with the materials, Tono warned his wife and children 'not even [to] touch it'. He believed it 'a trap'. He told me later in an interview:

> When I use those materials to start rebuilding a house, then they [the government] will put me in jail after I have finished. It is forbidden to build a house here, right, because this land is owned by the government. So, if I rebuild my house, then they have the formal right to punish me. They will tell me I have disobeyed governmental orders…[because] I am illegally occupying the riverbanks. The Indonesian government is like that; they seduce poor people into doing bad things so that they can take it out on them.

Ignoring the frequently expressed desire of his wife to rebuild a house in order to end their homelessness, Tono carried his bags of materials to the market and came back with his pockets full of banknotes. He had sold the materials to 'some rich Chinese man'. Tono planned to use the money to rebuild a house in another neighbourhood, he said. 'A safe place', he promised his eldest son, 'a house without floods, and without the bulldozers of the government waiting their turn'.

Yet the little money that Tono was able to earn by selling the building materials was not enough to build or rent a house in a different part of town, especially not in an area where land is registered and inhabitants live 'legally'. Tono knew all too well that he had earned too little to escape from his current 'illegal' status, nevertheless he seemed completely determined to fulfil his promise to his son. Often when talking to his children, he repeated that one day soon the boys would live in a 'villa'. He even visited potential new neighbourhoods by motorbike, pointing out to his sons and me where their school would be, and what a nice street they would live on. 'Can you believe that we will live here?' he said. 'Only the prospect of that makes me want to work harder'. In the two months that followed the flood, Tono tirelessly thought of new ways to quickly collect more money. One thing he tried was asking neighbours whether they could help him to find more or better-paid work, offering them his services as a jack-of-all-trades. When no jobs were offered to him by anyone, he was seen stealing stones and wood from the newly rebuilt houses of other flood victims, materials which he again sold at the market. Tono furthermore stole pieces of fruit from food carts of salesmen passing through the neighbourhood, and during a public gathering, I saw him taking the food boxes that were meant for other residents. He admitted to me later that he sold those to inhabitants of a nearby neighbourhood because he needed cash:

> I need much money to move house. So I must find ways to get it. It is bad, but in my opinion I have no other choice. It took me a long time to realize that there is no hope for me here. It is dangerous to stay in this neighbourhood! I need to take my family away from here. We must leave before they come and do us harm. We are like enemies (*musuh*) of the [Jakarta] government.

For similar reasons, Tono told me during an interview that he had decided to stop paying land taxes to the government, indicating that he planned to invest that money in a new house. At that point of the interview, a neighbour (widely known as an *orang ajar*) intervened in our conversation and spoke disapprovingly of this decision, arguing that Tono was behaving like a 'bad citizen' and that he should act 'normal' again. Tono, his body shaking from emotion, replied in an angry tone to him:

> Oh, I used to be like you, always obeying the government, paying them money. But what did I get back? No citizens' rights! No protection! So why would I try to be a good citizen, if the government neglects me anyhow? I won't obey them. I will fight them. I am prepared. You go to your friends and tell them so.

Fellow residents of Tono disapproved of all of Tono's actions, but they appeared truly bewildered when Tono decided to join an ethnic gang or civil militia group called Forum Betawi Rempug (FBR, Betawi Brotherhood Forum).

This organization was created in the year 2000 after inter-gang rivalries inten- sified in Jakarta between largely ethnic Madurese and Betawi-based gangs, the latter believed to be the indigenous population of Jakarta. In order to achieve their vision of a Jakarta dominated by Betawi strongmen, the FBR has used a number of controversial tactics and strategies. According to researcher Ian Wilson, these 'traverse the line between legal and illegal, ranging from classic extortion and stand-over tactics, to political lobbying, legitimate business ventures and entre- preneurial initiatives' (Wilson 2010: 252). FBR especially appeals to the poor in Jakarta society, and attracts a broad spectrum of local *preman* looking for a new organizational cover for their racketeering, as well as the unemployed and people working in the informal street economy, in particular *ojek* motorcycle taxi drivers. In Jakarta, an estimated 60,000 people have now become members (Wilson 2010: 252). In Bantaran Kali, the organization is especially popular in the residential segment where an FBR chairman occupies a double role as *Kepela RT*.

Tono joined FBR four weeks or so after the flood. In the following months, he assisted during all FBR meetings that took place in the wider area of Bantaran Kali; he consistently wore the black clothing of FBR's members; he practiced his fighting skills with other FBR members in a nearby FBR office and invested in a gun to 'protect myself and my brothers'. As was mentioned, the main aim of FBR is to fight for the rights of original Betawi inhabitants in Jakarta. Yet, Tono had his own reasons for joining the organization, as the following excerpts of an interview show. When I asked Tono why he became a member of FBR, he replied:

> Maybe FBR does bad things, but at least they care for poor people like me. If the government fails to protect me from floods, FBR will try and help me for sure. If the government sends bulldozers to my house, FBR members will help me fight back! We have weapons. We can unite and organize a large protest against floods, demanding the government builds a dam to protect us. We are also trained to become good fighters, so together we are strong against whoever wants to hurt us. I have no other choice than to be prepared in this way, right?

The behavioural shift that Tono made – from a 'friend' of the authorities to a man willing to fight them – is outstanding in its sharp distinction between past and present risk practices. Simply put, Tono used to trust the city government and now he distrusts them; by the time I met him, he trusted the FBR more to help him out in future times of need. His perceptions of the future also seem to have radically altered: while he used to envisage himself as an *orang ajar* for many years, cooperating with the government in the management of safety in Bantaran Kali, he later aimed to move to a legal, flood-prone neighbourhood and started aspiring to a completely new kind of life. Whenever he spoke about such changes, Tono emphasized the belief that he would be able to turn his hopes into reality soon, and often said that he would be willing to do what it takes to provide his family with a safer, better life. I will later show that Tono was not exaggerating when he said this. In order to fulfil his hopes of a safer future, he even went so far as to overtly protest the government, something which – as became clear in the previous chapters – not many people dare to do in Bantaran Kali.

Ratna: From orang susah to orang siap

Ratna is a young widow and mother of three. A few hours after the flood, she sat in the corner of the provisional shelter and wiped away tears that rolled down her cheeks and said:

> Everything is drowning [flooded] here. They [government bureaucrats] must be laughing behind their desks. This neighbourhood is becoming more and

more dangerous because of the floods, but they refuse to care for us. Instead, they like to make us suffer more by demolishing our houses. I have had enough. We must prepare to leave as soon as possible, and I am so confused because I don't know where we should go…Allah knows how we must save ourselves! I must be prepared.

Just like Tono did, Ratna accused the government of not taking effective measures to prevent Bantaran Kali from flooding. She also referred to the threat of an eviction, carried out by the Jakarta government. Obviously, Ratna did not believe that she would be provided with a new house by the government, indicating instead that she must find a new place of residence without knowing where.

Over the weeks that followed the flood, Ratna invested all her money, energy and time in leaving the kampong 'before the bulldozers come'. Ratna believed that she had to act quicker than the Jakarta government, so that:

At least I have the time to prepare and save what is mine. I can take along the building materials from my house to reuse them and I can take my children's school uniforms with me. If I just wait here until the bulldozers come, they will demolish all my possessions. I would be left without anything. And they might even put me in jail! Yes, they might actually do that, because they will say we had no legal rights to live here in the first place. If they make other promises to us, we must not be naïve and believe them. They are dishonest. Many years I trusted that they would make my life better. Now, look at me! I must prepare to leave as soon as possible.

Several times she travelled by public transport to three neighbourhoods just outside Jakarta that she had in mind for eventual resettlement. I accompanied her during two of these trips, and saw how she – shy but determined – asked residents whether she could live there as well and how high the rent would eventually be. In both cases, she was waved off by these residents, who told her their kampong was 'full', or who demanded a far too expensive rental price. Nevertheless, Ratna remained determined to accumulate as much money as possible so that she could soon move away from the riverbank.

There were several ways in which Ratna tried to accumulate money to move. First, just like Tono, Ratna received several bags of building materials from the *kelurahan*, and, just like Tono, she sold them immediately at the market, while she and her children remained homeless after the flood. Second, a few days after the flood she took her children out of school in order to save on their educational fees. Third, on the eleventh day after the flood, Ratna started begging, in Bantaran Kali and in a nearby neighbourhood. Finally, three months after the flood, she stopped paying land taxes to save even more money, as she was sure that the government would evict her any time soon now, and she felt therefore, 'there is no use in paying them anymore. They will chase us away anyhow'.

Similar to what happened with Tono, negative talk about Ratna's behaviour started circulating in the neighbourhood in the months following the flood, and neighbours appeared confused about the unfamiliar ways in which Ratna had recently started to act. Residents called Ratna a bad mother (for taking her children out of school), a bad neighbour (for begging) and a bad citizen (for not paying taxes for the land), but most often, she was called 'ungrateful' (*tidak berterimakasih*) for refusing the help of the *kelurahan*.

The latter idea that Ratna has turned 'ungrateful' has to do with the fact that Ratna used to be known as a typical '*orang susah*' in the kampong. In past years, she was one of the regular beneficiaries of the *kelurahan*. Several civil servants working in that institution told me that Ratna 'used to be a friend of ours' and that 'we have often helped her with her problems'. During the 2002 flood and the 2007 flood, Ratna indeed received relatively large amounts of financial support from the *kelurahan*.[1] Until recently, she also worked for the *kelurahan* in different side jobs: sometimes volunteering work for free, sometimes working in return for a small reimbursement or gift. One of the civil servants who volunteers in the *kelurahan* shelter during the flood still remembers working with her:

> Ratna? She used to work right beside my desk! Yeah, I gave her tasks to do, like putting my files in plastic covers. In return, she could lunch here in the office for free. She liked helping us, and me and my colleagues did not mind helping her a bit in return. Even though she lives in a slum she is diligent. Therefore we have helped her whenever she had difficulties in her life [...] Now she acts like she never knew us. It is ungrateful, in my opinion. But as she clearly feels too good to take what we offer her, she shall survive the next flood on her own.

Clearly, Ratna's unfamiliar behaviour upset not only her neighbours, but also her former patrons.

These mutual frustrations between Ratna and her former patrons came to a head when Ratna ran into two of her former 'friends' from the *kelurahan* one evening and attacked them. This happened about five months after the flood. By then, Ratna was still busy 'preparing', *siap*; hence, she was trying to collect as much money as needed in order to move away from the riverbank. Apparently, the fact that Ratna had turned into a beggar was known in the *kelurahan*, because, as Ratna sat in a *kios* late one evening, drinking sweetened tea, two female *kelurahan* employees passed by and whispered that she was a 'bad person' for asking others for money. Ratna answered that she had no other option, as no one was helping her with her financial struggles. One of the ladies replied that that was nonsense, as Ratna could try to find another job, and that she was a bad Muslim for asking other poor people for money. Ratna then jumped up and flew at the women, pushed them, scratched their arms and pulled their hair. She screamed that she would no longer be treated badly by the government, and that the way in which the *kelurahan* women acted towards her was 'unfair' (*tidak adil*). Her loud screaming was heard in the kampong and many residents approached to see what was going on. Ratna was grabbed by a fellow resident, and the *kelurahan* women were protected by others. Even though they threatened to inform the police, the kampong leader eventually became involved and convinced them to leave Ratna be. 'I explained to them that she has gone crazy', he said that evening. 'The police would punish her too harshly, we must pity her – and also, Ratna says she wants to move away anyhow, so no one will be bothered by her anymore'. Yet even if Ratna was spared this time due to the kampong leader's counsel, her behaviour did not exactly make her popular in the neighbourhood. Most people overtly disapproved of her behaviour, saying that Ratna was 'ungrateful', and that they wanted to have nothing to do with her.

Meanwhile, Ratna continued to overtly challenge the *kelurahan*. On her Facebook account, she started posting harsh comments about the *kelurahan* employees, for example stating that they are 'bastards' (*banjingan*).[2] When I asked whether she was afraid that this might cause her problems, Ratna replied that she had recently decided that she would, from now on, overtly protest the *kelurahan*:

> I am not afraid any longer to publically say something ugly (*pernyataan buruk*) about the government. I use the Internet to express myself; I do it for the [future of] my children. What kind of life do we have here? The Indonesian government treats poor citizens badly. I have been obedient for a long time. Now, whenever I have anger [inside me], I just let it out, I express myself.

Another way in which Ratna overtly challenged the *kelurahan* was by approaching fellow residents and asking them to join her in a protest against the Jakarta government. Ratna wanted them to become united, she explained, and 'fight the governor together because he is creating floods in this neighbourhood to chase us out of our houses'. None of them appeared interested in such a plan, and again, Ratna was told that they wanted to have nothing to do with her. Two months later, Ratna had left Bantaran Kali. I have since remained in contact with her through social media, and have been informed that the family lives in the street, begging, while still in search of a new home.

We will later examine Ratna's biography more closely to see precisely what made her alter her risk style as compared to previous years. Yet in order to sketch a more clear picture of what the *siap* risk style entails in Bantaran Kali, the next section relates the individual stories of Ratna and Tono to those of other *orang siap* in Bantaran Kali, exposing that *orang siap* have in common a set of characteristics that sets them aside from fellow residents in regards to their risk perceptions and practices.

Characteristics of the siap risk style

Most importantly, what *orang siap* have in common is their strong distrust of the authorities. It is for example clear from the narratives of Tono and Ratna that they regarded the city government as a danger to their personal safety and well-being, first because they believed that the Jakarta government did too little to prevent floods in Bantaran Kali, and second because they believed that the Jakarta government had a second agenda of slum clearance. This risk perception is again related to their belief in who can be trusted to support them in case of risk. A similar argument can be made for other inhabitants of Bantaran Kali that I got to know and who referred to themselves as *orang siap*. They all held extremely unfavourable (or distrustful) perceptions of the *kelurahan*. Not only did these people consistently reject the idea that the Jakarta government would solve the flood problem; they also believed that the Jakarta government would soon carry out evictions of the riverbanks.

Just like Ratna and Tono, these people indicated that they must therefore get prepared, *siap*, in order to protect their own safety vis-à-vis the government; and just like the case with Ratna and Tono, these people's distrustful and angry perceptions of the government was evident in their refusal to accept aid after floods from the authorities, or to evacuate to a *kelurahan* shelter during floods and other risk events.[3] Instead, during the flood in 2010, described in this book, they chose to remain in the provisional shelter or on the surrounding streets, and afterwards, most of them sold the building materials that they received from the government. Similar to Tono, these people were convinced that this gift was 'a trap', and that they would be punished as soon as they rebuilt a new house on the riverbank. They therefore tried to find ways to quickly accumulate money and to move in time 'before the bulldozers come'.

Narratives of *orang siap* indicated that they were highly distrustful of civil servants and accused them of having a 'second agenda'. More specifically, these people claimed that what was presented as charity by *kelurahan* actors was in fact a 'trick' that may have negative consequences for beneficiaries. The following excerpts were taken from interviews with *orang siap*:

> Floods are a big problem here because of the government. They like to see poor people flooded. Next, they act as if they offer us help, but one should never believe that. For example, if after a flood we lose our focus and we relax in the [*kelurahan*] shelter – for sure they will have demolished my house by the time I return. This is why I must get ready (*siap*).

> The government does not like it that we live here…So they use every…flood as a chance to evict us…If we are inattentive… *Vroooom!* [respondent imitates sound of large truck] They will come with bulldozers and evict us. So we better protect ourselves and act now, stay put and protect ourselves.

> If you ask me, we need to stay strong and compact together…we need to be prepared…because we have no evidence that we have rights to live on this land…even if we leave our land behind for a few days, they [the Jakarta government] will give us problems! […] In Indonesia…if the government does not like you, then they can do anything…they can chase you away or even torture you…they have killed people and started fires in poor neighbourhoods like this, sister…Yes! This is the way our government is!

During informal conversations in which the *orang siap* talked among themselves, similar distrustful opinions about the *kelurahan* could be overheard:

> They [the government] do nothing to protect us from floods. They could build a dam. Instead, they do nothing if we are flooded and just wait until we become so scared that we move out – after we have left they will create an amusement park here where elite people can bike or run.

If all houses are flooded and we have fled to shelters, then it is easier for them to turn this land into an apartment site…Yes, you better believe me! Rich people will come and live here and the government likes that better.

Such perceptions of distrust were expressed not only in the direct period after the flood when people had evacuated to the provisional shelter, but also in conversations with *orang siap* during later periods of my fieldwork. Whenever they spoke to me about the Jakarta government in relation to their own safety, they consistently expressed emotions of anger and fear. For example, when local newspapers headlined that riverbank settlers would be granted adequate compensation after eviction by the government (Haryanto 2011), these people dismissed the news as 'lies'. When the newly elected governor Jokowi visited the community and suggested that everyone would be displaced to a subsidized flat as compensation for eviction measures, it was once again the *orang siap* who accused the politicians of telling them 'lies' and 'tricking' them into something bad. These examples show that the narratives of *orang siap* consistently reflected a strong sense of urgency and anxiety whenever discussing the risk of flood or eviction – both risks that were perceived to be created by the city government. In order to protect themselves against these risks, these people were doing everything to become prepared, *siap*.

By contrast, many residents with other risk styles indicated that they had largely favourable (or trustful) expectations of the intentions of *kelurahan* actors concerning their involvement in the flood events that occur in Bantaran Kali. For example, in interviews, these respondents said that they expected that the *kelurahan* would either solve the flood problem sometime soon, or that their well-being would be protected by the *kelurahan* during large floods. For example, they often expressed the unfounded conviction that 'The government will build a dam to protect us against floods', or that 'The people of the *kelurahan* said that there will be no more floods because they only occur every five years and never in between, so the next year we will be safe anyhow'. Moreover, most of the people who expected that the problem of flooding will be solved in one way or another by the *kelurahan* also expected that the government would allow continuation of settlement on the riverbanks. Whenever they talked to me about evictions in interviews or informal conversations, they also appeared certain that the government would 'leave them be' and believed that any news about evictions was 'untrue', a 'myth' or 'a lie'. For instance, right after he had arrived in the *kelurahan* shelter during the flood, Kurdi explained to me that:

They want to help flood victims because they pity us. Even though the Jakarta government cannot prevent floods, they try at least to take care of us after we are flooded. It is a positive thing that the *kelurahan* takes up that responsibility.

Yusuf likewise believed that the *kelurahan* offers help to people for reasons of empathy and goodwill:

Those people [*kelurahan* employees] care for the inhabitants in Bantaran Kali, even though they do not like the fact that we live on the riverbanks.

Still, they know that many of us are their friends. So they feel that they should support us for reasons of humanity.

Underlying factors

From the past section it has become clear that a major factor underlying the *siap* risk style is 'distrust of other actors involved in the flood management of Bantaran Kali', particularly the government. But what, one should wonder, creates this distrust?

One part of the answer to this question has to do with the structural marginalization of the poor in the highly unequal society of Indonesia. Obviously, *orang siap*'s fear of being evicted or being discriminated against in other ways by the government is by no means unrealistic. Yet I want to argue that the other part of the answer points to another underlying factor of the *siap* risk style, namely a traumatic experience in people's lives that forced them to critically reflect upon their perceptions and practices of risk and trust.

It appeared from the interviews with *orang siap* that their 'typical' ways of perceiving and handling risks had significantly changed due to what they often called a 'trauma'. In hindsight, nearly all of the *orang siap* called themselves 'naïve' in the way that they used to respond to flood-risk warning messages during earlier years, while they described their recent responses to such messages as more appropriate, that is, 'safe' (*aman*). When asked about the reasons for their changed practices, almost all of these people defined a moment in their lives or a traumatic experience that made them realize that what they used to do was not safe enough – and that therefore, an alternative *siap* risk style was needed.

It seems, then, that we have come to the point in the analysis where it becomes relevant to reconsider the question that has popped up several times already in this chapter. 'What has come over them?' people wondered out loud about Tono and Ratna. My own research questions about heterogeneous risk behaviour are related to theirs. The impact of a general habitus is generally considered so strong that it is hard for people to challenge it or to act outside of it, so what is going on with these *orang siap* that they were, nevertheless, eventually able to develop a new risk style? How and why do people let go of a former risk style? Why did Ratna change from an *orang susah*, dependent on the support of her *kelurahan* patrons, into a person who calls herself '*siap*' and who exhibits defensive practices towards her former patrons? And how can it be that Tono's perceptions of risk and trust have altered so radically over time?

In order to answer these complicated questions, I propose to move beyond the sociological theory of habitus on which I have largely built my analysis so far, for even if this theory in principle allows for agentic moves, it offers little detailed insight into when such moves might take place and who might make them. Even more problematically, it tells us nothing about how people experience the alteration of their practices and perceptions. Therefore, it is more helpful to use Niklas Luhmann's theory of risk and trust, which was already briefly introduced in Chapter 3. While Luhmann acknowledges that perceptions of risk and trust are generally habitual, he also claims that this can only be the case as long as experiences with trusted actors remain 'relatively disappointment-free' (Luhmann 1985: 25). If, however, we experience too many events that challenge these habitual perceptions, our disappointments accumulate, until a certain point of no return has been crossed, and we need to radically change our habitual expectations and actions. In his own words, we maintain our habitual perceptions for a fairly long time, but only 'until one reaches a critical point, and from that moment on, a small event can bring about large changes' (1968: 96, my translation). So, after the critical point has been reached, we feel forced to change our perceptions and behaviour radically.

I will now present an analysis of the biographies of Tono and Ratna to define the precise critical moments in their lives when their critical point of no return was reached, or where we might say that their risk style was altered.

Tono's biography

Tono was born as the son of a garbage collector in Bantaran Kali. At the age of 12, he left school and started working different jobs, including as a cleaner in a cafeteria, as a jack-of-all-trades and, sometimes, as a waiter in restaurants. He was 22 years old when he married his wife Vita, who also grew up in the kampong. Vita gave birth to two sons, who were aged four and six at the time the fieldwork for this research project took place. Tono reflected about this period in his life as follows:

> I remember when my wife was pregnant from the second child, I told myself that this was the best time in my life. You must understand, I am only a man from the slums, and nevertheless I had a regular income from the restaurant where I worked back then. I had a wife, children, and also I had some friends here, even some friends who worked in the *kelurahan* [...] I was always helping them to teach the other people here about floods. I was also planning to buy a HT, so that I could help and protect other people against the floods. [...] It was a good time in my life, I think. I felt comfortable each day.

His youngest son was born in rural Java on the day in 2007 that a large flood would demolish Tono's house. Three days before the flood occurred, his wife had travelled to her family in the countryside to give birth there. So when Tono first heard that Bantaran Kali would be flooded, he was home alone with his eldest son, who was aged three at that time. Tono's son was obviously too young to swim, and Tono considered it impossible for himself to swim through strong currents of a flood while saving his son. Still, Tono felt certain that the two of them would stay safe during the flood, as he expected that one of his 'friends' would save them:

> I was close to [names of two *orang ajar*] back then, I was always helping them, so I just knew that one of them would help me evacuate or call in the rescue team of the *kecamatan*. When they informed me that a flood would come this

way, they asked me to assist them in their duties. So I really did not worry when I first heard that a flood was coming, because I knew I was going to be picked up by a boat....All of their friends are helped first during floods.

Therefore, instead of quickly evacuating, Tono decided to first assist the people known as *orang ajar* in the kampong by spreading the flood-risk message among his fellow residents, as he had done during former floods. With his son in his arms, he walked through the streets to check whether everyone had received the flood-risk warning message and he ordered them to evacuate to the *kelurahan* shelter. Meanwhile, the streets outside became inundated. After about an hour, Tono went back home and packed as many goods as he could carry. He took his time to collect all of his valuable goods, as he did not want to take a large economic loss if his house were to be flooded. He then spent about half an hour tying up his furniture with ropes so that his valuables could not be taken away by the currents, and he took some more time to barricade the windows and the door so that these would not be easily smashed by waves.

But Tono's positive expectations of the authorities were let down during the flood:

> I waited and waited. One hour...two hours...there was still nobody to help me and my son, but the water rose higher than what felt comfortable. I kept telling myself that they were busy and that they would come soon, but to tell you the truth, I became nervous, I did not like to wait that long. Finally, I called two of my acquaintances in the *kelurahan* on their cellphones, but they did not respond. I also texted [the name of an *orang ajar*], saying that I needed help and that nobody had yet come to evacuate us. After three hours, I was still standing in the water, holding my son above my head. Can you imagine how scared I was? The water was waist-high, and the current had become too strong for me to wade through. My son was crying. It was cold...I was so afraid to drown, so very afraid...Then! I could see a helicopter circling above my head. I was so happy! I thought that they [the Jakarta government] would finally save me and my son! I shouted: 'Help me, there are still people here!' But they didn't care about us; they left again. It felt like I froze, but it was not from the cold in the water, but from the cold in my heart. They could not care less that I was drowning.

About 20 minutes later, Tono's hopes rose again when he heard a voice shouting that a government rescue team had arrived with boats. But none of the boats eventually entered the water. 'Those people just stood there, next to their boats, and they did not even try to rescue me', Tono remembered:

> I finally decided to swim, holding my son high above my head. The water had risen as high as my chin by that time and my son was shivering from the cold. His lips were blue. I cried, then I started swimming. I had to risk

our lives and I was so happy when I reached a dry street. We could have
drowned! I was in shock to realize that I mean so little to the people [in the
local government] whom I have helped so often. Even though we called
each other friends!

The feelings of shock and disappointment that Tono experienced are reflected in
his next quote:

That time I came to understand that civil servants do not care so much about
people like me as they want us to believe. I think that they only care because
we help them with the radios [Handie Talkies]. But if they feel personally
threatened by a flood, yeah, they act as if we are strangers again.

This realization shuffled Tono's formerly structured set of favourable or trustful
expectations about the future actions of his acquaintances in the Jakarta government. While he had invested in his social network in past years and expected
personal benefits in return in times of need, the events of 2007 challenged his
habitual, trustful perceptions to such an extent that Tono's perceptions of the
intentions of government actors became much more negative. Tono realized in
retrospective that he was 'naïve to think that we were friends, when in fact they
did not care at all'.

He made a commitment to himself in the days after the 2007 flood that from
that moment on, he would act differently. He immediately started distancing
himself from *the orang ajar* in Bantaran Kali; he stopped investing his time in 'lecturing' other people about safety, and he decided he would not buy a radio set.
Instead, he started investing most of his time and energy in his paid work, and
set aside savings.

Years later, when Tono and I met during fieldwork, Tono's perceptions and
practices seemed still altered. We saw earlier in this chapter that he expected
that, during a future flood, government actors would not offer support to him.
Therefore, he exhibited defensive, *siap*, risk practices in the face of flood risk, and
expressed distrustful perceptions of the intentions of authorities.

And, as I have argued before, his unfavourable or distrustful expectations
regarding the intentions of the Jakarta government were not limited to the government involvement with the hazard of floods in Bantaran Kali. Rather, his distrust
of the Jakarta government can be related to the multiple risks that characterize
a context of normal uncertainty. In this way, we might also say that *orang siap*'s
distrustful expectations influence their broader worldview, and consequently also
their repertoire in practices towards covariate risks.

Because of these distrustful perceptions, formed and strengthened over the
years, Tono and other *orang siap* nowadays try to protect their personal safety, as
well as the safety of their family members, by using defensive strategies against the
Jakarta government – strategies that give them the feeling that they are prepared,
siap. For Tono, he has come to invest most of his time, energy and money into
defensive and violent risk practices, such as joining in FBR activities.

The next section offers another example of how a person might develop a *siap* risk style. I analyse the biography of Ratna to examine when and why her risk style was radically altered.

Ratna's biography

Ratna's parents moved to Jakarta from rural Java when she was only two years old. Her father found a job as bus driver in Jakarta, and, thanks to his monthly salary and the family's determination to accumulate their money for the education of their child, Ratna would become one of the few adult riverbank settlers in Bantaran Kali who would graduate from junior secondary school (SMP). When she was 21, she managed to find work as the secretary of a local politician at the *kelurahan*. About that time she remembered:

> I was grateful that I could get my school diploma and a good job in an office… Truly, I did everything to keep my boss satisfied. I knew this job was my best chance to get a good life for me and my family, and so I worked day and night.

That latter part of the sentence must be taken literally, as neighbours remember how often Ratna slept in the office. Ratna did not mind working overtime, she explained, as she received a lot of aid in return from her boss during floods:

> In 2002, my boss had only just recently hired me and my house was already flooded. I lost everything: clothes, money, documents…I was embarrassed, but I asked him for help nevertheless.

Her boss pitied his employee. For a couple of weeks, he provided her with three meals each workday. He also gave her 1 million Rupiah in cash to rebuild her house. Ratna reflected upon that gift as follows:

> I worked even harder for him after that. I took all the extra jobs, I offered to do things free of charge, just to show that I was grateful that he cared for me like a father.

Ratna and her husband had three children together, and the family became relatively well-off in the kampong. Ratna's husband made a living as a taxi driver, for which he took night shifts. Ratna received a fixed monthly income from her office job, and her boss sometimes treated her with small extras, which enhanced their financial situation. For example, he gave her school shoes for her children, and sometimes an extra meal for herself. Ratna recalled:

> My husband looked after the children during the day, while I did it at night. We hardly ever saw each other, but we were happy, nevertheless, because we knew that we could save enough money for our children to become educated. We also knew that we had friends at the *kelurahan* who would help us with problems.

Even a second large flood in 2007 did not affect the family's well-being too much, as Ratna's family members were again financially supported by the *kelurahan*. Ratna's trustful expectations were thus consistently fulfilled at this point in time. 'We were among the first to be evacuated', Ratna recalled. 'My boss had sent in a boat to get us. He also paid for our losses afterwards'.

But when Ratna's husband started suffering from heart problems, the family was faced with high medical costs, and it appeared for the first time that Ratna's patron would disappoint her. Ratna soon realized that she could not afford the recovery surgery that her husband needed and decided to ask her boss in the *kelurahan* to give her a loan. Instantly, her employer refused, which astonished Ratna:

> I was sure he would help me because my contract stated that employees' families have some insurance for health, but that existed on paper only. In reality, it was a lie, and they only paid for the first two days in hospital. After that, no one supported me, while my husband still needed much more treatment...he needed surgery or else he would die! I cried and I begged them, I reminded them of my good work during all past years, but...nothing.

Ratna's husband passed away after one week of illness. She was, of course, devastated by her loss. She was also disappointed by her boss' refusal to help her. But at the same time her biographical narratives indicate that she initially interpreted his response as a tragic, yet also somewhat understandable *exception to the norm* – the norm in which her patron was still regarded by Ratna as the one who cares for her 'like a father'. When Ratna reflected on how she felt in the weeks after her husband died, her narrative shows how she managed to maintain her trustful expectations towards her patron:

> First, I was upset because my friends in the *kelurahan* had not helped my husband. But then I also realized that my boss himself is not a very rich man. He is only averagely rich. So I realized that maybe he has only enough money to help me with floods, but he lacks money needed for surgery.

So, although she was let down this one time, she still trusted that he would continue to support her financially in future times of need. As we saw in Chapter 4, in situations of uncertainty, clinging to one's positive expectations of the intentions of other actors is a common way for people to maintain their sense of safety and calm. But several months after the death of her husband, it became more difficult for Ratna to maintain her trustful expectations. She started hearing more and more rumours of possible evictions of the houses on the riverbank. Left as a widow at age 29, with three small children to care for, Ratna feared that she would soon lose her house and her social network. She wondered whether the *kelurahan* employees that she knew so well would order this eviction, even if they knew that Ratna's house would then be demolished. After days of pondering, Ratna asked her boss whether the rumours were true and begged for a confirmation that he would protect her house. Without hesitance, he said the rumours were true and added that he could do nothing to save her house. Ratna recalled:

> I felt desperate, while he did not show any emotion. So I reminded my boss about the many reports that I had typed for him in the last weeks. Then I showed him my receipts for the land taxes that I had always paid the local government. But he said it was not worth a thing and he even said that I am illegally occupying the land of the government. Then he just left his office and he did not speak to me again. The next day a colleague told me they could no longer hire me. I had lost my job.

It is at this point in time that Ratna's point of no return seems to have been reached. She started to critically reflect upon her habitual expectations of her patron. Like Tono, in hindsight, Ratna now started to feel naïve about her former trustful perceptions. Thinking back of that time, she indicated that she felt betrayed by those she considered to be her 'friends':

> I always thought I was smart because I was educated, but it took me a long time to see how naïve I actually was! I had always ignored all of the stories of neighbours about how the government hates poor people. I just believed that they [*kelurahan* employees] were good people, and that we were friends. But they showed me well that we are not. They could not care less about me. In fact, they like to make my life more difficult!

As a result of this realization, Ratna started to perceive the government institution as distrustful and began taking defensive actions to 'prepare' and 'protect' herself from the *kelurahan*. While in former times of need Ratna still turned to her *kelurahan* patron for help, we have seen that, after the 2010 flood that was experienced by her at age 32, Ratna would not even accept the support that the *kelurahan* offered to flood victims, and that she tried to move away from the neighbourhood 'before bulldozers come'. Moreover, she was willing – literally and overtly – to fight her former patrons.

Tono and Ratna's biographies offer only two of many examples of people who have become highly distrustful of the Jakarta government, because their former favourable expectations have been let down. She was an *orang susah* with trustful expectations of acquaintances in the *kelurahan*; he was an *orang ajar* and trustful of the intentions of his 'friends' working for the local government. But over the years, both of them have changed so much that people nowadays wonder 'what has come over them'. What has come over them, I have tried to argue so far in this chapter, is that their expectations were dashed again and again, until it was just one time too many. A similar pattern is recognizable in the life histories of other *orang siap*.

From analysing their biographies, I learned that other *orang siap* had their own reasons for moving from positions of trust to distrust of the *kelurahan* or other political institutions of the Jakarta government that are involved with flood management – I provide two brief examples below.

Almost all *orang siap* defined a particular moment in their lives that made them see that what they used to do in situations of risk and uncertainty was not safe enough – and that, therefore, an alternative *siap* risk style was needed. As did Tono and Ratna, *orang siap* would often describe this particular moment as a trauma or an emotional shock. For example, one male *orang siap* (28 years old) who moved to the neighbourhood in 2000 from rural Java told me that he had always trusted the *kelurahan* to financially support his family after floods because he was the nephew of a secretary who had been working in the institution's office for over 20 years, and that he felt let down when, suddenly, in 2010, this did no longer happen:

> I was always joking to my aunt that she must work hard and be diligent, so that the *kelurahan* likes our family. They were like our insurance, you know? [laughs] My aunt always comforted me, saying that if there were ever a flood, for sure we would be helped again by the *kelurahan* because she worked as hard as she could. Then! The flood [in 2010]! My house completely flooded, we lost everything we had! My son got very ill afterwards, I spent all my money on his medicines. And you think that we got any support from the *kelurahan*? Not one Rupiah, while before…we always received enough to recover! But this time, without any explanation, we got nothing. My aunt said she did not understand it either…I got deep into debt. It was a shock for me that the *kelurahan* did not want to support a family member of a loyal employee, and even now, when I tell you about it, I feel betrayed.

As did Tono, this man became a member of FBR and announced that he was ready to 'fight the government'. Whenever the civil militia group had a meeting during my fieldwork, his wife catered for them free of charge, and the couple emphasized that as soon as their son turned 15, he should also become an FBR member. For this respondent, the FBR seemed a better institution to help one become *siap* than was the *kelurahan*.

Another riverbank settler who called herself an *orang siap* told me that she had been trying to get support from the *kelurahan* for many years, but she never managed to get it. Despite her volunteer work for this institution and her socializing efforts with employees, she was never accepted as a beneficiary. When she noticed over and over again that fellow residents received financial support from the *kelurahan* while she did not, she – in her own words – 'went crazy because of the shock'. She started publically offending civil servants whenever they passed by the neighbourhood, screaming that they did not care for her and that she hoped that they would lose their jobs, falling into poverty. And, as did Yati, she started posting offending messages about the institutions on her Facebook wall.

The above narratives from *orang siap* show that their experience of 'shock' and 'trauma' is specific, but what binds all their stories is their feeling that this experience was unfair or unjust.

On perceived unfairness, protest and rebellion

James C. Scott emphasizes the crucial role of feelings of unfairness and unjust in instances of protest and rebellion. In his famous book *The Moral Economy* (1977), Scott analyses different mass protests in Asia and concludes that these were always the product of people's conceptions of social justice; hence, what they deem morally right. Even if it is true that many of these instances in which protests were organized were marked by objective poverty, Scott emphasizes that rebellion is not just a response to objective circumstances. This is an interesting observation because it underlines the subjective experience of people's circumstances, while it somewhat plays down the role of these objective circumstances. Scott implicitly warns us that not everyone who is marginalized – objectively speaking – radicalizes. On the contrary, there are many other non-violent ways which marginalized people find to cope with poverty and disenfranchisement. People only start to protest and rebel, so Scott claims, if they feel that these objective circumstances are unfair and unjust. This is what Scott calls the 'moral economy': people's notions of economic justice and their working definitions of exploitation. He writes that 'violation of these standards could be expected to prove resentment and resistance...not only because needs were unmet, but because rights are violated' (Scott 1977: 6).

Scott's observation is helpful for understanding why *orang siap* radicalized while others in their neighbourhood did not. *Orang siap* do not simply act defensively because they are living in a poor, flood-prone and eviction-prone neighbourhood. Neither do they necessarily protest their objective marginalization in wider society. After all, they have been living with such risks and marginalization for a long time and did not seem to experience this as 'unfair'. That was because, during these times, they believed that they had 'friends' or patrons who would support them, and this idea offered them a sense of safety and calm. What was regarded as unfair in later stages of their life, then, is that this support had at some point in their lives stopped, and that unwritten agreements of reciprocal obligations were thus unmet by the other party.

Horgan (2008) adds to the analysis several other 'predisposing factors' that highlight why one person may try to challenge structures and the other may not when they are both exposed to the same conditions. Here, I will discuss only the factors that seem most relevant for the case of the *orang siap*. Horgan regards personal victimization as one very important contributing factor towards protest. He furthermore emphasizes the 'presence of some emotional vulnerability, in terms of feelings of anger, alienation...and disenfranchisement' (Horgan 2008: 85). Put differently, people must be upset and feel powerless or marginalized in order to finally rebel. From the biographies of Tono and Ratna and other *orang siap* in Bantaran Kali, it became clear that this certainly is true of them. Next to the fact that they feel betrayed by their patrons, formerly perceived as friends, they express anger, grief and frustration about what they now perceive as their vulnerability.

Furthermore, Horgan clarifies that people who radicalize often experience a strong dissatisfaction with the activities that they had in the past used to reach a certain goal. People might, for example, have expressed their discontent with their marginalization by engaging in symbolic resistance, but then realize that such practices are not forceful enough to change their situation. Or people might have been engaged in political or social protest, until years later, they comprehend that this practice does not lead to a fulfilment of their goals. Hence, they become convinced that more radical action is absolutely necessary (2008: 84–85). This dissatisfaction with former activities is also visible in the biographies of Tono and Ratna. Although they used to believe for years that their *ajar* or *susah* risk style was an effective way of staying safe in Bantaran Kali's context of 'normal uncertainty', after several disappointing experiences, they became convinced that their former practices and social investments were in fact not guaranteeing them protection against risk. In hindsight, they call themselves 'naïve' and feel that they must strategically change their risk practices in order to become prepared, *siap*, to face the risk.

One final question that needs be answered in this chapter is: does the newly acquired risk style of *orang siap* help them to challenge unequal structures, and hence to decrease their personal risk of floods, eviction and poverty? Or, framing that question differently, we might ask: is becoming *siap* a more effective strategy for escaping the trap of risk and poverty than the other risk styles discussed in this book? I argue in the final section of this chapter that it is not necessarily successful in decreasing people's risks and problems.

The (in)effectiveness of a siap risk style

One reason why a *siap* risk style does not necessarily decrease the personal risks that *orang siap* encounter has to do with their social isolation. It is problematic that not many fellow residents join the overt protests of Ratna and Tono. For any protest to have even a slight chance of making a change, larger-scale organization and mobilization would be needed, or at least a shared sense among participants of what is wrong and what needs to be changed (Scott 1977: 250; Gramsci 1977/1980: 144–145). These demands are not easily fulfilled in the fragmented society of Bantaran Kali. This is because, as has become clear throughout the empirical chapters, many inhabitants of Bantaran Kali cooperate in a patronage system with elite actors, through which they receive small incentives in return for large investments in time, money and energy.

We might say that these strategies function as patchwork solutions for the marginalization of riverbank settlers, while they make it hard for the inhabitants of Bantaran Kali to alter the social structures that underlie the risks of floods, poverty and eviction. This problem is also noted by James C. Scott, who writes that marginalized people generally deal with exploitation and poverty through short-term patchwork solutions that tend to reduce the likelihood of more direct and violent solutions, rather than overtly protesting these issues (Scott 1977: 192). That is because, if one is dependent on a patron, then one cannot protest him or her without running the risk of losing this support. For the people in Bantaran Kali who regard their current patronage risk style (the *orang susah* and the *orang ajar*) as somewhat effective, and who still hope and believe that their current practices are their best option to stay safe, it is hardly attractive to disturb these social relations. Therefore, rather than challenging the social structures in which they live, river-bank settlers generally try to maintain their reciprocal relationship with patrons, thereby reproducing the social structure as it is.

The fact that most people prioritize their own interests of course does not nec-essarily mean that they disagree with Tono, Ratna and other *orang siap*. It might very well be that some of them have experienced similar feelings of injustice towards the elite. However, these feelings are apparently not pressing enough to risk losing the benefits that they may enjoy now.

In contrast, *orang siap* have become engaged in overt, provocative and public pro-test. This puts them in a very vulnerable social position in the riverbank settlement: they dare to speak up, but they are not backed by fellow residents – at least not overtly. Therefore, they cannot link their personal sense of injustice to a broader-felt class consciousness, from which larger-scale protests could be organized.

Admittedly, Tono and several other *orang siap* have found some support through the civil militia group, FBR; but even though they might feel that this social network will help them stay safe, it is questionable whether it actually can. Remember that FBR attracts members from the lowest socioeconomic classes in Jakarta society: those who are often unemployed, marginalized and relatively powerless. If it is true that FBR membership brings *orang siap* in contact with other members of this civil militia group, it also needs to be acknowledged that the power of FBR members in wider society is generally limited. FBR membership itself thus seems insufficient for helping *orang siap* escape from their living context of normal uncertainty.

Therefore, even though Tono promised his children a 'safe' house, in daily practice, we have seen that he nowadays loses all his time and money to his FBR membership, and seems unable to accumulate an amount of money that would be needed to move. At the same time, Tono made enemies among people who have the power to discipline or control disobedient, 'crazy' or radicalized individuals. He also isolates himself from neighbours, thus risking exclusion from local safety networks.

Ratna's situation is even worse: she wanted to move and tried to accumulate money for that goal, but as a widow with three children, expelled from a social net-work in Bantaran Kali and without a patron to help her with her problems, *susah*, Ratna is not able to buy a legal and safe piece of land, let alone to build a house for her family on top of that. Therefore, she and her children ended up alone – on the streets of Jakarta.

Afterword: Siap risk practices outside of Bantaran Kali

The foregoing empirical chapters showed that people's perceptions of risk and trust are generally habitual; however, the biographies of *orang siap* that were presented in this chapter make clear that people's risk styles are not completely determined by structured cognitive dispositions. They are also strongly influenced by dynamic processes in daily, immediate experiences. This chapter examined in detail those critical moments in time in which people reflect and adapt habitual actions and perceptions. An in-depth analysis of the biographies of key informants helped to show that although a general habitus of poverty predisposes people's perceptions of risk and trust, this habitus can be reflected upon and altered after traumatic experiences. For *orang siap* we saw that, after their trust was disappointed and they had an experience of personal grief and injustice, they chose to take actions that go against their former, habitual risk style.

This all means that the group of people I described in this chapter are not inherently trustful or distrustful, nor are they 'natural risk-takers', but they can become that way through agentic reflection on past experiences and by acquiring a specific habitus in lived experience. The same can of course be said for the people I have introduced in former chapters. If the labels and nicknames that circulate in Bantaran Kali suggest that riverbank settlers are born with preformed and static perceptions and actions (remember from former chapters that Yati holds that she 'just is' an *orang susah*, while Edi is an *orang antisipasi* 'like that' according to his neighbours), this chapter has underlined the temporality of people's risk styles: Tono and Ratna's perceptions of risk and trust slowly but steadily changed, until finally they became convinced that they needed to alter their former risk styles, and turned into *orang siap*. Local nicknames and labels thus suggest a fixedness of human behaviour that I did not necessarily recognize in the field. In the final conclusion of this book, I return to this point by elaborating on the usefulness of the concept of 'styles' for an analysis of risk that allows for both reproductive and innovative aspects of human risk behaviour.

Let me end this chapter with pointing out that several characteristics of the *siap* risk style resemble the behaviour of a group of people locally known as the *orang nakal* in East Java, a term which might best be translated with wayward, madcap or naughty types of people. In a paper from 2001 that was based on his PhD fieldwork, Nooteboom explains that *orang nakal* are people who violate mainstream norms and values of society, and deliberately take excessive risks such as gambling, machismo, engaging in extramarital relations and speculating. Just as is the case with *orang nakal*, *orang siap* do not follow mainstream norms and values of society, and they also take huge financial risks. However, one big difference between these two behavioural patterns has to do with the factors underlying their risk styles. For *orang nakal*, a risky lifestyle is simply an attractive alternative to compliance to the village norms and social pressures urging for huge investments in social security and reciprocal relationships (Nooteboom 2001: 9). In contrast, I have shown that *orang siap* have developed their style after they experienced a trauma or emotional shock that resulted in distrust of authorities.

Notes

1 Not all of the information about financial aid was registered in the *kelurahan* registration. Therefore, the incomplete *kelurahan* data was checked three times for this analysis: with Ratna herself, with the kampong leader in Bantaran Kali and with two different neighbours who were aware that Ratna was offered financial assistance after the flood. I provide more detailed information about the aid that Ratna received later in this chapter.
2 Facebook is extremely popular in Indonesia (Grazella 2013). Even in the slums of Jakarta, people who could read and write often used social media to keep in touch with acquaintances. They would access it in nearby Internet cafes, which charge Rp 1,000–3,000 per time.

For my research, this popular use of Facebook offered a great opportunity to keep in touch with respondents after I had left the field. Ever since I have left Bantaran Kali, I have remained in close contact with several key informants through daily chats, personal messages and Facebook wall posts.

3 It is relevant to know that *orang siap's* decision not to evacuate to the *kelurahan* shelter did not just take place during the 2010 flood described in this book, but also during other disasters. When a fire damaged a large number of the houses in Bantaran Kali during my fieldwork, it was these same *orang siap* who set up a provisional shelter and who refused to seek shelter with the *kelurahan*. And when another large flood inundated the kampong again in 2013, none of the *orang siap* registered with the *kelurahan*. Instead, most of them stayed in the streets surrounding their houses until the water had receded enough for them to return home. Some *orang siap* stayed in a shelter that was set up and maintained by FBR.

References

Baan, M. E. (2008). Fear appeals als risicocommunicatiemiddel bij overstromingsrisico's. Een onderzoek naar relevante factoren voor het gebruik van fear appeal als risicocommunicatiemiddel bij overstromingsrisico's [Fear appeals as risk-communication tools in relation to flood risk. A research about relevant factors for the use of fear appeals as risk-communication tool in relation to flood risk]. Unpublished Master's thesis, University of Twente, Enschede.

Eagly, A.H. & Chaiken, S. (1993). *The Psychology of Attitudes*. Orlando, Florida: Harcourt Brace Jovanovich Inc.

Gramsci, A. (1980). Gramsci e Noi 1937–1977 (M. Jorn, trans.). In V. Gerratana, & G. Matteoli (Eds.), *Grondbegrippen van de Politiek. Hegemonie, Staat, Partij [Fundamental Notions of Politics. Hegemony, State, Party]*. Nijmegen: Socialistiese Uitgeverij Nijmegen (original work published 1977).

Grazella, M. (2013, June 18). Facebook has 64m active Indonesian users. *The Jakarta Post*. Retrieved from www.thejakartapost.com/news/2013/06/18/facebook-has-64m-active-indonesian-users.html, last accessed 25 October 2015.

Haryanto, U. (2011, February 24). Flood-hit Jakartans wary of relocation offer. *The Jakarta Globe*. Retrieved from www.thejakartaglobe.com/archive/flood-hit-jakartans-wary-of-relocation-offer, last accessed 25 October 2015.

Horgan, J. (2008). From profiles to pathways and roots to routes: Perspectives from psychology on radicalization into terrorism. *The Annals of the American Academy of Political and Social Science*, 618, 80–94.

Human Rights Watch. (2006). *Condemned Communities. Forced Evictions in Jakarta*. Retrieved from www.hrw.org/sites/default/files/reports/indonesia0906webwcover.pdf, last accessed 24 October 2015.

Luhmann, N. (1968). *Vertrauen. Ein Mechanismus der Reduktion sozialer Komplexität [Trust. A Mechanism to Reduce Social Complexity]* (4th ed.). Stuttgart: Lucius & Lucius.

Luhmann, N. (1985). *A Sociological Theory of Law*. London: Routledge & Kegan Paul Plc.

Mariani, E. (2003, November 29). Govt to evict hundreds to build shopping mall. *The Jakarta Post*. Retrieved from http://groups.yahoo.com/neo/groups/beritabhinneka/conversations/topics/73819, last accessed 25 October 2015.

Nooteboom, G. (2001). *Wayward and Wagering: 'Orang Nakal' and Risk Taking in Rural East Java*. Paper presented at the 3rd EuroSEAS conference, London (September 3–6).

Scott, J. C. (1977). *The Moral Economy of the Peasant: Rebellion and Subsistence in Southeast Asia*. Yale: Yale University Press.

Wilson, I. (2010). The biggest cock: territoriality, invulnerability and honour amongst Jakarta's gangsters. *Indonesian Studies*, Working Paper No. 13. Retrieved from http://sydney.edu.au/arts/indonesian/docs/USYD-IS_Wilson_BiggestCock.pdf, last accessed 25 October 2015.

Conclusion
A revelatory risk approach

In the Introduction to this book I argued that if we want to make sense of diverse risk practices, we have to understand from a bottom-up and holistic perspective which circumstantial and psychological factors underlie them. In this chapter I reflect on how a focus on 'normal uncertainty' and on 'risk styles' has helped me to recognize important circumstantial and psychological factors underlying heterogeneous risk behaviour in Bantaran Kali. After briefly elaborating on these factors, I explain how these findings add to our academic knowledge and introduce a new perspective on disaster that can help to improve understanding of the heterogeneous ways in which human actors handle risks in their daily lives.

Normal uncertainty and risk styles

In this book I have presented an integrative study that views the topic of risk from below and embeds human risk practices in the cultural and social environment. As such, this study departs from the more common method of centring on a particular risk towards an approach that embeds risk in a context of what I refer to as the 'normal uncertainty' of people's daily lives. Instead of narrowing the focus of research down to one isolated risk, namely flooding, this study took into account the different pressing risks that shape daily life for riverbank settlers, a living situation that is both uncertain and normal at the same time. Viewing people's practices in the face of risk through this normal uncertainty lens, I was able to recognize that behaviour that is exhibited in the face of one risk may well be associated with *another* risk. For example, some flood victims in Bantaran Kali refuse support and advice that is offered to them by the local government *not* because they underestimate the threat that a flood poses to their well-being nor because they principally disagree with formal safety advice, but because they highly distrust the intentions of the government institution that offers them help during and after a flood event, but is also involved in other issues in people's lives, such as evictions and healthcare. Had this study taken into account only the *flood* hazard, then no explanation for the differences in their risk strategies might have been found. Instead, my more holistic approach reveals that risk practices related to the hazard of flooding must not be understood as responses to an isolated hazard but rather as cultural and individual adaptations to everyday life experiences in a context of normal uncertainty. This finding may help to improve academic understanding of risk and human risk behaviour. It may specifically be useful for scholars pursuing studies of risk and disaster, as it suggests scholars must widen their lens much more than is currently the norm.

My holistic approach shows that people's risk behaviour was typically influenced by their trust in other actors, their habitus of poverty, their self-efficacy and individual life experiences. Therefore, I claim that people's risk practices are much more than 'just' disaster responses. Rather, they give us an insight into the ways in which they view their world and their position in it: their chances, opportunities and future outlook. If these factors are crucial in determining risk behaviour, they are generally overlooked in anthropological/sociological risk and vulnerability analyses. This suggests that future research on heterogeneous risk handling should look beyond the material aspects of risk and vulnerability, towards psychological and individual factors that underlie risk behaviour. If risk styles are guided by individual preferences and opportunities, it also became clear from my analysis that these preferences and opportunities are shaped within structural boundaries. Therefore, in future analysis of risk styles, both circumstantial and psychological factors need be taken into account. I briefly elaborate on the most important of these factors below.

Further, by introducing an analytical framework to define and interpret heterogeneous risk behaviour, I was able to distinguish four major behavioural patterns or types of risk behaviour that are used by inhabitants of Bantaran Kali in relation to the different risks that shape their normal uncertainty. People were categorized on the basis of an analysis of their observed risk behaviour, their narratives on risk, and the local nicknames and descriptions of risk that circulated in the research area. If the four risk styles that I defined in Bantaran Kali are for a large part context-bound (for example, practices typically associated with a *susah* risk style are related to the aid institutions present in Bantaran Kali), I have also shown that characteristics of each style overlap with the risk behaviour of people in other regions of the world, by comparing my findings to those of scholars working on risk in other contexts.

Psychological factors: Perceptions of risk, trust, self-efficacy and a habitus of poverty

By focusing on styles, I was able to recognize that an early-acquired habitus of poverty generally has a huge impact on people's present-day risk practices. Life experiences shape people's perceptions of risk and trust, thus influencing their risk behaviour. This became clear, for example, in the case studies of the *orang antisipasi* and the *orang ajar* in Bantaran Kali, who seem unable to aspire to a life radically different from their marginalized existence on the riverbank. The idea that such radical change could never occur for 'their type of people' reflects early-acquired ideas about themselves and society that are internalized and experienced as natural and 'true'.

Despite the fact that habitus can have – and generally does have – a great impact on people's practices and perceptions, my focus on styles also helped me to examine and recognize the moments in which people reflect upon their former habits and convictions and are able to challenge or even alter these. While most perceptions and practices of risk and trust were acquired at an early stage of life, after which they were internalized and became habitual, it is also evident from the case studies presented in this book that more recent daily life experiences can alter habitual perceptions and practices, and that, in some instances, people may at some point in their lives gradually or radically shift their risk styles.

A first example of this mechanism was given in the case study of the *orang susah*: in Chapter 4 I showed that this group of people shifted their risk style from being more or less autonomous to being largely dependent on a patron. This shift occurred through the new opportunities that floods offered riverbank settlers. It entailed not just a change in people's practices but also, and importantly, in their perceptions of risk, trust, and self-efficacy. While in earlier phases of life, these people seemed still to regard themselves as capable of handling flood risk without external support, their more recent experiences – in which they were supported by a patron – seem to have 'taught' them that they need others to survive floods, and that they are 'weaker' and more 'troubled' than are their fellow residents. Hence, their older, general habitus differed from their later-acquired, specific habitus. Their recent experiences of risk, however, have not altered their deep-rooted views of the world and their own position in it. This became clear from the fact that most of these people's aspirations remained humble and located in the context of their current flood-prone neighbourhood. Moreover, even if some of these people might dream of a 'better life', they were unable to imagine such a life without the support of their patron – suggesting that their trust in other actors had become high, while their self-efficacy was low. As a result, they felt forced to stay living along the riverbanks out of fear of losing their patron's support.

Perhaps an even clearer example of the ways in which habitual perceptions can be reflected upon and altered came from the case studies of the *orang siap*. An analysis of their biographies showed that these people radically altered their perceptions of risk and trust after they had been disappointed over and over again by formally trusted 'friends'. These disappointments forced them to critically reflect upon their former habits and beliefs. In retrospect, these people call themselves naïve, and they have consciously shifted their practices towards a more defensive risk style. These people became convinced that they had a chance of a better life, as long as they 'prepare'. These beliefs were reflected, for example, in their concrete plans to move house. But, as was shown through case studies presented in Chapter 5, their future hopes did not always accord with actual opportunities to make change. Hence, while sometimes they perceived a chance for themselves to improve their safety, it remains questionable whether this perception is realistic. This is because of their extremely marginal and vulnerable position in both the kampong and in wider society. As most other risk styles in Bantaran Kali tend to reproduce unequal structures, adversaries from it generally do not press hard enough to challenge the deeply embedded unequal structure of the society in which the riverbank settlers live.

Besides the factors that seem to emphasize the internal dynamics of riverbank settlers' practices – habitus and people's perceptions of risk, trust and self-efficacy – this book shows that the social dynamics as products of unequal structures of power and economy also have a large impact on risk styles.

Circumstantial factors: Class, power and inequality

People are always bound in their decisions and actions by social or cultural norms, structural power relations and material options. The narratives that were presented in this book about people's practices in relation to floods and other risks made clear that their risk perceptions and practices come about in highly unequal structures of economy and particularly power. Therefore, it is relevant to discuss the underlying factors of class, power and inequality and explain how they impact risk behaviour.

Riverbank settlers are often portrayed by the elite as the creators of floods, but this book has underscored that they should in reality be seen more as the victims of a highly unequal society. They run a higher flood risk than do most of the inhabitants of Jakarta, due to their economically and politically marginal position in society. Their marginalization has driven them to occupy the unregistered and cheap land along the riverbanks, where they face not only recurrent flood risk but are also threatened by eviction due to their illegal status.

In recent years, the DKI Jakarta government has tried to decrease the city's flood problem by taking physical and technical measures such as widening and clearing the riverbanks, but little is done to address the vulnerability of slum dwellers to floods. As a result, after each flood, the vulnerability of these people continues to increase. Furthermore, in the name of flood management, riverbank settlers have already been and threaten to be evicted without sufficient options for relocation. However, as I have argued throughout this book, this does not solve the problem, only moves it: many slum dwellers will return to other flood-prone and/or 'illegal' areas, because they have few alternative housing options that are available and affordable in the city. I will return to this topic of government failure later in this conclusion, but here let me emphasize that power inequalities in wider society mean that riverbank settlers are exposed to a relatively high flood risk, that this is first and foremost the result of their marginalized and disenfranchised position in wider society, and that this limits their repertoire in risk practices.

It also became clear that within kampong society there are highly unequal divisions of power that impact people's repertoire of risk practices. Some residents, such as the *orang antisipasi*, are exploited by more powerful residents. This limits the repertoire of action of *orang antisipasi* because, for example, they are forced to share part of their income with these more powerful actors or because they fear surveillance and discipline and therefore adapt their behaviour to the needs and wishes of these powerful actors. Out of fear of being monitored or corrected by *orang ajar*, many people in Bantaran Kali overtly obey their wishes. At the same time, I have also claimed that even the most powerful actors in kampong society are themselves limited in their risk repertoire, due to their being subject to elite actors in wider society. For example, while the *orang ajar* have relative power within Bantaran Kali, it is clear that they operate according to elite cultural hegemony and hence they act in ways that benefit the elite. Due to their cooperation with political elite, *orang ajar* make it hard – if not impossible – for fellow residents to organize any large-scale protest against unequal structures in Indonesian society. Thus, they help to reproduce elite cultural hegemony, as well as the unequal structures maintained by this hegemony, which places riverbank settlers – including *orang ajar* themselves – in a situation of relatively high flood risk. A few people are able to exploit the flood problem for their own benefit, but it is clear that the social mobility and hence the risk repertoire of most people remains strongly limited as a result of social interaction that arises in the face of recurrent floods.

I wish to underscore that it is not the flood itself that creates all these dynamics or determines people's practices. Instead, the flood only renders visible the social processes and structural divisions that would have, perhaps, remained latent. Flood events brought these to light because they created so much damage and indeed opportunity in the kampong. Due to floods, *orang ajar* and *orang susah* get to interact with elite actors; due to floods, *orang antisipasi* Edi can create a thriving business; due to floods, riverbank settlers can be monitored, lectured and disciplined; due to floods, kampong leaders can be bypassed; due to floods, people are forced to critically reflect on their habitual beliefs and risk practices. Thus, on the basis of these observations, I propose a new research approach to risk and human risk behaviour, which I call a revelatory disaster approach.

A revelatory disaster approach

This study sprang from a normal uncertainty perspective in which floods were not regarded as exogenous events but rather as part and parcel of daily life, in which people have to overcome many different dilemmas and hazards. Consequently, people's practices in the face of floods were not interpreted as reactive to the isolated flood risk; instead, they were regarded as an expression of daily life practices. Taking this point of view, it became clear that flood risk often accelerates and lays bare social dynamics that are already existent in kampong society. We might thus say that flood risk offers us a lens through which we can understand these social dynamics, and the impact that these social dynamics have on people's practices.

This, I argue, implies a completely new approach to risk and its human handling. I am proposing that we turn the lens upside down. Instead of looking at how an agent responds to a flood, as is commonly the case in the field of risk research, it seems to me much more helpful to use risks, hazards or disasters as lenses that provide opportunities to understand and perceive the social structures in a given society, and how these are reproduced or challenged by human actors. I call this a revelatory approach.

My proposal for the revelatory approach is inspired by an analysis that was carried out by Jaqueline Solway in Botswana. Looking through what she calls a 'revelatory lens', she showed how a drought allowed for a shift in communal entitlements and hierarchies. For example, the drought provided a point of entry for already powerful local actors to engage in new and expanded ways in the lives of citizens (1994: 472). Furthermore, the crisis enabled wealthy cattle owners in society to deny family members the rights they had based on kinship to access their property. If the situation had been 'normal', these wealthy farmers might have felt a social obligation to share; but now they saw an opportunity to use the situation to their own benefit. The drought proved to be a perfect scapegoat for these powerful actors: the crisis allowed them to easily justify their behaviour as necessary and strategic. Solway argues that these social dynamics were not arbitrary. Instead, the crisis of a drought accelerated dynamics that were already in progress. It laid bare the structural contradictions and societal conditions. In addition, the crisis disrupted conventional routine sufficiently to allow actors to undermine normative codes and create new ones (1994: 471).

I claim that floods, just like droughts, might be considered an avenue for agency and social change to interact. Therefore a revelatory approach to risk can help scholars to view the dialectic between agency and structure that shapes people's practices. Above I concluded that the risk styles of riverbank settlers comes about from a mixture of individuality (habitus, interpretations of risk, perceptions of self-efficacy and trust, lived experience) and sociality (unequal structures and social interaction therein between riverbank settlers of different power positions, and between riverbank settlers and elite actors from outside the kampong). Therefore a revelatory approach can function to expose socioeconomic dynamics during a flood event in the area under study. It seems to me this is useful, because it is clear from my analysis that people's habitus often reflects their social position. A similar argument can be made about people's interpretations of risk. In my study I found that these perceptions appeared not to be based on their objective risk cognition but had everything to do with their subjective perceptions of trust and self-efficacy, which were framed and altered in social interaction. It follows, then, that the actions of people in the face of flood risk cannot be assumed to be completely predictable, but neither are they random. Rather, they are to a great extent extensions of structural contradictions. They reflect social structures or are responses to them – responses whereby people make use of them or aim to alter them. Therefore, I argue that if we want to understand why people act as they do in the face of risk, and especially if we want to understand heterogeneous practices in the face of risk, then we need to study risk differently than is currently being done in studies of risk and disaster.

I have argued above that in far too many of today's risk studies, the persisting focus remains on the hazard, as if it is cut loose from 'normality'. As a consequence of this view, these studies come up with conclusions that suggest that people, whenever faced with hazard, are also cut loose from all the social pressures, norms and interests that otherwise shape their daily lives. All of a sudden, the focus of the scholars shifts towards the individual and the risk – and nothing else matters than the individual's response to that risk. But a lot still matters, I wish to underscore, even in a riverbank settlement where people are constantly flooded. This study, therefore, suggests that people do not respond solely to a flood, but rather to life. They exhibit practices that are related to power structures, influenced by local habits, cultural norms, and individual and social interests.

Based on these observations, I propose a revelatory approach to consider risk and disasters as points in time that expose unequal structures and also have the potential to change practices that reproduce social inequalities and power relations. In order to understand the links between structure and agency, we need to analyse change in terms of the structural conditions in which change takes place and also with regard to the actions taken by individuals and institutions. As such, to study a social group from a revelatory approach forces us to try to understand risk practices in the triangular interrelationship between structure, agency and social change.

Observing social action around a risk event is revelatory for a social researcher, both for what it reveals of social processes and for the questions it poses for comparative purposes. This case study of Jakarta is an insightful first step towards such a revelatory approach, but of course is by no means sufficient. Future research would be needed to investigate whether similar social dynamics are to be found in other places or during different risk events. In such future studies, a revelatory approach would help shed light on the relations between power structures, social dynamics and risk styles. My analysis does not answer these questions but points to the need to consider them in any analysis of risk and human risk handling.

Policy implications

In the Introduction to this book it was noted that, in fast growing megacities, an increasing number of poor inhabitants are becoming more and more vulnerable to natural hazards. In many of these cities, policymakers find great difficulty in decreasing this risk for inhabitants, not only because natural hazards are often caused by a wide range of complex interacting natural and societal factors, but also because implementing effective and coherent policies to handle risk has proved difficult. This is because people tend to handle risk in highly heterogeneous ways. At present, little is known by policymakers about the factors that underlie such heterogeneous risk practices. As a consequence, policies are most often based on assumptions about the relationship between risk cognition and risk behaviour. Thus homogenizing policies are implemented in communities that respond to risk in heterogeneous ways. These tendencies become visible, for example, in the fact that the Jakarta government has been concerned in recent years with educating riverbank settlers about flood risk, for example by spreading one type of information brochure. This has had little effect until now, and this study has helped to show why. I emphasize again that it is not a lack of cognition that determines risk practices, but a complex interplay of factors which may seem unrelated to floods in the first place.

The impact of these factors may differ from actor to actor, as they come about from habitus and lived experience. However, for all four major risk styles it appeared that a habitus of poverty and people's self-efficacy, as well as people's trust in external actors from aid institutions and political institutions, significantly affected risk practice. This latter factor of trust seems most relevant for policy implications; therefore I elaborate on it below.

In Bantaran Kali, a flood shelter that was set up by a political institution remained largely empty because many of the flood victims distrusted the intentions of this political institution. For similar reasons, inhabitants sometimes refuse to make use of externally provided aid that could potentially decrease their vulnerability to risk. This shows that for policymakers trying to decrease the vulnerability of urban inhabitants, it is not enough to offer support in times of disaster. Instead, relations of trust between citizens and the state need be built and maintained. In the case of Jakarta, however, such a goal seems far out of reach.

My scepticism exists for two main reasons. First of all, my study indicates that the flood problem may be even harder to solve for the Jakarta government than bureaucrats are already aware of. That is because, as I have argued, risk behaviour is influenced by non-tangible factors, such as mistrust of the government, power inequalities and marginalization. Clearly, no governor or President can solve such complex problems within a term or two. Hence, it is questionable whether the current policymakers responsible for Jakarta's flood management will even try to address them; they may, instead, chose to take populist measures that satisfy the large group of voters from the middle class and the elite and thereby secure their political position.

Second, the political decisions that have been taken by the current Jakarta government offer ambiguous signals and do not exactly seem to improve trust relations with slum dwellers. Systematic evictions of poor neighbourhoods have recently been carried out in the city. In the North and East of Jakarta, the 'illegal' houses of hundreds of families were demolished. The Jakarta government took these actions despite NGOs' protests that the evictees had not received adequate compensation, and despite the fact that there were still not enough relocation options available. Thousands of other Jakarta inhabitants living in flood-prone areas are expected to be evicted in the near future, including the inhabitants of Bantaran Kali.

There, preparations for evictions have already started. During the last time I visited the neighbourhood, in September 2015, many inhabitants reported that civil servants had visited their houses in order to check whether they possess documents for the land or house; others were warned by local politicians, who claimed that evictions will start 'soon'. In some parts of the neighbourhood, buildings and trees were marked to indicate that they would be demolished.

The issue of compensation remains unclear: while subsidized apartments are currently being built in Jakarta to provide housing for some of the evicted poor at cheap rental rates, there is by far not enough room for all evictees. This means that many of them will be homeless and fall deeper into poverty, especially those without identity cards for Jakarta – according to the city government, they have no right to relocation (Yusuf 2008). Another problem concerns the flat apartments themselves. NGOs and local residents fear that the rents will be too expensive for the poorest, and hence remain only accessible to the relatively wealthy (Desyani 2013; ACHR 2013). Even if spokespersons of the Jakarta government claim that they are taking care of relocation issues (Yusuf 2008), it seems that in practice most evictees are left by their government to their own devices.

The Jakarta government does not make a serious effort to tackle the underlying root problem of social inequality: it moves rather than solves these problems. The structural inequality and marginalization of the poor in Jakarta leaves them no option other than to reside in dangerous places – only to be chased from one such place to another. The situation of normal uncertainty which confronts the poor is clearly not of their choosing; it is a product of inequality, as well as of political denial and neglect of poverty-related problems by the city government. The poor, who are most in need of social security in a fast-modernizing country that is prone to natural hazards, have to live with more insecurity.

This failing of the state suggests that the poor in Jakarta will have to continue to seek out strategies that enable them to protect their own safety and well-being, whether through clientelist relationships with powerful actors in society or by exhibiting autonomous practices that cross the line of what is legal. While to outside observers these relationships may appear to produce dependency and disempowerment – and hence go against liberal, individualist conceptions of citizenship – it must be acknowledged that for riverbank settlers these relationships also create access to vital resources and safety.

References

Asian Coalition of Housing Rights (ACHR) (2013). *ACHR/DPU Junior Professionals Reporting from the Field*. Indonesia, Ariel. [Weblog comment]. Retrieved from https://achryoung-professionals.wordpress.com/jakarta-ariel, last accessed 25 October 2015.

Desyani, A. (2013, May 31). Pluit residents hold protests in fear of eviction. *Tempo*. Retrieved from http://en.tempo.co/read/news/2013/05/31/057484743/Pluit-Residents-hold-Protests-in-Fear-of-Eviction, last accessed 25 October 2015..

Solway, J. S. (1994). Drought as a 'revelatory crisis': an exploration of shifting entitlements and hierarchies in the Kalahari, Botswana. *Development and Change*, 25, 471–495.

Yusuf, W. S. (2008, November 17). Pluit Dam eviction planned this month. *The Jakarta Post*. Retrieved from www.thejakartapost.com/news/2008/11/17/pluit-dam-eviction-planned-month.html, last accessed 25 October 2015.

Glossary and abbreviations

Bahasa Indonesia acronym or concept	Meaning in English
Ajar	Abbreviation of the verb *mengajar*, meaning 'teaching' or 'lecturing'. In Bantaran Kali, the notion *ajar* is mostly used to refer to the risk-handling practices of *orang ajar*. See Chapter 3 for more information on these notions.
Antisipasi	In Bantaran Kali, *antisipasi* means something like 'autonomously overcoming one's own problems'. An *orang antisipasi*, then, is someone who uses 'antisipasi' risk-handling practices. See Chapter 2 for more information on these notions.
Arisan	*Arisan* are regular social gatherings for purposes of saving money. They are a popular form of microfinance in Indonesian culture and an essential form of credit in poorer social circles, funding an otherwise unaffordable business venture, wedding, or large purchase.
BPDB	*Badan Penanggulangan Bencana Daerah Tingkat Kabupaten/Kota*: The Indonesian National Disaster Management Agency, the institution that coordinates and mitigates disasters such as floods on the city level.
Dangdut	An Indonesian music genre with influences from Indian, Arabic and Malay music, which has traditionally been popular with the working classes and lower income groups.
FBR	*Forum Betawi Rempug*: The Betawi Brotherhood Forum, an ethnic gang or civil militia group which operates in Jakarta. The FBR claims to represent the interests of Jakarta's ethnic Betawi, portrayed as the indigenous population of Jakarta.

HT	Handie Talkie: Radio sets used in Bantaran Kali for communication between riverbank settlers, sluice-gate keepers in Manggarai and Depok, and KORAMIL (see below). The communication is facilitated by the *kecamatan* (see below).
Jamu	A traditional herbal medicine venerated by Indonesians of all ages for its power to heal ailments or enhance one's beauty, strength or stamina. *Jamu* is made by an *ibu jamu* or *jamu* maker, from herbs, spices, fruits and plants. Sometimes rice wine or palm wine is also added to the drink.
Keamanan	Safety, often abbreviated to '*aman*' – meaning 'safe'.
Kecamatan	Administrative sub-district, positioned between the municipality (*wali-kota*) and the kampong administration (*kelurahan*). All three institutions serve under the Provincial Government of Jakarta.
Kelurahan	Kampong administration, the lowest level of government administration.
Keras	Tough or hard, often referring to a person's character.
KK	*Kepala Keluarga*, head of a household.
KORAMIL	*Komando Rayon Militair*: The military sub-district command involved in Jakarta's flood-management and security unit.
Kumu	Slum
Lonton	A dish of steamed rice in banana leaves.
Nasi kuning	A dish of rice, boiled in coconut milk, prepared with turmeric, cardamom, cinnamon and cloves. Usually served on festive days and events.
Nasi telor	A dish of rice with egg.
Orang Betawi	Inhabitants born in Jakarta, also sometimes referred to in Bantaran Kali as '*orang asli*', *asli* meaning 'native' or 'original'.
Orang bodoh	*Bodoh* means stupid. In Bantaran Kali, '*orang bodoh*' refers to people who lack valued knowledge and/or education.
Orang politik	Politicians.
Orang rendah	'Low people', people with low social status, often contrasted in narratives with '*orang tinggi*' (see below).
Orang tinggi	'High people', people with high social status.

Pendatang	Newcomers, people who, unlike the '*orang Betawi*' (see above), have not been born in Jakarta but who came to live there in search for a job.
Pengamen	Beggar singer or street singer; someone who sings in the streets for money, often while playing a guitar, but sometimes also with a help of a karaoke set and microphone.
Petai	Stink beans.
Preman	Thug or gangster.
PBB	*Pajak Bumi dan Bangunan*: Taxes for land and buildings that must be paid by residents to the DKI Jakarta government.
RASKIN	*Beras untuk Orang Miskin*: A subsidized rice program for poor families which provides 10 kg of rice per poor households at the price of Rp 1,000 per kg.
Reformasi	A period of political and societal transition that began with the fall of Suharto in 1998. With the ending of three decades of the New Order period, a more open and liberal political-social environment ensued.
Rentenir	Moneylenders, people who lend out money to others in return for (usually high) interest rates.
RT	*Rukun Tetangga*: neighbourhood
RW	*Rukun Warga*: community. Each RW consists of a number between 5 and 20 RT (see above)
SD	*Sekolah Dasar*: primary school. Children start attending SD at age six and can continue to SMP (see below) at age eleven.
Simpan pinjam	A *simpan pinjam* is an example of an Accumulating Saving & Credit Association (ASCRA). In a *simpan pinjam*, a group of people join together to contribute money to a loan fund from which they can disburse sizeable loans, for example, for investments in a new business. They can resemble small banks, such as the one that the municipality runs in Bantaran Kali, or they take more informal forms.
SKTM	*Surat Keterangan Tidak Mampu*: A card that, until 2014, could be issued by the *kecamatan* (administrative sub-district) to the desperate poor. In 2014 the card was replaced by Indonesia's Health Card (*Kartu Indonesia Sehatan* or KIS) as part of a new healthcare plan for Indonesia, which should guarantee affordable healthcare for all 240 million Indonesians by 2019.

SMP	*Sekolah Menengah Pertama,* or middle or junior secondary school. SMP education takes three years and follows elementary school. SMP may be followed by three years of senior secondary school (*Sekolah Menengah Atas* or SMA).
Susah	In Bantaran Kali, the term *susah* means 'difficult' or 'hard'. It is mostly used to refer to a risk-handling practice of the so-called *orang susah,* who emphasize their difficulties and problems in order to claim aid. See Chapter 5 for more information.
Tukang kredit	A creditor, a person of whom one can buy goods on credit and pay back the debt in daily installments – which mostly include an interest rate of 5 to 10 per cent per day.
Uang Bencana	Best translated as 'disaster money'. Money saved for the goal of being used in case a disaster strikes and brings along high costs, such as a flood or illness.
Uang jajan	Pocket money – a small amount of cash, just about enough to buy sweets, a drink in the street or other small purchases.
Uang rokok	Best translated as 'cigarette money' – a small amount of cash, just about enough to buy one or more cigarettes.

Index

For Product Safety Concerns and Information please contact our EU
representative GPSR@taylorandfrancis.com
Taylor & Francis Verlag GmbH, Kaufingerstraße 24, 80331 München, Germany

www.ingramcontent.com/pod-product-compliance
Ingram Content Group UK Ltd.
Pitfield, Milton Keynes, MK11 3LW, UK
UKHW021610240425
457818UK00018B/483